'A great contribution towards healing the deep wounds of our dreaming soul at the present time ... A boo~ ~ ~ nating guide both for those ~ dre~~~~ a~~ ~~ose w~~ose ~~ea~~ ~~e is an unexplored country.' **Anne Baring Ph.D., author of** *The Dream of the Cosmos: A Quest for the Soul*

'A valuable guide on your journey through the wondrous world of dreaming. Melinda Powell provides the full spectrum to help you understand the scientific, psychological, artistic, spiritual and colourful nature of your dreams.' **Bob Hoss, past president of the International Association for the Study of Dreams and director of the DreamScience Foundation, author of** *Dream Language: Self-Understanding through Imagery and Color*

'This book is a great encouragement to a world that is rediscovering the importance of dreams. Melinda Powell covers the benefit of dream work from the psychological and scientific as well as the therapeutic and spiritual perspectives, showing how dreams are a source of guidance, inspiration and wellbeing.' **Bob Haden, founder and former director of the Haden Institute, author of** *The Soul's Labyrinth*

'Melinda Powell beautifully explains how dreams can shed light on our fears, inviting us greater freedom in choosing consciously how we wish to be in our relationships and in the world.' **Diane Greig, Ph.D., founder of the Pacific Northwest Dream Community, Canada**

'Exploring the depths of dreaming with an experienced guide like Melinda Powell will bring you closer to your heart, your purpose and your truest self. An exceptional book for those listening to the wisdom of their dreams! Highly recommended.' **Robert V~** ~~ ~~ ~~ ~~~~~~ ~~~~~~~ *~teway to the Inner Sel*

D1584343

The Hidden Lives of Dreams

What They Can Tell Us and How They Can Change Our World

MELINDA POWELL

Published by Lagom
An imprint of Bonnier Books UK
Wimpole Street
London
W1G 9RE

www.bonnierbooks.co.uk

Trade paperback 9781788702386
eBook 9781788702393

A CIP catalogue of this book is available from the British Library.

Designed and set by seagulls.net
Printed and bound by Clays Ltd, Elcograf S.p.A.

1 3 5 7 9 10 8 6 4 2

Every reasonable effort has been made to trace copyright holders of
material reproduced in this book, but if any have been inadvertently
overlooked the publishers would be glad to hear from them.

Lagom is an imprint of Bonnier Books UK
www.bonnierbooks.co.uk

To my beloved Andrew,
my dearly loved family,
and for a world in need of dreams.

The world is a dream, you say, and it's lovely,
sometimes. Sunset. Clouds. Sky.

No. The image is a dream. The beauty is real.
Can you see the difference?[1]

– Richard Bach

Contents

Acknowledgements

In my early forties, I had a dream in which a man leads me into a room where my parents, brothers and others close to me have gathered. He tells them, 'I know Melinda's life may not have turned out as you might have thought. But that's okay because her life had to be this way for the dreams.' The man who appeared in the dream has also written the foreword to this book. That makes sense because the psychotherapy centre he set up in the 1980s has provided a 'home' for dreams and dreamwork both for me and for many others. For this, my profound thanks to Nigel Hamilton.

In my twenties. I decided to let my dreams guide my waking life. I thank my dreams for leading me to this present moment in which I look through my study window at a cluster of yellow roses that remind me of my dear mother. She has long since passed from this life, but her presence in my dreams has been a continuing source of encouragement. I also wish to remember and thank my father for instilling in me from childhood both soul stamina and a deep love for the wonders of Nature – the coastlines, canyonlands, deserts and mountains of my homeland.

Such natural beauty features in the photographs by Chris Nassef. Thank you, Chris!

Next, my thanks to the many people who have walked the paths of my life and dreams with me. You know who you are and when you read these words, you will know they are for you. In particular, I thank Sajada Taylor, my dream guide, whose wise counsel has led me through many dreams. I would also like to thank Dave Billington, my colleague at the Dream Research Institute, London, for his hands-on help in bringing dreams into reality.

To the many people referred to in these pages, whose thoughts and experiences form part of an ongoing conversation about life and dreams, I thank each one of you.

To the readers of this book, as I share with you my thoughts and dreams, I express my gratitude for your interest and openness. May your dreams, likewise, lead to your heart's innermost treasure.

And to my editor, Oliver Holden-Rea of Bonnier Books, who commissioned this work, and to his team, my warmest thanks.

Here, my thoughts turn with loving thanks to my husband, Andrew, whose steady hand, warm heart and lucid mind move tenderly through my life, dreams and the revisions of this book.

With humble thanks, I offer these pages to the spirit that moves through dreams and rustles among the treetops.

In my life, dreams have shone like living Presences of light against the backdrop of the dark, sacred night. Like bright stars, dreams have guided and filled me with a deep sense of gratitude and awareness of grace. The stars shine for all of us. The earth beneath our feet, the wind upon our cheeks, the touch of a loved one – these entwine with the light of our dreams, enriching life. For all this, I give heartfelt thanks.

Foreword

This unique book by Melinda Powell fills a gap in the available dream literature. Namely, it extolls and illustrates the vital importance of the Imaginal Mind as a bridge between our human and spiritual natures. Melinda's book shows how dreams reveal the limited perspective we have on our problems, on ourselves and on life in general – due to our overly conditioned capacity to look at how we see the world and our place within it. As Melinda demonstrates, dreams act as mirrors, revealing our wounds, our defences, and our illusions. Yet if we can clear our minds of old impressions and heal ourselves, our Imaginal Mind becomes a mirror, one in which dreams reveal the treasure of our hidden spiritual nature.

Melinda suggests in a very readable and carefully researched way that dreams could become one of the major frontiers of a new psychology of mind – moving the mental focus from a purely cognitive or neuro-cognitive model to embrace a multidimensional view of the mind's creative potential. She shows how, by revisiting our dreams and consciously interacting with them, we are able to explore the wonders of the universe within. According to the mystical traditions, these wonders are mirrored in the beauty of the natural world around us. Conversely, as Melinda persuasively argues, the messes and tangled complexities that we create in our minds, and which are reflected in our dreams and nightmares, bear remarkable similarities to the devastation we see today in the polluted wastelands humanity has created in the outer world.

My first memory of Melinda recalls her volunteering to work with one of her dreams – a dream of great importance – during her training programme in transpersonal psychotherapy. I had no idea what would emerge from this Waking Dream exploration – the experience was powerful and initiated dramatic change in Melinda's life. As a result, she began to explore more deeply her extraordinary capacity for dream lucidity.

The remarkable lucid dreams that followed described increasingly beautiful landscapes representing the subtle realms of consciousness. Light and 'Black Light' appeared regularly in the imagery. Over the course of hundreds of lucid dreams, Melinda learned to surrender ever more deeply to the experience of the 'Black Light', a phenomenon St John of the Cross and other mystics have spoken of as the prelude to profound spiritual awakening.

I encouraged Melinda to attend and speak of her dreams at the annual conference of the International Association for the Study of Dreams (IASD). By then, Melinda had begun to refer to her conscious attitude in these 'Black Light' experiences as 'Lucid Surrender', a term she coined professionally, as a path to spiritual awakening.

Since we both shared the same views regarding the significance of transpersonal dream exploration, we discussed the need for an institute that promoted dream research. This culminated in the setting up of the Dream Research Institute (DRI) as part of the expanding work of the Centre for Counselling and Psychotherapy Education (CCPE) in London, with Melinda as co-founder and director.[1]

Melinda had also taken on the role of directing and reviving one of CCPE's student psychotherapy practicum placements, HELP, a charity originally started by Richard Branson as a phone-in advice centre more than 40 years ago.[2] Over the years, the service evolved into a charitable counselling centre to help people in need of psychotherapeutic support. Given Melinda's education and experience, her dedication and integrity, the charity blossomed to become a largely self-funded service offering short- and long-term psychotherapy to hundreds of people every year.

Much of what has emerged in Melinda's dreams and through her work as a psychotherapist has been combined and presented in this book. She has clearly illustrated the possibilities of human development by working with dreams.

To sum up, this much-needed work shows how the ineffable human spirit that resides within all of us beyond the conscious mind can help to harmonise and enhance the relationship between our human and spiritual natures, as well as our shared humanity and the natural world of which we are part.

Nigel Hamilton, Ph.D.

Director, Centre for Counselling and Psychotherapy Education

Co-Founder, Dream Research Institute, London

Author of *Awakening Through Dreams:*
The Journey Through the Inner Landscape

Author's Introduction

Let Nature be your guide.[1]

Epigram 42, Michael Maier
(physician and alchemist, 1568–1622)

Why write or read a book on dreams at a time when environmental crises threaten life on Earth, a time when children ask, 'Why go to school to learn facts when the most important facts about the planet are not taught?'[2]

We might also ask why one of the essential aspects of our existence, our ability to dream, does not appear on school curricula or in our daily conversations. Dreams tell us about ourselves, our relationships with others and the natural world we inhabit. Dreams play a vital role in our physiological and personal development. Like myriad leaves that link a tree to the light-filled atmosphere and which, by means of photosynthesis, breathe life into the world, dreams bridge our inner, subjective experience and the outer world, breathing new life into us. When we ignore our dreams, we disregard the nature of our consciousness, rooted, as it were, in planet Earth.[3]

Our vision sees for the Earth, our voices speak for it, and our hands extend its reach. In our sleep, Earth dreams.

And each night, if we pay attention to our dreams, we awaken to new potentialities both in ourselves and the mysterious ground of life itself. Our appreciation of the dream world hallows our awareness of life.

In modern life, we have little time for reflection, for sleep and even less for dreams. We have become accustomed to living without regard to the natural rhythms of night and day, seasonal change, or the balance between taking and giving, doing and being, mind and heart, body and soul. The day begins out of step with Nature when we waken unnaturally to the sound of the alarm clock – the only species that does so![4]

The accelerated warming of the planet reflects our 'overheated' lives. Pollution of the natural world parallels a profound imbalance of the human psyche. The desecration of Nature mirrors the unthinking worldview of humankind towards both the waking and dream worlds. Cultural neglect of the inner world becomes a living nightmare as it finds expression in the decimation of the Earth's natural landscape.

Consider how the global deforestation of Earth reflects a collective one-sidedness in our species' approach to life. Before the Industrial Age, forests covered half of the planet. Now, less than half of those forests still exist, and only one fifth remain untouched.[5] As the human population increases and the pace of our lives and our technologies speed up, so does the pace at which we deplete the planet's resources, especially trees, putting ourselves and life on the planet at risk. Each tree absorbs up to 48lb of carbon dioxide per year.[6] Without trees, we lose Nature's most efficient way to counter the increasing levels of carbon dioxide that contribute to global warming. Yet we continue to fell trees at an ever-increasing rate. With an estimated 800 million of us in the 'developed world' struggling with poor sleep health,[7] might these alarming statistics correlate with a symbolic 'felling' of dreams, a destruction of the very environment needed to nurture our dream life – in other words, a good night's rest?

In such a world, should we be surprised that by 2016 doctors in the United Kingdom were writing more than 64 million prescriptions a year for antidepressants, a 108 per cent increase over the ten previous years?[8] Globally, one in seven people have a diagnosed mental health or substance abuse disorder – an estimated 1.5 billion of us in 2019.[9] In developed countries, mental health expenditures and losses in productivity represent at least 4 per cent of the Gross National Product,[10] some £100bn for the UK economy alone.[11]

In 1983, scientists first hypothesised that life on the planet keeps the Earth's atmosphere at a dynamically steady state, primarily by mediating levels of carbon dioxide.[12] By 2001, 1,000 scientists boldly declared:

> The Earth System behaves as a single, self-regulating system comprised of physical, chemical, biological and human components. The interactions and feedbacks between the component parts are complex and exhibit multi-scale temporal and spatial variability. The understanding of the natural dynamics of the Earth System ... provides a sound basis for evaluating the effects and consequences of human-driven change.[13]

Dreams provide one of Nature's most effective ways to recognise our need for balance.[14] We have only just begun to appreciate the contributions of sleep and dreams to our personal wellbeing and, on a larger scale, to that of the Earth. In 1954, one year after the first scientific studies that linked rapid eye movement in sleep to dreams,[15] and long before brain imaging studies revealed important links between dreaming and healthy human development, Carl Jung, the founder of analytical psychology, proposed that the psyche acts as a 'self-regulating system that maintains its equilibrium just as the body does'.[16]

In this book, I ask you to imagine how our lives – how we treat ourselves, others and the Earth – would change if we drew on our dreams to live more gracefully. A prayer of the Native American People's implores, 'May I walk in balance.'[17] To this we might add, 'May I dream in balance.' By attending reflectively and appreciatively to our dreams as we would to a tree newly planted, we learn how to restore balance in our lives as we move towards the collective harmony so badly needed by humanity.

Gratitude towards the gift of dreams engenders gratitude towards life. Research has shown that if a depressed person writes down three things for which they feel thankful, even just once a week, then before long, they will feel markedly better for it.[18] Imagine a world where everyone included dreams on their list of what they feel thankful for! Yet so often people discount their dreams or feel frightened of them, thereby losing out on the positive gift therein.

We can illustrate the modern tendency to neglect both dreams and the natural world with an African legend, retold by the mythologist Joseph Campbell, of a boy who returned to his village from the forest with a small bird. The bird sang a beautiful song and the boy listened attentively. One day, the boy left the bird in his father's care. But the father resented having to feed what he saw as a useless bird and so he killed it. A moment later the father also died. As Campbell tells us, this tale warns that when we kill the song, we kill ourselves.[19] I recall a dream in which Bob Dylan appeared to me saying, 'Songs are dreams sung.' When we silence our dreams by dismissing them or simply treating them purely as bio-chemical phenomena, we risk 'killing' the dreams' songs of life within us.

On a similar note, the Jungian analyst Anne Baring retells the story of a king who receives gifts on a daily basis from those seeking his favour.[20] Day after day, a beggar approaches the king's throne and leaves a different fruit – an apple, orange or pear – asking for nothing in return. Each day, the king receives the beggar's humble gift as decorum dictates, but then orders his servant to throw the offending fruit away. After many years, when the beggar has become an old man, a monkey sitting on the shoulder of an envoy from another land jumps down, steals an apple, takes a bite and tosses the fruit on the floor in front of the king. Everyone gasps as a ruby, hidden in the apple's core, shines. The king's servant rushes down to the cellar where for years he had thrown the unwanted gifts. There he discovers a pile of jewels: rubies, emeralds and diamonds left in the wake of the decayed fruit.

This story highlights that gratitude, considered to be one of the highest virtues, also requires humility. Hand in hand with humility, gratitude opens the heart to the rich qualities of the inner world, to the grace that develops our capacity to receive gratefully and, in turn, to give. This book asks us to approach our dreams in the same spirit. As the story of the hidden treasure intimates, dreams, so often neglected or feared, can potentially give us insights of great value.

As a dream researcher, therapist and dream guide, I study dreams, write about them and help people discover the gift of their own dreams. But if someone asks me what I do and I tell them that I co-founded a dream research institute, often the other person will look slightly confused, nod their head, and quickly move on to another topic! Yet, from time to time, someone I hardly know takes me aside, lowers their voice and says, 'You know, I had a dream last night…', or else a person will clutch my arm and, in a hushed, anxious voice, tell me about the nightmare that plagues their sleep.

I remember one such man in his twenties who told me in passing about a bear that rose up nightly in his dreams to attack him. He described how the bear, a grizzly, stood towering over him. I remarked that the Native American Indians viewed the bear as a powerful spirit guide and sought such a bear in their visions. Mastering their fear, they would face the bear, speak to it and receive its message. I added that if it felt hard to imagine doing this on his own, then, when he was ready, he could meet his bear with the help of a dream guide. He went quiet for a moment, then said he had not thought of the dream that way and it encouraged him to think he could do so.

When we share a dream, the dream becomes alive for those who hear it.[21] If that had been your dream, would you be ready to meet the bear? What might the bear have said to you or given you? If you can imagine the bear without fear, you will find that doing so puts you in touch with the bear's powerful, instinctual energy – energy you can draw on to recharge your life. The bear's message will give you what you need to move confidently into what life holds for you.

These days, the bear may well be telling us, 'Wake up! You, too, are a child of Nature. Your home, like mine, has come under threat.' I picture the bear echoing the words of the Native American Chief Seattle in a letter he wrote to the United States government in the 1850s:

> This we know: the earth does not belong to man, man belongs to the earth. All things are connected like the blood that unites us all. Man did not weave the web of life, he is merely a strand in it. Whatever he does to the web, he does to himself.[22]

If by chance I met you at a gathering, what dream might you choose to share with me? I recall at a dinner party some years ago, when I spoke about my work with dreams, a fellow guest asserted, 'The world needs dreams. It's good you're doing that', upon which the conversation around the table thoughtfully quietened. His unexpected words encouraged me greatly, just as I would like to encourage you, the reader, to discover your dreams anew and cherish them, both for yourself and for a world in need of dreams.

Chapter One

The Sea of Dreams:
An Exploration of Hidden Depths

The sea does not reward those who are too anxious,
too greedy, or too impatient. To dig for treasures
shows not only impatience and greed, but lack of faith.
Patience, patience, patience, is what the sea teaches.
Patience and faith. One should lie empty, open,
choiceless as a beach – waiting for a gift from the sea.[1]

– Anne Morrow Lindbergh

I invite you to begin this exploration of your dreams by picturing yourself at the seaside. There, you walk barefoot along the shoreline, scanning the receding waters for shells. Many tantalising shell fragments catch your eye as the waters carry them back into the sea. Occasionally, a fragment, its colour, texture or shape, may tempt you to pick it up and examine it more closely. Most likely, you will find a shiny shard of a mussel, the broken fan of a clamshell or the inner spiral of a conch, its outer husk worn away or broken off by the motions of the waves. These fragments hold a certain beauty and may evoke memories of the past or a sense of wordless longing.

With luck, the waves will toss a shell, complete in its mathematical precision, at your feet, causing you to wonder at the beauty encasing the hollow emptiness where a sea creature once lived. Sometimes, as you search, an unseen wave may rush up unexpectedly, dousing you in cold, salty water. Yet, for seemingly no particular reason at all, searching for shells brings pleasure, putting you in touch with an intimate part of the immense, unknown sea that stretches out before you.

The shell in your hand holds a particular meaning for you. It is true that a knowledge of science may certainly enhance your appreciation of each shell, the intricacies of its form, the strength of its exoskeleton, the creature it housed, its role in the sea. Yet, you don't need to be a collector to know that combing the beach for shells does you good, focuses your mind, and puts you in a more contemplative state.

A scientific appreciation of how the action of the waves generates negative ions that benefit our mood, activate our immune systems, stimulate our appetite and create brainwaves that bring us increased awareness will deepen your understanding of why you might like to walk by the seaside and look for shells. But, unless you go to the sea, take your shoes off, get your feet wet and breathe in the wave-filtered air, you won't truly know what you've been missing. The same holds true of our dreams: science can tell us about our dream processes and purposes of dreaming, but you alone can relate the subjective reality of your dreams – what it felt like to be in your dream and what it might mean for you.

Research has shown that during sleep, dreams come with wave-like regularity across the sleep cycle. Yet, given that we spend nearly an astonishing third of our lifetime asleep and a total of six years dreaming, much about the purpose and benefits of dreams remains unchartered territory. The first study of the flickering eye movements indicative of dreaming associated with Rapid Eye Movement (REM) sleep took place in 1953.[2] Subsequently, measurements of fluctuations in brain activity using the electroencephalogram (EEG) during REM sleep provided more evidence that dreaming occurs. But because the EEG confines the exploration of the nocturnal brain to electrical measurements close to the brain's surface, the scientific exploration of the deeper neurological substrates of dreaming remained mostly inaccessible until the mid-1990s.

The evolution of computer technology has enabled researchers to penetrate ever deeper into the neurophysiology of the brain. Magnetic resonance imaging (MRI) can map the hidden depths of the brain in both dreaming and dreamless states at ever-higher resolutions in three dimensions. Functional MRIs (fMRIs) reveal not only where brain activity occurs but also the brain processes involved *in real time*, recorded while the research subject dreams. Remarkably, computer algorithms used in conjunction with fMRI scans of brain activity during REM sleep can now be used to map dream imagery[3] – if you dream of a seashell, the computer potentially recreates this.

Over recent decades, the scientific knowledge about dreams, especially the physiological and psychological benefits they offer, has deepened. Key findings from empirical studies on the purpose of dreams, particularly since the turn of the 21st century, have demonstrated that dreaming, both in REM and non-REM sleep, helps to promote and maintain neurological health across the lifespan of humans and other mammals.[4] Significantly, as the neuroscientist Matthew Walker has pointed out, humans spend up to three times longer each night in REM dreaming than do primates, which appears to have given our species an evolutionary advantage.[5]

Dreams, it seems, generate scenarios wherein we can rehearse for waking life, enabling learning,[6] insight,[7] problem-solving and decision-making.[8] They are thought to initiate the neural networks that transcribe experience into memories,[9] balance our emotional life[10] and help us to recognise and attune to emotions in others, particularly through the recognition of facial expressions.[11] Dreams may inspire creativity[12] and, importantly, lay down the foundations of self-awareness and reflection:[13] conceptualisation, reasoning, intuition, insight and volition. Crucially, and for the benefit of the human species, dreams can potentially increase our capacity to master our more instinctual reactions of fear and anger and to express the deeply felt emotions essential for real relatedness and intimacy, including empathy.[14] All these possibilities we will be exploring throughout this book.

Thanks to cross-disciplinary approaches to the study of dreams in neurology and psychology, sleep and consciousness studies, we have learned a great deal, yet further unexplored depths remain, particularly in the area of lucid dreams – dreams in which the dreamer becomes conscious that they dream.

Research first carried out in the late 1970s and early 1980s demonstrated the phenomenon of lucid dreaming.[15] In these experiments, lucid dreamers successfully used pre-agreed eye movements during REM dream sleep to signal their lucidity – sending a sign from a previously hidden dimension of consciousness. Nevertheless, the world at large remained sceptical that lucid dreaming really existed until as late as 2009, when neuroimaging began to map the brain activity of the lucid state.[16] Yet, the development of reflective awareness in dreams already had a long history within esoteric traditions. Tibetan Buddhism, for example, has developed a highly developed practice of 'dream yoga', refined over centuries,[17] while Judaism, Christianity and Islam have also explored the revelatory aspects of reflective dreaming for spiritual purposes.[18]

Whereas neurological maps have revealed the features of the dream terrain, the qualities and emotional textures of the dreamscape exist in the infinitude of the imagination and the dreamer's subjective experience of their 'inner landscape of dreams'.[19] Even though a computer may one day recreate your dream shell perfectly, only you can say what the shell means to you: that it might remind you of your first trip to the sea, the sound of the ocean, a powerful storm-tossed sea, or a calming turquoise-blue cove, and how that shell might put you in touch with qualities or feelings that you might have forgotten or not yet realised in yourself, a loved one, or the natural world. Only you can give an intimation of the dream shell's personal value.

Dreams may yet be shown to be 'the purest form of the imagination'.[20] As such, alternative modes of knowing – analytical and experiential, biological and autobiographical, rational and poetic, left brain and right brain together – give us the most complete 'imaging' of the dream. In this book, these complementary perspectives interweave to help you engage with your dream life to enrich your waking life.

Why have I written this book on dreams? My answer, at heart, is simple – because of a dream! The dream came in my mid-twenties at a time when I had to decide whether or not I would take the opportunity to move to Europe from southern California near the Pacific Ocean, where I had grown up. I had completed my postgraduate studies and had been teaching for a few years. I deeply desired to go and do something practical and purposeful in the 'real world' that would benefit others.

During this time, the Berlin Wall dividing West and East Germany had fallen, leading to the opening of former Soviet Bloc countries to the West. The United States Peace Corps was recruiting volunteers with postgraduate degrees to set up teacher training colleges for foreign-language teachers in Eastern Europe. I applied and was offered the chance to go to Poland. Suddenly confronted with choosing whether to stay in the States or to move abroad, I was feeling rather despondent at the thought of leaving my family. I took a long walk along the foothills, where I stopped to take inspiration from a view of the blue Pacific, shining in the distance, and to pray for dream guidance – the first time I had asked for this for myself. (As a child, I knew from biblical stories that people can obtain guidance from a dream, but it had never occurred to me that such requests could apply to ordinary people like me.)

That night, in my dream, I found myself walking at the base of the California foothills along the coast, where I wandered through crowded carnival grounds, feeling alone.

I longed for a friend to join me. The crowds jostled around me, pushing me out towards the hills, where a man approached me saying, 'I've heard you've been looking for a friend.' His gentleness reassured me, and I felt that I could trust this stranger whose blond wavy hair touched the shoulders of his royal-blue poet's blouse. His fine features and form radiated beauty.

As we walked in the hills, we communicated without words. The sea-washed breeze cooled us. I asked him his name and he answered, 'Gabriel.' I turned to face him and said, 'You know that name means "child of God"?' He smiled and said, 'I know.'

We walked together for a long time. Then he invited me home to meet his family. There, his elderly parents and three sisters greeted me warmly. A gentle fire burned in the hearth. They fed me freshly baked bread and fresh milk. As I ate, the meal seemed to make me whole and gave me new life. After supper, Gabriel told me that we would be taking a journey into the night. Since childhood, I had been terribly afraid of the dark, but now, with Gabriel, the darkness felt friendly and safe. I got into his invisible 'car' and together we moved into the velvety blackness at an incredible speed. Then I awoke.

This dream held great import for me because, at the dream's end, I understood 'Gabriel' to be an angelic presence. In the Christian tradition in which I was raised, Gabriel heralded a clear divine message. Although the Gabriel of my dream did not signpost the direction I should take, his loving presence nonetheless imparted an abiding sense of inner guidance, one that has accompanied me throughout my life.

At the time, I intuited the dream as indicating that I had the inner strength needed to take a leap of faith into the unknown and to make the move to Poland, that I wasn't alone and didn't need to feel afraid. Now, some 30 years later, I recognise even more importantly that such dreams remind us that we 'belong to more than ourselves'.[21] They intimate that we are loved, not for what we know, possess or do, but simply for who we are as 'children' of a star-studded universe, alive with 'more-than-human-consciousness'.[22]

Given my Christian upbringing and my personal exploration of other wisdom traditions, I use words such as 'God', 'the numinous', 'the Mystery', 'a Divine Presence', 'the Beloved', 'the Essence', 'a Higher Wisdom' and 'the transpersonal' when referring to this all-encompassing consciousness. Such consciousness deeply moves us and broadens our appreciation of life, awakening our minds *and* hearts to the animating principle that moves soulfully through all of creation in its abundance of form. Such appreciation in its many different manifestations expresses our human spiritual nature.

The root of the word 'spirit' is found in such words as 'respire' and 'inspire', having to do with the intake of breath that gives us life. For each of us, what makes us *fully present* to life is unique. It might be observing a religious ritual or taking a walk by the sea. At the same time, I have learned from my own experience and that of my clients' that dreams can serve this valuable purpose when we become attentive to them.

Prior to my 'Gabriel' dream, I could never have foreseen that turning to my dreams for guidance would lead me from my country of origin, where I had studied literature and language, to Europe, where I would do research in the Psychology of Religion and go on to train as a psychotherapist specialising in dreams. Nor could I have imagined that my dreams would help me to direct educational programmes, a charitable counselling service, and to co-found the Dream Research Institute (DRI) in London – a rare place where researchers study how dreams influence the wellbeing of mind, body and spirit.[23]

Among our projects, the DRI has undertaken research on how dreamwork supports the emotional wellbeing of patients suffering from autoimmune disease;[24] how therapeutic dream re-entry facilitates positive changes in mental wellbeing long-term;[25] how dream guidance facilitates creative development over time;[26] and how the appearance of light, symmetry[27] and colour in dreams,[28] as well as directional movement in the lucid dreaming space,[29] promotes therapeutic processes – topics that this book covers. In a later chapter, I describe how my numerous lucid dreams led me to explore what happens when the lucid dreamer takes a receptive attitude in lucidity rather than attempting to 'control' the dream, a therapeutic process I have called 'Lucid Surrender'.[30]

Many learned books on dreams already exist. Rather than elaborating on dreams from a purely theoretical angle, my approach has been to contextualise dreams within the natural world and our daily lives. I am grateful to the many people who have given consent to have their dreams included in this book – colleagues, friends, clients, students and contributors from archived collections. The dreamers and their dreams have been anonymised for reasons of confidentiality. Where I present a full case illustration or more extensive reflections on a dream and its therapeutic value, I have given the dreamer a pseudonym.

Please remember that no matter what I may have to say *about* a dream, nothing has more authenticity than the dream itself. Only the dreamer can tell us what happened in a dream's depths and what it felt like to be there. We cannot separate the dream from the reality of the person who dreamed it, particularly as a dream comes fully alive through how it changes both the dreamer and waking life.[31] Further, a dream when shared can change others too.

With this in mind, I have selected sample dreams that clearly foreground a particular feature of dreams. These first-hand accounts speak to our individual and collective experience as human beings and have been gleaned from my many years of working with people and their dreams. Wherever possible, I have included the dreamer's own understanding of the dream's intent, and the accompanying reflections which appear in quotations have been written by the dreamers themselves. However, I also invite you, the reader, to approach each dream account *as if* it were your own.

Dreams, when viewed from a detached stance, lose their vitality. And so, throughout this book, I invite you to imaginatively interact with the sample dreams as we reflect on each in turn. However, if you are feeling emotionally unstable or have a been diagnosed with a mental illness, then I would recommend considering each dream or visual exercise as an observer, rather than as a direct participant. Doing so will help give you distance from the dream's emotional content.

You can also seek out a therapist who works with dreams to provide extra support and guidance.[32]

In my presentation of dream material, I have endeavoured to be true to the dreams from the 'inside-out' in order to help us understand what it feels like to enter into relationship with our dreams. This has required the personal courage to share more intimately of my own experience. I decided to include my own dreams to show how I, too, had to learn to trust my dreams, listen to them and appreciate how they heal and guide. My learning helps to point the way; your dreams give you the opportunity to learn from your own experience.

This book draws on both the science and art of dreaming, with a special focus on the therapeutic benefits of dreams, their capacity to renew us, reveal our nature and restore balance to our lives. For this we also need an understanding of our human psychology and spirituality. While it is good to know about the science of dreaming, the facts of brain circuitry alone can never explain the revelatory nature of a dream and what we can learn as we contemplate it. Nor can any understanding be complete, for, unlike the sea, dreams have infinite depth.

The purpose of this book is not only to impart a deeper understanding of dreams but also to engage you in learning to trust your dreams and to respond to the guidance dreams bring to waking life. Thus, the style, theme, content and structure of the chapters interweave to amplify a particular element of the dream experience. Because of this, I would read the text from start to finish. Readers who follow the book's natural progression, rather than dipping into chapters that hold particular interest, will find that each chapter, while complete in and of itself, contributes to a foundational understanding for what follows.

This chapter and chapters Two and Three introduce knowledge about the study and nature of sleep and dreams, guiding the reader to become more attentive to the reciprocity between dreams and life. Chapters Four, Five, and Six direct the attention to underlying principles that dreams share with the natural world and the ways these reflect both human and more-than-human consciousness. Chapters Eight, Nine and Ten then consider the nature of presence, will and awareness – including self-awareness and transpersonal awareness – within dreams. These latter chapters bring ideas introduced and attitudes cultivated in previous chapters to fruition.

Each chapter includes references to scientific research, philosophy, religious traditions, the creative arts and alchemical teachings. Chapter notes, while not required reading, provide further details and extensive resources – a veritable dream library – for those who have an area of interest they would like to have evidenced or deepened. In instances where I provide examples of research in a particular field, I have selected one or two key studies of especial relevance and accessibility.

As this book will show, dreams, whether felt to be positive or negative, memorable or inconsequential, fragmentary or complete, serve to connect us to a transformative energy that, like the power of the sea when harnessed, can change our lives and the world around us. Even as we sleep, the brain's intricate neurology connects us to a mysterious 'sea of dreams' – vast 'domains of potentiality'.[33]

While much of the good our dreams do us happens without our full awareness, to benefit fully from our dreams, we need to bring our attention to them – no matter whether we recall a dream as a whole or only in wisps – before the dream recedes into the forgetfulness of sleep or the distractions of waking life. We need to wake up to our dreams!

Listen to your own dreams and those in this book to decide for yourself. Be aware that by reading these dreams and learning about the art and science shaping them, your perspective on your dream life and waking life will change, while your relationship to your dreams – and thus to yourself – deepens. By choosing this book, you have already taken the first step. Now, you need only to pause, pick up the dreams like shells in your hand, turn each one over in your mind and reflect on them with me as we experience the transformative power they hold.

Chapter Two

The Science and Symbols of Sleep and Dreams

That we come to this earth to live is untrue.
We come but to sleep, to dream.[1]

– Aztec poet

This chapter takes us into a creative investigation of the sleep cycle. Drawing on a dream-based narrative to portray the relationship between sleep and dreams, we first move imaginatively through real-world knowledge of sleep health and disorders to dreaming states, including an introduction to lucid dreaming. We then look more closely at what advances in research suggest about how dreaming helps to shape our sense of self, from the womb through to the end of life. In light of this research, we consider how therapeutic dreamwork enhances our emotional life by enabling us to re-access our dreams and to apply the energy and learning held in them so as to transform our waking life. A series of my own dreams, appearing in chronological order throughout the chapter, brings to life the concepts discussed and also gives you a personal sense of the points I am making.

Let us begin our creative exploration of sleep and dreams by imagining ourselves sitting next to a stone-ringed campfire on the shore of a still lake on a warm, moonlit summer's night. Here we sit, companionably watching the play of firelight and shadows as we talk about the nature of sleep and dreams. As fireside conversations invite storytelling, to prepare you for an exploration of the sleep cycle, I will tell you one of my own dreams as a story, one that gives a picture of the relationship between sleep, dreams and the imagination:

A young man and woman in their twenties stand looking out over a mountain lake set in an immense, granite basin. The lake's shiny pitch-black surface does not appear to reflect the moonlight. Naked, the young man dives joyfully into the water, calling out for the young woman to join him. Suddenly, she finds herself naked too, and dives into the black waters.

Upon diving in, she feels surprised to see shafts of golden light illuminating the lakebed, where large squares made of copper carved in intricate patterns, like the designs of Islamic prints, cover the ground. Through the backdrop of the design, more darkness appears, suggesting that the lake has further depths. As the woman admires the beautiful squares, the young man swims over to her, laughing, and then swims on playfully. She swims after him, aware that she can breathe underwater. Then she awakes.

Reflecting on the dream now, I associate the young man with the ancient Greek god of sleep, Hypnos, enticing us into the depths of sleep and dreams. Born of the goddess Nyx (or night), Hypnos has a sweet, playful disposition, a natural innocence, in contrast to his twin brother, Thanatos, who portends Death. Yet, in our nightly sleep, we do, in one sense, 'die'. We die to consciousness of the waking state as we enter other realms, whose characteristics and benefits we have only recently begun to understand. This symbolic 'death' takes us out of the routine and stress of the work-a-day world into the 'Imaginal World' of sleep and dreams.[2] Imagination in this 'world' acts as an 'image-making, form-giving, creative activity', rather than a superficial fantasy.[3]

No matter how much we may try to evade the nightly call of Hypnos, distracting ourselves with endless to-do lists, diversions and detours, or taking stimulants to keep us going, ultimately we must become stripped of our waking consciousness and surrender nakedly to sleep.

Returning to our lakeside campfire, we leave behind the night-defying artificial light of the urban world that dims the stars and moon and instead look up and wonder at the incandescent stars. We can rest our eyes from the incessant glare of technologies that obscure our natural light–dark cycle, our body's circadian rhythm, as the fire's hypnotic flames and glowing embers calm us. Our circadian 'clock', set over 4 billion years to the spinning timepiece of the earth's rotation, pivots between the sun and moon. Every cell in our bodies responds to the cycle of day and night, sleep and waking, as does all life on Earth, hardwired to respond with extraordinary biological sensitivity to the daily cycle of the planet's 24-hour circadian rhythm. Awake and alert by day, by night we sleep for seven to nine hours, not uniformly but in 90-minute cycles, four to five times a night, with momentary periods of waking between cycles.[4] Living close to Nature, we follow the natural pattern of sleep in accordance with our internal body clock.

However, many of us living in the 'developed world' regularly attempt to circumvent this rhythm by staying up late. A 2016 survey revealed that 75 per cent of Britons go to bed after 11:00 pm and routinely get only five to seven hours' sleep – a loss of one whole night's sleep a week and resulting in a 20 per cent loss of dream time![5] Overriding the evolutionary forces that determine our sleep/wake cycle has proven to be seriously detrimental to public health. In 2007, the World Health Organization included long-term 'circadian disruption' as a possible cause of carcinogens in humans, particularly breast and prostate cancer.[6]

The body takes the forced pace of modernity literally to heart. Chronic, work-related sleep disruption has been linked to coronary heart disease – a bruising, 12-hour-plus work shift increases the chances of heart problems by as much as 40 per cent.[7] When we work longer to get more done, far from achieving more, we increase our chances of making errors on the job threefold, dulling the very qualities we need to be truly productive: concentration, recall, accuracy and decisiveness.[8]

In 2016, the Royal Society for Public Health (RSPH) noted that by the year 2000, sleep disturbance had already been identified in the United Kingdom as 'the most common expression of mental ill-health for men and women over the previous 15 years.'[9] Hoping to wake us up to the health benefits of sleep, the RSPH has compiled an eye-opening list of risks associated with sleep deprivation, with no less than a total of 36 potential ill-effects linked respectively to our physical and mental health, as well as to our behaviour and performance.[10] In addition to the increased risk of cancer and heart disease, loss of sleep weakens the immune system, causes metabolic imbalances and adds to weight gain. Poor 'sleep health' destabilises our emotional equilibrium, contributing to depression, anxiety, outbursts of anger and, tragically, an increased risk of suicide. Losing out on just one hour of sleep not only detrimentally effects our performance at work, but also interferes with getting to and from work, contributing to an estimated 20 per cent of road traffic accidents.[11]

Accordingly, the RSPH recommends the inclusion of sleep health in the school curriculum and the creation of a 'Slumber Number', a national helpline for sleep advice. The UK's National Health Service (NHS) now posts helpful tips for 'Sleep Hygiene' online, advocating regular sleeping hours, a gadget-free hour to wind down before bedtime, a warm bath, a sleep-friendly bedroom – one without a television – and a sleep diary to track sleep patterns.[12] To this can be added avoiding stimulants like alcohol, nicotine and caffeine, especially in the evening, when the body and mind are meant to shift from the daylight focus on *doing* to the nocturnal emphasis on *being*.

Following these guidelines, along with other suggestions found throughout this book, will also improve your 'Dream

Health'. Perhaps one day, the addition of dream health programmes to school curricula as well as a 'Dream Dial' helpline will also be recommended! The simplest prescription for a good night's sleep would be to 'listen to your body'.[13] Thankfully, most of us recognise that we feel better after sleeping for at least seven hours a night. I recall a dream of mine that reminded me of this:

> *I am in a room with two women, the one on my left*
> *a hard-headed, sophisticated businesswoman, and the*
> *other, on my right, a gentle and sweet artistic type.*
> *We talk about work and what needs to get done.*
> *The young woman on my right teaches a choir full-*
> *time and says that she does so on Saturdays as well.*
> *Thinking of how I also end up doing dreamwork*
> *over the weekend, early in the morning hours, after a*
> *full week at my day job, I exclaim, 'Six days a week!*
> *You'll wear yourself out!' She comes over to me, her*
> *eyes deep and round, and says, 'I want to introduce*
> *ever more people to the Holy Choir.' She says this with*
> *incredible sweetness and musicality in her voice.*
> *With this, I awake.*

The dream invites me to redirect my efforts towards what matters most to me. Only upon waking does the dream's dramatic irony strike me – I have given the woman in the dream the very advice I don't follow myself! The dream warns me that by overworking I am putting my health at risk, no matter how laudable my intentions. Here, it is important to dispel the myth that we can make up for sleep that we have lost. Sleep specialist Matthew Walker states this in stark terms: 'The brain can never recover all the sleep it has been deprived of. We cannot accumulate a debt without penalty, nor can we repay that sleep dept at a later time.'[14]

Having acknowledged the importance of sleep to our wellbeing, let us now come back to our lakeside fire, a million miles away from the reality of 24-hour-plus round-the-clock 'days' fuelled by artificial light and the frantic economics of the modern world. Here, as we meditatively watch the hypnotic flames, photosensitive cells in our eyes respond to the soft wavelengths of firelight and the encircling darkness. These receptors signal the pineal gland to increase production of the hormone melatonin that induces and maintains sleep. Our natural tendency towards sleep/wake homeostasis brings us into balance with the circadian cycle, and we begin to feel sleepy. Hypnos has arrived. Night's coolness cocoons us in still darkness. As our core body temperature begins to fall, additional thermosensitive cells within the brain also induce a rise in the melatonin levels that prime our internal systems for rest.[15] Sleep becomes irresistible.

Drifting off, it is as though we have dived into a lake whose surface waters, illuminated by moonlight, reveal strange hypnagogic forms. Within a few minutes, we pass through the initial shallow stage of sleep towards deep sleep, in which our brains begin to fire up with electric charges. These charges form sharp wave-ripples in the deep brain structure of the hippocampus, in which recent events are consolidated into long-term memories. Thalamocortical sleep spindles sift, filter and transform the sensory input from our waking life into memories and help constellate our sense of self. For the next 50 minutes or so, as more spindles flare up across the grey matter of our brain, we become increasingly able to process new information from the preceding day.[16]

The spindles also protect us from external sounds that might otherwise waken us, so that, shielded, we move into the furthest reaches of what neurologists call non-rapid eye movement (NREM) sleep. In this state, the brain operates at one tenth of the speed it does while we are awake,[17] while it regulates essential physiological processes at a cellular level. Our body temperature falls by two to three degrees, and the pulse slows, allowing cerebrospinal fluid to wash away the waste products of cell metabolism.[18]

Importantly, this fluid appears to wash out the protein beta-amyloid thought to be responsible for the shrinkage of grey matter found in patients with Alzheimer's disease; thus, a chronic lack of deep sleep may significantly contribute to an increased risk of Alzheimer's.[19] Also, in deep sleep, the pineal gland secretes the restorative human growth hormone (HGM), which activates tissue repair in muscles and bones through cell regeneration. This hormone facilitates neuronal repair, key to the neuroplasticity inherent in healthy brain tissue.[20] If we miss out on our delta sleep, then we become moody, injuries take more time to heal and the immune system weakens.

Our deep sleep has healing properties for our body and mind. However, during the sleep cycle, the body's lowered temperature makes it vulnerable, especially during the REM state wherein our body's inner thermostat loses its capacity for regulating our body temperature.[21] To protect us from the dangers of hypothermia, if the temperature of the atmosphere becomes too cool (or too warm), we will wake up before entering the REM state. An ambient temperature of 65 degrees Fahrenheit (18 degrees Celsius), like that of a pleasant summer's eve, proves ideal for sleep and for dreaming.[22]

As we move into REM sleep, where the extended narratives characteristic of REM dreaming occur, our heart begins to beat faster and our breathing rate increases. Our brain activates in ways surprisingly similar to the waking state, while our body musculature, apart from that involved in respiration and eye movement, becomes immobilised.

Towards the end of each 90-minute sleep cycle, we embark on ever-longer REM dreaming sessions, from around five minutes in the first 90-minute cycle to some 30 minutes of dreaming in the final cycle of the night. But for the healing balm of nightly sleep across both NREM and REM stages, before long a person would develop signs of mental distress: depression, anxiety, paranoia and, not least, hallucinations.

Thus, whenever the long-distance runner Dean Karnazes ran 100 miles over a period of three days and nights *consecutively*, he began to hallucinate. Karnazes inherited a genetic characteristic that – combined with his extensive training regime – inhibits the accumulation of lactic acid in his muscles. After running continuously for 72 hours, he had to stop, not because of muscle fatigue, but because he would experience hallucinations.[23]

It seems likely that both NREM and REM sleep work synergistically in laying down memories that serve to underpin our sense of self.[24] This process is thought to begin before birth, during the third trimester, when we spend most of our time asleep in the womb. New technology has vividly shown that the eyelids of a baby asleep in the womb flicker in ways similar to REM sleep.[25] We might wonder about what kind of dreams are taking place: auditory impressions from the orchestra of sounds made by the mother's digestive, respiratory and circulatory systems, the rhythmic pulse of her heart, feelings sensed via the mother's nervous system, the muffled sounds of conversation, the mother's voice, her singing, fragments of music, modulations of lightness and darkness. During this period, half a million neurons are laid down *per day*, until at eight months the brain has formed 100 billion neurons – comparable to the number of stars in our galaxy!

Babies born prematurely need to sleep up to 75 per cent of the time, and studies tracking the EEG of premature infants suggest a positive correlation between the proportion of REM sleep and better cognitive outcomes.[26] Consequently, neonatal units have taken steps to improve the quality of the infant's sleep: lights dimmed in the night, routine procedures completed around wake times, and, touchingly, 'kangaroo care', whereby the baby sleeps at an upright angle, lying on the parent's bare chest.[27] Newborns spend nearly half of their sleep time in REM sleep compared with 20 per cent for adults.

If we look at the neurochemistry of the dream state in adults, we find a curious paradox: as areas of the brain involved in processing emotional memories become 30 per cent more active than in the waking state,[28] there is a surprising drop in the level of the chemical noradrenaline, normally associated with the body's fight-or-flight response.[29] Based on these findings, Walker has proposed that dreams comprise a 'Biological Theatre' for 'overnight therapy'.[30] He hypothesises that the fall in noradrenaline during REM dreaming dampens down our emotional reactivity, thereby allowing us to work through painful emotions, for the most part without waking.[31]

The nocturnal therapy of dreams can be compared with psychotherapy, where, with the support of the therapist, we can safely recall and re-engage with deeply emotional memories. At the same time, the therapy encourages a reflective awareness that gives us a more objective perspective on life. Drawing on language of the theatre, Carl Jung remarked that 'if the observer [the dreamer] understands that his own drama is being performed on this inner stage, he cannot be indifferent to the plot and its denouement.'[32] As 'Biological Theatre', the dream, coupled with subsequent dreamwork, provides a new and therapeutic perspective on challenging emotional content, enabling us to better integrate the emotion of the dream scenario and to work more confidently with its meaning.

Sometimes, however, the dreamer can feel overwhelmed by the emotional pain of a real-life trauma revisited in a dream, especially a recurring dream that awakens the dreamer repeatedly, as happens in cases of post-traumatic stress disorder (PTSD). In this condition, due to the intensity of traumatic flashbacks, noradrenaline levels become unusually heightened. The drug prazosin, normally used for treating high blood pressure, additionally supresses the effect of noradrenaline. On the basis of his research on REM sleep, Walker trialled the use of prazosin in cases of PTSD, and it is now recognised as an approved treatment for recurrent nightmares.

Therapeutic dreamwork, which has also been shown to be successful in the treatment of PTSD patients, gives people a sense of mastery over their nightmares without the use of medication. This matters because two thirds of those who have distressing nightmares mistakenly believe they can't do anything to change them.[33] One of the most widely recognised interventions, Imagery Rehearsal Therapy (IRT), focuses on re-scripting a person's dreams, thus transforming the experience. Essentially, the person having nightmares rewrites the dream narrative by changing the dream in any way they would like and rehearsing this new version in their imagination at brief interludes during the day and before sleep.

One of the groundbreaking studies in this field, which looked at the dreams of PTSD patients who had suffered sexual abuse, reported dramatic improvements; not only did the participants' nightmare severity and frequency lessen, so did their PTSD symptoms.[34] Nearly 50 per cent of those who completed the study reported using imagery for dealing with problems in waking life.[35] Researchers have attributed the participants' sense of mastery over their nightmares as being at the 'heart' of the therapy's success.[36] As we shall see in Chapter Nine, 'Nightmares: From Fear to Freedom', mastery *over our own fear* also proves key in facing nightmares.

For a small number of people, vivid or frightening dreams give rise to strange or out-of-character behaviour while still asleep, including, rarely, acts of self-harm or violence towards others.[37] Such sleep disorders, known as parasomnias, some-times stem from brain lesions or chemical imbalances. If your dream life drastically interferes in unwanted ways with your sleep and your waking life, a medically qualified specialist can help you rule out or identify biological causes that may require specific treatment.

In contrast to the parasomnias, normal REM dreaming provides for neural networks to reconstruct emotionally significant events,[38] the theme of a dream often reflecting emotions from the previous day, while details of the dream hold important personal, symbolic meanings.[39] Here we can pause in our journey through the sleep cycle to consider how this might play out in an actual dream. I will illustrate this process with a dream of my own that I had shortly after my marriage of 18 years ended in divorce:

> *I dream that I own an open-plan, two-storey log cabin. One of my brothers has come for a visit. He suddenly tells me the house in on fire, so we have to get out, but that I have time to get a couple of things. I feel sad, but also glad to think, 'Well, I can start over again.' The only 'thing' that I want to take is my doll Honeybunch that had belonged to my mother. My brother and I are on the second floor, and I can see the flames lapping up from floor to ceiling, but do not feel their heat. I begin to feel worried about how we will get out if the stairs are on fire. Will we have to jump? Then I awake.*

Honeybunch has been part of my life as long as I can remember. When my mother was seven, she received Honeybunch as a gift from her own mother for Christmas. At that time, my grandparents had lost their family home because of financial losses during the Great Depression. Grandmother cut off her long thick curls and sold them to buy each of her three daughters a doll. She had a dollmaker weave strands of her cut hair to make each doll's cascading curls.

Honeybunch has always felt precious to me, but since my mother's death, she gives me a tangible connection not only to my mother but to all the women in my family tree. She also puts me in touch with the innocent ideals of childhood.

The spontaneous appearance of Honeybunch in my dream connected me to a quiet sense of loving confidence, exactly the feeling that I needed to be reminded of at a time in my life requiring me to take yet another life-changing leap into the unknown. Her silent presence acts as a symbolic reminder of where I have come from, and of my need to remain close to an earthly sense of time and place, as well as a heavenly sense of hope for what is to come.

In the dream, my mind seemingly sifts instantly through all my belongings and their meaningful associations as I discern what choice I need to make before the fire consumes my belongings. I remain calm, for I feel the fire not only destroys but also purifies. Curiously, the fire does not feel hot. Somehow, my dreaming mind created this scenario, along with actors, actions and symbols, scripted perfectly for me. In the short term, this dream helped to lift my mood. In the long term, the dream, and others on a similar theme, supported my emotional recovery from the divorce. This experience of mine anecdotally supports research by Rosalind Cartwright suggesting that, over time, REM dreaming of a specific emotional trauma such as divorce can help to resolve the feelings associated with the waking life event.[40]

As the dream foregrounds, the highly charged emotional content of a dream can be a powerful catalyst for decision-making. How would it be if we could only use formal logic to list, categorise and organise data? We would endlessly weigh up every course of action without being able to draw on the intuitive 'gut feelings' we need when deciding to take a course of action in the world.[41]

Having to make do without the guidance of 'gut feelings' occurs in people who have damage to the basal ganglia, located in the brain's limbic system, fundamental to process-ing emotions. Studies have shown that such people suffer from a neurological condition called auto-activation deficit (AAD) that causes them to be apathetic, lacking in imagination and emotional range.[42] Nor can they take initiative or make decisions. Upon being awoken from REM sleep in the sleep laboratory, people with AAD report unimaginative dreams, with only basic representations of actions and an absence of feelings. In contrast, when the basal ganglia function normally, the limbic system works in tandem with areas of the brain associated with cognition and intuition, enabling dream imagery to facilitate decision-making processes.[43]

In lucid dreams, when we become aware in a dream that we dream, decision-making comes powerfully to the fore. Research indicates that over half of us will recall having had a lucid dream at least once in our lives, but that fewer than a quarter of us will regularly have lucid dreams.[44] Later, in Chapter Ten, 'Journeys into the Deep: Lucid Dreaming and Lucid Surrender', we shall see that our capacity for lucid dreaming can be cultivated.

Importantly, in lucidity the dreamer can explore the nature of dreams consciously and in 'real time'. Lucid dreams provide a dream laboratory for exploration of our personal psychology and of transpersonal awareness. As Jung observes, 'The dream is a little hidden door in the innermost and most secret recesses of the soul, opening into that cosmic night which was psyche long before there was any ego-consciousness, and which will remain psyche no matter how far our ego-consciousness extends.'[45]

Prefiguring this vision of the transpersonal, as early as the sixteenth century the alchemist Heinrich Khunrath called the visionary dream space 'The Theatre of Secrets'.[46] In Khunrath's view, the dream 'theatre' served as both an alchemical laboratory, where the dreamer could experience the 'labours' associated with the features of everyday life, and as an 'oratory', a hallowed space, in which the sacred quality of human spiritual nature could be realised.[47]

Such has been my own experience in lucidity, as in the following dream in which I become fully aware that I dream and so make a conscious choice:

> *I swim in a deep pool of golden water. Although I*
> *swim underwater effortlessly, I suddenly become*
> *concerned about my breathing. In a panic, I try to*

get up to the water's surface. But as I become lucid,
I recall that in the spiritual teachings of Emanuel
Swedenborg, water symbolises spiritual knowledge.
Then I understand that what appears to my mind
as 'water', a kind of liquid amber, actually is Spirit,
expressed in golden light. I remind myself how when
we use 'inner breathing'[48] in the 'Spirit' we can breathe
in this 'water'. With this in mind, I realise there should
be no problem in breathing, for the water itself is no
less than the inner breath of the Spirit. Suddenly, I can
begin to breathe calmly again, and so I swim in the
depths of Being with a feeling of absolute delight,
until I awake.

In this dream, my recognition of the essential, spiritual quality of the 'water' frees me to overcome my fear and to stay in what becomes a healing, rather than frightening, experience.

In ancient Greece, on the entrance of the Temple of Apollo, the words 'Know Thyself' were inscribed. Dreams invite us to enter into this knowing. Laden with feelings and meaningful subjective qualities, dreams can feel more real than 'real'. In dreams, we come alive in ways that may beguile, frighten, enliven, inspire, puzzle, empower, guide and heal us. We wake up to the mysteries of Being!

When we begin to pay attention to our dreams and learn how to feel at home in their subtle domain, it feels as though we can begin to 'breathe' underwater. Unconstrained by the usual earthly limitations of time and space, our dreams may seem irrational from the perspective of the logical mind and yet, paradoxically, their creative interplay helps to maintain the 'rational' consciousness of everyday reality by consolidating memories, modulating our emotions, and effectively shaping how we construct a personal sense of our self with a past, present and future.[49] Whether we are conscious of it or not, the process of dreaming thereby contributes to our sense of who we are.

Having undertaken our creative exploration into the depths of nightly sleep and dreams, we can now swim back up through the waters of the realm of sleep towards the surface, where, above us, the light of waking consciousness dances. As the levels of melatonin in our blood decrease and the surge of nocturnal neuro-chemistry in our brains subsides, we move steadily towards full wakefulness, then gently open our eyes and awake from sleep, bringing with us the rich potential of our dreams, to know ourselves more feelingly and to live our humanity more fully.

Chapter Three

Dreams, Trees and Their Roots in the Imaginal Mind: Transforming Waking Life

> *The greatest achievement was at first and for a time a dream. The oak sleeps in the acorn, the bird waits in the egg, and in the highest vision of the soul a waking angel stirs. Dreams are the seedlings of realities.*[1]
>
> – James Allen

Do we dream or is there a dream dreaming us? In response to this question, I have chosen trees – what we know about them from the sciences, philosophy, religious traditions, alchemy and the arts – to open the way to an experience of the creative imagination expressed through dreams, what I shall refer to as the Imaginal Mind. The philosopher Ludwig Wittgenstein asks, 'Can someone teach me that I see a tree? And what is a tree? And what is seeing?'[2] We can ask the same questions of dreams as we consider how to see our dreams anew. Learning to become attentive to the Imaginal Mind – in which the intellect and sense perception meet – deepens our understanding of dreams and life. The Imaginal Mind invites us to enter into relationship with Nature –

rather than observing it at a distance, as an object outside of us, a 'thing' apart.

To give you an example of what I mean, I ask you to picture a tree in your mind's eye. It may be an actual tree that you are familiar with, one on whose branches you climbed on or played under as a child, or one in whose shade you rested in as an adult. Alternatively, you can choose whatever tree comes to mind – a willow bent tenderly towards a river; an apple tree bearing humble gifts; a weathered oak embracing the sky; a majestic redwood whose tip pierces the highest heavens. As you look at the tree, take a deep breath and exhale, then give yourself a moment to experience the tree's scent, its touch and texture, the coolness of its shadow, the colour of its leaves. With each exhalation, focus on the qualities the tree holds for you – its grace, simplicity, strength, determination. With your in-breath, draw those qualities deeply into yourself.

Now imagine yourself stepping into the tree and taking on its form – your feet rooted in the ground, your body extended upward as a trunk, your arms branched out, your thoughts unfurled like leaves, sensitive to your environment. How does it feel to become a wakeful tree? How does your viewpoint change? When you are ready, imagine stepping out of the tree and looking at it afresh.

By re-imagining the tree in this way, you may have become more aware of the tree's rootedness in time and place, the uniqueness of its shape, its symbiotic relationship to its environment or possibly the threats the environment posed. Perhaps the tree stood alone and felt self-sufficient, or maybe desired companionship. Perhaps it aimed to reach higher than the trees around it or felt unprotected, battered by recent storms. Did the tree seem healthy or in need of water and light? Did you see the tree with new eyes? Whatever you sensed in the tree, before you read on, take a moment to consider how that tree relates to your own concerns, hopes and dreams, how becoming the tree can heighten the way you feel about yourself, your life – and trees!

A waking-life visualisation, such as our reflections on a tree, enables us to access the liminal state of dream-like consciousness. The word 'liminal' derives from the Latin *limen*, associated with a threshold such as a doorsill or windowsill, delineating where worlds appear to touch – the shoreline, where the sea and land meet; dawn and dusk poised between day and night; moments between sleep and waking; transitions of life and death. When we reflect on a dream or re-enter it imaginatively, we re-engage with the consciousness animating it. Moving in and out of such liminality through imagery comes more naturally to some of us than others, but it can be learned with guidance.[3]

As we enter this liminal state mindfully, what we normally perceive as inanimate objects may take on a life of their own. We imagine ourselves as a tree and we ourselves are re-imagined. In his moving book *I and Thou*,[4] the philosopher Martin Buber observes that when we consider a tree we can look at it as an object to be classified, owned or used, or we can enter into relationship with the tree in a *gestalt* awareness of the tree's 'form and structure, its colours and chemical composition, its intercourse with the elements and the stars...'[5] Through mutual relation, something we generally think of as inanimate, or a person we may have depersonalised, becomes a 'Thou' to which we relate, rather than an 'It' that we simply objectify, unaware of our deep-rooted interconnectedness. The same applies to our dreams.

Trees have literal roots, whereas our human 'roots' are metaphorical, yet they intertwine in the Imaginal Mind. Both need nourishment, as the following dream, had at a time when I felt creatively 'blocked', suggests:

*I dream of a tree planted in a large wooden tub
on the street where I grew up. The tree, of a good
size, looks rather beleaguered and the soil dry.
The container too small. A woman looks on and
comments on how the tree needs a great deal of
water. But she has poured something dark on it.
'What's that?' I wonder. 'Did you pour cola on it?'
'Yes,' she replies, 'the caffeine and sugar will wake it
up.' I strongly disagree with this as I can see the soil
is dry and needs turning. I get a bucket of water and
pour it into the container. Then, I turn the wet soil
over with a trowel. While doing this, I am surprised
to notice some clothes and linen tangled among
the tree's roots. Up come objects from my past, all
associated with a difficult time in my life. I wonder
that the tree could live with its roots blocked by these
things. But most of all, I sense the tree's gratitude at
having the soil watered, turned and cleared. I realise
that I now need to find a more spacious place to
plant the tree so that it can continue to grow.*

The dream indicated to me that I was literally drinking too much caffeine and had become dehydrated! But when I dream of a need for water, this also suggests to me a need for a more soulful, less pragmatic, 'living-waters' perspective – time to rest, reflect and recharge. Through the dream, I was reminded that, earlier in the day, I had felt rather sorry for the trees planted in a stand on a London pavilion, but, even so, had thoughtlessly poured my leftover tea into the planter as there was nowhere else to empty it. Immediately, I winced at the memory, aware that I had not helped the tree at all! The dream reflected my own thoughtless behaviour. I hadn't given the tree or myself what was needed.

The dream tree also mirrored my personal need to have good deep soil in which to put down roots. Reflecting on the dream imagery, I realised that some leftover thoughts from the past limited the tree's growth as well as my own. As a whole, the dream presented me with a psychological task: to 'clear out' old ways of thinking about the past and myself in order to make space for new, creative growth in fresh soil. Just as I had sensed the dream tree's gratitude for being tended to, I, too, could be grateful for the dream's guidance.

When we reflect on our dreams using our creative imagination, elements of our personal history and psychology, woven into the dream imagery, come alive with the meaning and mutuality of relationship, opening the door to the Imaginal World, the *Mundus Imaginalis*, of dreams.[6] The French philosopher Henry Corbin proposed this term to refer to a dimension of experience described by Islamic mystics as the *'alam-al-mithal,* the World of the Imagination, entered in dreams. This 'world' arises from the interaction of our inner awareness with our human physicality, creating a bridge between our subjective reality and the 'objective' world. The Imaginal World of our dreams, in contrast to how we use imagination in the waking state, has a heightened reality all its own, yet speaks directly to our lived experience.[7]

Studies in the area of perception and insight hint at why dreams may feel even more real than the merely imaginary. In the first instance, to understand how visual perception works in dreams, researchers compared the way the eye moves during REM dreaming as it follows an object in a lucid dream with how the eye moves in an imagined scenario in waking life. In the physical world, when we visually follow an object, such as a leaf blowing in the wind, our eyes move in a smooth movement, but when we simply imagine the same sequence when awake, the eyes move in tiny, saccadic jerks. The results suggest that in REM dreaming the eye moves as it does when tracking objects in the waking world,[8] contributing to an experience of a 'world' we visually perceive as 'real'.

In the second instance, to investigate claims that the consideration of dreams results in personal insights, researchers compared the power of insights gained from dream recall versus the recollection of a waking-life event. The research indicated that when people consider a recent dream in a therapeutic process, they gain *more* personal insights than when they reflect on a recent event from waking life in a similarly therapeutic context.[9] These findings could lend credence to the idea that the increase of activity in areas of the brain associated with the emotions during REM dreaming, coupled with the decrease of sensory input, gives dream content more immediacy than merely imagined or recalled events.

As part of a study on visual imagery in dreams by sleep researcher Helder Bértolo, volunteers were asked to draw scenes from their dreams. One participant sketched what he had seen: a beach where two children played in the sand sheltered from the sun by a palm tree, while gulls flew overhead and a boat passed in the distance. This scene might seem unremarkable until we learn that the dreamer had been congenitally blind since birth. This prompted Bértolo to question how it could be possible to have such visual imagery without visual perception.[10] While recognising that the blind draw on other sensory input to create mental representations, Bértolo wondered whether the level of detail of the pictorial representations signified a *visual experience* as well as spatial properties.

According to subsequent research, because those born blind lack the visual input needed to create visual memories, they have dreams that mostly feature the senses of sound, touch, smell and taste.[11] However, dream-based depictions drawn by the congenitally blind raise fundamental questions about the nature of visual perception without visual input and how we 'see' in a dream. A person born blind may experience themselves as 'seeing' in a dream – as one participant in Bértolo's study testified, he felt reluctant to tell people that he could see in dreams because he had previously been told that he 'didn't see things, he just felt them'.[12]

Further research has confirmed that the dreams of the blind and sighted primarily share similar types of emotional and thematic content.[13] It would appear that both the blind and the sighted share 'inner sight', perceived by the 'eye' of the creative imagination in dreams. The feeling-toned, relational quality of the Imaginal Mind draws on forms of knowing that are deeper than the mere products of sense perception. As we consider the nature of dreams, we will, as Buber advised, 'keep to the meaning of the relation', remembering that in dreams, as in waking life, 'relation is mutual'.[14]

Rather than thinking of dream scenarios as bizarre because they bend our ordinary experience of space-time and befuddle our expectations, we can appreciate how our dreams challenge us to think *and* to feel 'outside the box'. We can do so by attending to our right brain's metaphoric and associative qualities, characteristic of the intuitive, creative mind, rather than the left brain's more linear and rational approach.

The neuroscientist and psychiatrist Iain McGilchrist calls 'the right-brain's understanding of the world' one that arises from 'empathy and intersubjectivity as the ground of consciousness'. He notes that when we look at the world with a right-brain perspective, we hold an awareness of 'the importance of an open, patient attention to the world, as opposed to a wilful, grasping attention'.[15] Describing the 'fundamentally asymmetrical' differences between how the brain's right and left hemispheres perceive the world, he observes, 'These are not different ways of *thinking about* the world: they are different ways of *being in* the world.'[16] This statement holds just as true for dreams.

Since the right brain becomes more active during dreaming,[17] along with areas of the brain associated with the processing of emotions, it follows that we can usefully learn to access a more right-brain *way of being* by re-engaging with our dream-feelings through dreamwork. Sigmund Freud, in his classic work *The Interpretation of Dreams*, refers to dream images as 'dream-thoughts'.[18] I prefer to use the term *dream-feelings* to highlight our emotional response to dream imagery.

On the subject of dream imagery, Joseph Campbell has explained: 'In dreams things are not as single, simple, and separate as they seem, the logic of Aristotle fails, and what is *not-A* may indeed be *A*.'[19] A similarly metaphoric way of thinking enabled Einstein to imagine travelling along a beam of light, relativise time in a space-bound elevator, and envision the fabric of space-time curved like a trampoline weighed down with a bowling ball.[20] When Einstein was asked if he trusted more to his imagination than knowledge, he answered: 'I am enough of an artist to draw freely upon my imagination. Imagination is more important than knowledge. Knowledge is limited. Imagination encircles the world.'[21] Such intuitive knowing has significant implications not only for how we view our dreams (and trees) but also for how we share the earth with them and with each another. For, as the psychologist James Hillman reminds us, the 'imagination is not merely a human faculty but an activity of soul to which the human imagination bears witness.'[22]

Long before the recognition of the 'observer effect' in quantum physics, in which the mere presence of an observer changes the experimental outcome, alchemists of old recognised the influence of their state of mind upon the objects of investigation. In their pursuit of gold – a quest both material and spiritual, and one that would grant immortality – alchemists explored the intersection between the human imagination and the world of matter. The seminal alchemical text the *Emerald Tablet*, or the *Tabula Smaragdina*, attributed to the legendary Hermes Trismegistus, enigmatically states: 'What is above is like what is below, and what is below is like that which is above.'[23]

This verse expresses the alchemical axiom of correspondences between subjective experience and objective 'reality'. For the alchemists, the spiritual world literally enlivens the material world, the human capacity for creative imagination mirroring that of the Supreme Creator's divine or 'theophanic' imagination.[24] The alchemist Heinrich Khunrath boldly claimed: 'He who denies true dreams, speaks in a dream.'[25] Dream revelations, according to Khunrath, can reveal the secrets of the created universe. Experiential knowing garnered from the Imaginal Mind gives insights and a deep reflective awareness in dreams no less than life.

In a modern society heavily focused on productivity and outcome measures, the liminal state has struggled to maintain its historical status as an important means of healing body, heart and mind. Yet this imaginative faculty, with roots deep in our shared humanity, remains essential to our wellbeing. For example, during the visualisation of your tree, had you been connected to a HeartMath device that monitors your heart rate variability, you would most likely find that as your breath slowed and deepened, your heart rhythm became more 'coherent'.

Your heart sends these signals to your brain through nerves, hormones and, importantly, its biomagnetic field (an estimated 5,000 times stronger than the brain's).[26] These impulses in turn synchronise or 'entrain' your brainwaves with your heart's rhythm,[27] quieting your thoughts and lowering cell-damaging levels of stress-induced cortisol and oxidants. Such research lends support to Blaise Pascal's insight made over 400 years ago that 'the heart has its reasons which reason does not know.'[28]

The researchers who developed HeartMath have described the heart's intelligence this way:

> ... the intelligent flow of awareness and insight that we experience once the mind and emotions are brought into balance and coherence through a self-initiated process. This form of intelligence is experienced as direct, intuitive knowing that manifests in thoughts and emotions that are beneficial for ourselves and others.[29]

The heart/brain connection helps us find solutions where the logical mind has reached a dead end,[30] including through the 'direct, intuitive knowing', the 'heart intelligence' gained when we slow down and breathe deeply, taking time in our daily life to work imaginatively with our dreams and the feelings they arouse.

Additional research has shown that in sleep, our breathing gradually slows up to 10 per cent over a period of several hours, whereas in meditation, the rate decreases by 20 to

40 per cent in few minutes.[31] Such changes in breathing rate could be one reason that when a person meditatively does a visualisation or reflects on a dream, it can feel as if they are dreamed rather than dreaming.

The liminality between dreams and waking life is revealed in a biblical dream from nearly 3,000 years ago, recounted by an ancient king of Babylon. The dream puzzled the king, so he asked for his court magicians to discern its meaning:

> *Here is my dream; interpret it for me. These are the visions I saw while lying in bed: I looked, and there before me stood a tree in the middle of the land. Its height was enormous. The tree grew large and strong and its top touched the sky; it was visible to the ends of the earth. Its leaves were beautiful, its fruit abundant, and on it was food for all. Under it the wild animals found shelter, and the birds lived in its branches; from it every creature was fed...*

> *I looked, and there before me was a holy one, a messenger, coming down from heaven. He called in a loud voice: 'Cut down the tree and trim off its branches; strip off its leaves and scatter its fruit. Let the animals flee from under it and the birds from its branches. But let the stump and its roots, bound with iron and bronze, remain in the ground, in the grass of the field.*

Let him be drenched with the dew of heaven, and let
him live with the animals among the plants of the
earth. Let his mind be changed from that of a man
and let him be given the mind of an animal, till seven
times pass by for him.[32]

Let us take a moment to consider the tree itself, radiant with life, and then imagine it struck down, reduced to a stump bound in metal. What kind of outside forces strike down trees? The 'holy one' in the dream gives no reason for the destruction, but, viewed from the perspective of this day and age, we can reflect on the human forces that have driven the destruction of Earth's natural environment and consider how these might relate to our individual experience.

In this biblical account, the prophet Daniel tells the king that the dream has come to reveal the thoughts of his heart.[33] He then gives the king a remarkably psychological interpretation – 'Your Majesty, you are that tree!' – thereby warning the king to be less prideful, to be kind to those he had oppressed and to acknowledge his dependence on a power greater than his own.[34] The king does not follow the advice and a year later loses his reason, spending seven years living in the fields, before regaining his health and kingdom. Traditionally, the king is seen to suffer because of his pride. However, in the 21st century, the dream also reminds us of the imbalances that cause destruction to individuals and the environment when humanity forgets that the mind is meant to serve the 'heart'.

Conversely, in our waking life, as in dreams, a tree, when perceived through the lens of the Imaginal Mind, can reflect something to us of our individual psyche, inviting us to connect our innermost self with the external world. The German poet Rainer Maria Rilke takes up this theme:

> … Oh, I who long to grow,
> I look outside, and within me grows the tree.[35]

Now, let me introduce you to a secluded grove on Hampstead Heath in London where there stands the 'Hollow Tree'. She has grown up at the end of a line of seven beech trees seeded in the late 1800s. Her hollow trunk is large enough to hold a few adults. To have a hollow of this size, she must have suffered a major wounding that exposed her heartwood. Yet she survived.

I have visited this tree during times of upheaval and exhaustion in my life. When in the tree's hollow, I press my open palms upon the swirls of time-smoothed ridges in her belly and instantly feel safe, soothed, re-energised, encompassed in a being whose lifespan will extend for generations beyond my own. The beauty of her hollow brings home the truth that wisdom is the fruit of suffering. From her empty womb comes new life, a feeling of rebirth. Now that I live too distant to visit the Hollow Tree regularly, a photo in my study reminds me of her. I simply recall her presence, and I feel better. In an embodied way, this tree centres me. In my mind and dreams, I often return to her. Her creative stillness speaks to me of my deep need for contemplation and creation. Her hollowness reminds me of my longings to have a child and the many other ways we bring life into the world out of emptiness.

The author Richard Powers, in his novel *The Overstory*, explores how trees shape our environments as active protagonists in our lives, possessing intelligence and personhood. Reflecting on the generosity and bounty of trees, especially the Douglas fir, whose roots bequeath its remaining store of nutrients with other trees before it dies, the narrator calls our arboreal cousins 'giving trees'.[36] A finely tuned individuality harmonises each tree into an interdependent system that far outreaches their individual limits.

Likewise, in the delightful book *The Hidden Life of Trees*, to which this book's title is an affectionate allusion, the forester Peter Wohlleben shares the discovery of a 'wood wide web'. This 'web', comprised of tree roots interwoven with fungi that can network an entire woodland, enables trees to transmit information about pests, dangers and food supplies.[37] More than this, older trees can support younger ones, and trees of different species help care for one another by sharing nutrients.[38] Through root systems that stretch well beyond their crown, trees can be said both to communicate and extend their social connections much as we do through the interconnectivity of our technology. Scientists in Finland and Hungary have found that trees also 'sleep'.[39] We might well wonder, 'Do trees dream too?'

Keeping in mind the maxim 'As above, so below', such earthly imagery serves as an apt analogy for the Jungian understanding of dreams as tapping into a collective unconscious psyche. Every night, our dreams mend and shape us, and, in turn, shape us all. While we sleep, our dreams breathe into us, transforming us in countless ways people long ago knew – ways that we, in our modern world, need to relearn. In dreams, we experience the properties of the Imaginal Mind, extending our range of thinking, feeling and action to include a realm of possibility that goes beyond the mind as generally perceived. As Jung noted, 'Everything that acts [on us] is actual.'[40]

Einstein's Theory of Relativity tells us that as space expands balloon-like around us, the centre of the universe coalesces around our individual perception; wherever we are *is* 'here', the centre – a viewpoint that, if taken to an extreme, can result in a dangerously egocentric focus. At the same time, as Einstein observed, the notion that we are separate from one another, and from the universe, comprises an 'optical delusion'.[41] This idea appears in a medieval teaching, most likely from Rabbinical sources, that describes 'God' as a being whose centre is everywhere and circumference nowhere.

Jung proclaims a similar message as regards dreams: 'All consciousness separates; but in dreams we put on the likeness of that more universal, truer, more eternal man dwelling in the darkness of primordial night.'[42] In a like manner, a dream reconsidered by the light of our creative imagination can give us the sense of being centred in ourselves and yet part of the entire universe. The Jungian analyst Edward Edinger shares one such dream had by a woman who, after many years of personal struggle and therapy, overcame her bitterness through acceptance:

I see a tree which had been struck by lightning.
However, it seemed that it had not been destroyed

completely, but that something of the electric power
had gone through the tree and into its surroundings
where it causes unusual fertility.[43]

Such dreams remind us that for all that we know about the universe, fundamental attributes such as space, time, light, consciousness, dreams, and even trees, remain mysterious to us.

The term 'Dreamtime', originally coined by ethnographer Francis Gillen,[44] is used to describe the Aboriginal people's sense of time as an eternal 'everywhere', a continuum in which the past lives in the present through relationship to the ancestors.[45] In this tradition, through dreams and ceremonies, Dreamtime can be accessed and lived. This perception of time offers what Mircea Eliade, a historian of religion, describes as a 'mode of being in the world', a 'sacred history' out of which humanity emerges.[46] In the words of one Kalahari Bushman, 'There is a dream dreaming us.'[47] Among the indigenous peoples of Australia we can find the belief that, prior to a child's conception, the spirit-child must appear to a parent in a dream.[48] Dreams, in a very tangible way, become 'the seedlings of realities'.[49]

In the Aboriginal cosmology of 'The Dreaming',[50] features of the natural landscape that mark important trails or locations take their shape from the form or actions of the ancestor who once walked and rested there. Thus, they believed that the Baobab tree, with its elephantine upper branches and swollen base, had been turned upside down by an angry god. The shamans of Australia, when sacrificing to the god of vegetation, kept the image of an inverted tree beside their altar.[51] The inverted tree graphically depicts creation as originating out of invisible forces and powers.

Similarly, trees have been used across cultures to represent consciousness. One of the earliest Hindu scriptures, *The Katha Upanishad,* describes an inverted tree, the Banyan Fig, whose extensive branching network, festooned with filaments of aerial roots, grows exponentially to contain 'all the worlds in it'.[52] Tradition has it that the Buddha extinguished the distractions of the mind under the heart-shaped leaves of the Bodhi Tree, a sacred fig tree, and so attained enlightenment. Medieval Jewish mystics imaged the relationship between the unity of *Ein Sof*, the Infinite Absolute, and the world of multiplicity as an inverted tree, the Kabbalah, the Tree of Life. Of this tree, the 13th-century *Book of Zohar* declares: 'Now this Tree of Life extends from above downwards, and is the sun which illuminates all.'[53]

Before humans developed fuel-dependent technologies, ancient cultures turned to trees not only for their usefulness – wood to warm and build, or bark, seeds and fruit to heal and sustain life. They also felt drawn to trees for a perceived connection to the spirit realm through the 'Tree of the World', the 'Cosmic Tree' at the centre of existence, a hallowed space.[54] The tree's trunk served as a representation of the *axis mundi*, the central axis of the world, with roots reaching to the Earth's core and branches to the highest heaven.

To this day, the *axis mundi* of the Cosmic Tree enables shamans to take a journey beyond the bounds of space and time, wherein the physical body becomes supplanted by a subtle body capable of bio-location, healing, and travel to other worlds. Siberian shamans access this tree as eagles, where they fly down to the underworld or ascend to the sky world. The shaman practices his or her vocation through two essential means: that of drumming and dreams. The shaman makes their drum out of wood from the sacred tree. The drumming, like the steady beat of the heart, puts the shaman into a trance state of liminality wherein visions and dreams occur, taking the shaman on ecstatic, spiritual journeys to find and heal their patient's soul.

Mircea Eliade, in his comprehensive work *Shamanism: Archaic Techniques of Ecstasy*, recounts the dream of one initiate who, ill with smallpox, dreamed he was taken to an island where he came upon a young birch tree:

> .... *It was the Tree of the Lord of the Earth. Beside it grew nine herbs, the ancestors of all the plants on earth. The tree was surrounded by seas, and in each of these swam a species of bird with its young. There were several kinds of ducks, a swan, and a sparrow-hawk. The candidate visited all the seas... After visiting the seas, the candidate raised his head and saw men of various nations... He heard voices: 'It has been decided that you shall have a drum (that is the body of a drum) from the branches of this tree.' He began to fly with the birds of the sea. As he left the shore, the Lord of the Tree called to him: 'My branch has just fallen; take it and make a drum that will serve you all your life.' The branch had three forks and*

the Lord of the Tree told him to make three drums
with it, to be kept by three women, each drum for a
special ceremony – the first for shamanizing women in
childbirth, the second for curing the sick, the third for
finding men lost in the snow....[55]

According to the mindset of classical physics, such dream journeys can be dismissed as nothing but imagination. Yet dreams have a reality all of their own, no matter how strange or surprising. We can be more accepting of the bizarre character of dreams when we take a look at the counterintuitive world of quantum mechanics, where sub-atomic particles exist everywhere and nowhere at the same time. Defying the laws of classical physics, particles pass through matter, influence one another at a distance and, when perceived or measured, change form. Such phenomena help us make sense of otherwise inexplicable scientific findings – for example, the discovery that photons of light can behave both as particles and waves, depending on how they are measured.[56]

Science acknowledges that the worlds of classical physics and quantum mechanics co-exist, though how they do so, remains a mystery. Yet, in our dreams, particularly lucid dreams, these worlds seemingly combine as we effortlessly walk through walls, defy gravity and fly, travel at the speed of light or even faster, influence other objects at a distance, and change our form.

Such experiences figure in a lucid dream shared with me by a man in his thirties, Michael, who had taken on a new and challenging position at work:

I am in a car driven by my friend driving through
sunny, autumnal, remote countryside – yellow leaves
on all the trees around us. She takes a turn to the
right and goes up a massive ramp and the car goes
flying vertically up into the air. Knowing we must
come crashing down, I escape from the car in mid-air.
Then, I realise I can control the direction of my fall,
and I swoop over towards some very tall trees. They
appear to be towering pines at first, but then the
one I go towards is like a giant dream-like weeping
willow. I grab onto its mostly bare reddish branches
and they lower me gently towards the ground.

Michael became aware that the usual laws of classical physics did not apply in dreams and so acted accordingly. His dream awareness helps him to think 'outside the box', even as it reflects a corresponding openness to new possibilities. He awoke from this dream feeling that, no matter the challenges ahead, he would have a 'safe landing'.

In the evocative poem 'Two Trees' by William Butler Yeats, we are invited to gaze into our hearts, where 'the holy tree' stands.[57] Yeats bids us to look upon this tree rather upon the 'bitter glass' that reflects all which makes us weary of life. At times when we despair, dreams can help remind us of the 'holy tree' that Yeats described in very actual ways. One such dream came at a time in my life when I suffered personal grief, having to accept that I would not be able to have a child. In the dream, I become lucid, aware that I am dreaming, leading to a heightened sense of clarity and beauty. The dreamscape disappears, and it feels as if I am carried a vast distance across an endless space of shimmering black light:

> ... *spread across an infinite expanse of shining*
> *darkness there emerge concentric rings of intense*
> *red. A desire to immerse myself in the red takes*
> *hold, and I wonder if the colour green will appear*
> *next. But instead bands of deep purple fill the*
> *outer rings. 'Red and purple,' I think to myself.*
> *'These are the colours of royalty: This is the*
> *Divine!' But then, rather than staying focused on*
> *the wondrous feelings aroused by the light form,*
> *my thoughts turn towards wondering what will*
> *happen next! I know from many previous lucid*
> *dreams that when I think about what is happening,*
> *doing so often breaks my concentration, thus*
> *ending the dream, but if I can direct my mind*
> *towards a focus on the deep feelings present in the*
> *dream, the lucid dream continues. As I struggle*
> *to focus my mind by singing a sacred song and*
> *breathing deeply, from the centre of the concentric*
> *rings there emerges a branching tree of red. 'The*
> *Tree of Life!' I exclaim inwardly. The branches rise*
> *up and reach out to include me in their reach until*
> *I feel lifted up on the red leafy branches and the*
> *blackness into another dream.*

This dream heralded an upsurge of creativity in my own life. I literally felt supported and energised by this dream's branching imagery, which evokes the 'holy branches' so beautifully described by Yeats. The experience renewed my hope in life. The emotional intelligence of the heart enlivens this dream and helps to focus my mind, throwing into question René Descartes' famous dictum, 'I think, therefore I am' – a statement that treats the mind as separate from the body and feeling.

In the provocative book *Descartes' Error*, Antonio Damasio draws on discoveries in neurology to challenge this dualism. Instead he argues for the inclusion of the bodily sensation of feelings – refined by learning and experience, and thereby shaping our emotional response – as the essential basis of our reasoning power.[58] In this case, perhaps it would be better to say to ourselves: 'I am conscious, therefore I am' – understanding consciousness as including not only perception, memory and cognition, but also, importantly, emotions, feelings, creative imagination and dreams.

Cultivating our capacity for creative imagination is enhanced by our dream life. For myself, most mornings I get up early to make a cup of tea and return to bed, where I spend time writing down my dreams and reflecting on them. If you don't already keep a record of your dreams, then choose a notebook and, each morning, before getting started on the day, take a few minutes to write your dreams down, even if you only recall dream fragments – an image, colour or feeling. If you can't recall anything, note how that feels or reflect on a dream you had in the past and think about how it might relate to the present. You can also consider a recent event in waking life *as if* it were a dream.

By daily reflecting on your dreams, you gaze into your heart. First note down how you felt when you awoke from the dream – the questions the dream causes you to ask and the questions it might answer. Describe the scene, setting and atmosphere – the emotional qualities, sequence of events, your sense of self, of others, and the dream imagery, including light, colour and darkness. Consider how the dream might mirror the day's events and emotions, as well as those from the past and possible future. Do you wish you had acted differently in the dream? Is there a part of the dream you would like to revisit and engage with again? If so, what might happen if the dream continued? Were there moments of dream awareness when you recognised how something in the dream corresponded to or differed from waking life? The chapters that follow will give you new ways to consider each of these questions with more clarity and consideration.

When you attend to your dreams, you will begin to see a reciprocal response from your dream life.[59] As you work through their psychological content, not only will your dream recall become clearer, your dream content will also become less confused and more readily understandable.

Like a tree whose extended roots stabilise and draw nutrients from the soil into branching leaves, the deep emotional connection and expansive insights that a dream inspires reinvigorate and transform life. Given the myriad correspondences between how we perceive trees and dreams when we view them with the attributes of the Imaginal Mind, perhaps the best answer to the question posed at the start of this chapter, 'Do we dream or is there a dream dreaming us?', can be stated as a paradox: We *both* dream *and* are dreamed into being.

Chapter Four

The Language of Rocks, Stones and Minerals: A Case Illustration

Cleave the wood and I am there;
lift up the stone and you shall find me there.[1]

– The Gospel of Thomas

Have you ever had a dream that filled you with such emotion, you awoke in the middle of the dream with the dream 'unfinished'? Waking up may momentarily relieve the tension, but the interrupted dream leaves a residue of feeling that lingers, and might even have left you wondering, 'What would have happened if I hadn't woken up?' An unfinished dream seeks resolution like a stone that will roll downhill until it comes to rest.

We have been hardwired to wake up from sleep when we sense an emergency, whether from within a dream or from an external source. Waking up at moments of extreme emotional tension in a dream happens often. Whatever emotion the dream evokes, we need to pay attention to the feeling – whether anger, sadness, anxiety, guilt, or even ecstasy – because our response has shown us that the emotion feels hard for us to bear. When we resist the feeling, it blocks our life energy, the pressure building up until it breaks through in a powerful surge of emotion portended by dream imagery. Typically, in order to avoid facing the difficult feeling, we wake up, as happens in the course of the following dream brought to me by a middle-aged man called Mark:

I stand opposite a dark, ominous rock face of granite hundreds of feet high. Unseen flood waters gather behind the rock, the water's force threatening to split the rock face down the middle. People I feel responsible for have gathered in passageways carved into the cliffside. I wave my arms and shout in a desperate bid to shepherd them all to a safe distance, for I know the rock will give way and the waters will engulf them all. Just then, I wake up, my heart pounding!

An unfinished dream like this one calls for an awakening to our inner state and beckons us to acknowledge deep feelings and so find emotional balance. By working with a dream guide in the waking state we can re-enter the dream imaginatively, undertaking a 'waking dream', exploring associations and allowing the dream to play itself out.[2] I invite you to engage with this dream experience, as did Mark, with my guidance.

Like the rock face in the dream, collapsing or dissolving forms, particularly those associated with permanence, cause great emotional distress if we associate their impact with personal loss, extreme vulnerability, or physical death.[3] When we understand such dreams therapeutically, the intense feelings focus our attention on what needs to shift in our lives and points towards the life-changing energy that can be freed up when we do. The more powerful the natural force depicted – floodwaters, a tidal wave, an avalanche, a mighty wind or fire, the more potential life-energy it contains. How to harness and transform that energy remains our challenge.

In this instance, Mark associated the rock face with his fear of feelings that might overwhelm him, leaving him and those he cared for vulnerable. Viewed from a psychodynamic perspective, the rock may symbolise a defence against the natural flow of feelings that, if allowed, could also bring a creative influx of life energies. Mark had recently met a woman to whom he felt drawn, yet he was resisting the attraction. If the rock face in the dream could speak, it might well say, 'Let your heart open under the influence of love. You don't need to be afraid.' The presence of 'living waters' breaking through the stone in the dream suggests that a profound inner change had already been initiated, a softening of the heart. This dream heralds the alchemical injunction, 'Perform no operation 'til all be made water.'[4]

Jung drew on the teachings of the medieval alchemists to explore how alchemical processes reflected the transformative power of dream imagery. The alchemists were fascinated by the formation of iron, gold and diamonds within stone. By heating base metals from the solid to liquid state, they sought to assist nature by accelerating this natural process of transformation, thereby freeing Nature from its base aspect to a more subtle spiritual state. The alchemists, in spiritualising matter, also believed they could work a similar transformation on their own being.[5] Their operations aimed to spiritualise matter and materialise spirit. While working to perfect Nature in this way, the alchemists were completing the *Magnum Opus*, the Great Work of alchemy, on themselves. Although to the modern mind this endeavour may seem archaic, from the standpoint of modern physics it can be found mirrored in the words of the British physicist Sir James Jeans, who compared the creation of the universe to 'the materialisation of thought'.[6]

In the alchemical model proposed by Jung, we follow a similar path when we work with the emotional content of our dreams. In this model, the dissolving of old ego-structures represents a recognisable stage of our inner transformation – a *darkening*, to use an alchemical term – when our mental conditioning and complexes – our hardened identifications and defensive positions – no longer serve us. This darkening involves the transpersonal journey of 'breakdown to breakthrough'. The 16th-century alchemist Gerhard Dorn articulates a comparable idea when he states: 'Transform yourself from dead stones into living philosophic stones.'[7] This entails opening ourselves to a deeper understanding of our essential nature.

Developmentally, life events that force our hearts to expand – even if painfully – ultimately forge positive ends because they increase our capacity to feel deeply and to face our fears. What we perceive as a shattering crisis – a splitting open of the rock, as in the dream – holds the opportunity for inner growth and creative life change by requiring us to develop qualities and skills that have remained latent so that we can work through the crisis and rebuild our lives. The discovery of this new capacity can be compared to the alchemist's quest for gold.

Even changes that we may think of as positive, such as having a child or falling in love, can shatter our normal ego identifications. To the ego, such change, requiring the 'death' of a way of being, can feel life-threatening – and no wonder! But we must remember every such 'death' brings new life, a 'resurrection'. The historian of religion Mircea Eliade explains:

> Every 'death' is at once a reintegration of cosmic night and pre-cosmological chaos ... darkness expresses the dissolution of forms, the return to the seminal stage of existence. Initiatory death and mystic darkness thus also possess a cosmological significance; they signify the reintegration of the 'first state', the germinal state of matter, and the 'resurrection' corresponds to the cosmic creation.[8]

In how we respond to this process, Jung noted that the degree of fear, the intensity of the 'feeling-tone' present, indicates the proportion of energy or effort required to shift our conscious attitude for real life-change to occur.[9] A Jungian therapist might see in the dark rock face pictured in the dream a representation of what Jung calls the Shadow,[10] a repository for all those painful feelings and thoughts that we supress from consciousness. There, out of our awareness, they harden like stone. Then, a dream may come that says, as the prophet Ezekiel taught, 'I will give you a new heart and put a new spirit in you; I will remove from you your heart of stone and give you a heart of flesh.'[11]

Surprisingly, the simple act of acknowledging our fears dissolves their power. This recognition marks an important first step towards transformation. In the case described here, taking this step enabled Mark to see how his overwhelming sense of responsibility took precedence over his capacity to stay with his feelings, which, like the unseen water in the dream, felt threatening. The loosening of the rock in this dream presents a challenge common to all: risking giving up our safe, habitual way of life, our conditioned modus operandi – in order to allow a new way of life to flow naturally.

The rock face speaks not only to Mark's personal psychology but also to a universal mystery. Mark described the rock as dark and ominous. 'Ominous' has its root in the word *omen*, meaning a portent of good or ill. The stone cliff tells us of a tremendous, unknowable mystery, greater than Mark himself – an ultimate reality, yet one in which he takes part. Like the bluestones of Neolithic monuments, the rock face takes on the power of a *numen*, the spirit of a place, an absolute presence. As such it had a *numinous* quality. As Jung noted, dream encounters with a numinous presence can be experienced as a defeat for the ego, especially when we take them to be omens of ill.[12]

A teaching of Hazrat Inayat Khan, the founder of Sufiism in the West, exhorts: 'Shatter your ideals on the rock of truth.' We don't have to give up our ideals; we only need to be less possessed by them so that they don't set us apart from our humanity. 'What closes the heart,' as Khan wisely observes, 'is fear, confusion, depression, spite, discouragement, disappointment, and a troubled conscience; and when that is cleared away, the doors of the heart open.'[13]

Focusing on our 'defeat' – the confusion, shame, anger or guilt we may feel when we approach the numinous – we may easily forget that the numinous is there to remind us of qualities against which we have become hardened. When cut off from Nature and locked into an uncertain world that seeks facts and certainty, we lose sight of our sense of mystery, the playfulness, tenderness and loving-kindness of our soul nature. We forget what makes our heart sing.[14] For instance, when asked to set aside his fear and recall what memories he associated with the rock face, Mark remembered summer holidays as a child with his family, when he played happily among the rockpools in sandy coves at the base of encircling coastal cliffs. The memories put him in touch with a lighter, more carefree spirit.

Through our dreamwork, Mark realised that the dream which had initially frightened him actually called upon him to open up in a radical way to the more playful and light-hearted feelings he would need for the next phase of his life: a new relationship built on trust, openness and love. Far from being an ill omen, his numinous dream portended good. The 'real therapy', as Jung observed, 'is the approach to the numinous', and inasmuch as we attain an experience of the numinous, we are released from 'the curse of pathology'.[15]

Like rock, unhewn stone may appear static, but, having been shaped by powerful forces, holds a great deal of energy. The most common types of stone, formed from *igneous* rocks, have an association with fire, as revealed by the Latin root, *ignis*. Igneous rock arises from molten magma that cools either deep in the earth over thousands of years (forming granite of quartz and feldspar) or on the earth's surface, where the magma cools more quickly (hence pumice, basalt and obsidian). Like stones, we too are made up of powerful forces that began long before our birth and will continue beyond them. When we access the emotional energy a 'stone' holds for us, we free up that psychic energy to reignite our lives.

The solidity and stability of stone makes it a symbol for the enduring nature of our inner Being: the Self. Stone evokes 'movement in a repose',[16] a quality sculptors have delighted in over the ages. But when we become too rigid in our positions and habits, stones may signify that we have become inflexible and unyielding. Yet even our most hardened positions remain subject to the workings of time and the elements of daily life, as the psychic heat and pressures of our lives and dreams shape each of us differently, forging a core of strength with us – the *lapis philosophorum,* or philosopher's stone, once sought by the alchemists.

The alchemists understood every individual to be a microcosm, each of us a miniature world. They enigmatically advised, 'Explore the inner things of Earth and by distillation you will find the hidden stone.'[17] Dreams are made of those 'inner things', and working with them is a distillation that enables us to know ourselves – 'the hidden stone'. For this reason, Jung said of a dream that, 'if we carry it around with us and turn it over and over, something almost always comes of it.'[18] This 'something' reveals the aims of the unconscious to us, thus setting our lives in motion again. One of my own dreams speaks in a direct way to the mystery of the elusive stone:

> *I am surprised to find myself driving a black London cab on a dirt road in the desert. The road is quite challenging, and I think how well those past years of practice off-roading in the desert have served me. The landscape has a ruggedness akin to the Badlands of the Anza-Borrego desert in California, and I feel how much I have been missing such vistas of my childhood. After crossing the desert, I drive through a passageway, carved out of a massive pink quartz boulder. In the dream, I am taken aback to see that the boulder has a heart shape. Driving through the narrow passage requires all my concentration. I am not sure how I squeeze through. I can see that beyond the quartz gateway the landscape becomes a green, lush valley, and I think, 'Yes, this is what we need!' The beauty of the green, its lightness and openness remind me of the Spirit's renewal…*

Working associatively with the dream, I recalled a small pink quartz my eldest brother gave me before he moved out of the family home. I was only 11 and felt heartbroken at his leaving. I have kept the stone all these years, and it now forms part of a miniature Zen rock garden. It reminds me of the heart's capacity for love. This memory gave added meaning to the dream. The dream showed me what was lacking and what needed to be restored.

When I revisited the dream with my dream guide, we tracked the cab journey movement through my body, beginning in my head, which was full of dry, arid thoughts and strategies for dealing with life's rugged terrain. Once I had squeezed between the rocks, my heart gave way to a more spacious quality of being, portrayed by the 'greening' of the landscape.[19] The Jungian analyst Robert Johnson relates how the verb 'to treat', meaning 'to pull or drag' in Latin, comes from an ancient healing practice in which the healer would actually pull a person through smaller and smaller holes carved out of series of stones.[20] In just this way, it felt as if the dream pulled me through the narrow space in the stone to a place of rebirth.

The quartz also spoke to me of evolutionary transformations. Between the ages of 16 and 22, I hiked down the Grand Canyon four times with my father. Time has spent over 6 million years carving out the canyon. In the process, it has created a vast abstract work grounded in geological reality. Sandstone, limestone, shale and granite form the canyon walls. Sediments recount tales of water and wind carving hours into the earth, the majestic iteration of forms creating a strangely intimate feel as you realise that your fingertips and the earth's surface share a similar imprint.

Our dreams likewise lay down a sedimentary history in our psyches. Seen from an evolutionary perspective, the content of our dreams can be said to be part of 'an evolved mechanism' by means of which we lay down new memories.[21] If you keep a record of your dreams, you will note that images and themes repeat. How these repetitions differ over time has great significance.

For instance, in my early twenties, I dreamed of a photograph of Yosemite National Park, a breathtaking valley carved out by glaciers eroding the softer earth from around massive igneous rock formations and sculpting the deep valley now overlooked by the sheer-faced cliffs of Half Dome and El Capitan. The valley's expressive rifts call to mind the words of Khalil Gibran: 'The deeper sorrow carves into your being, the more joy you can contain.'[22] In the dream, I felt so drawn to the landscape, I seemed to pass through the photo and into yet another artwork, this time a painting…

> *An underwater nymph in diaphanous white swims in blue-green waters. She holds a white stone. She and I swim together in a blue-green sunlit sea. The white stone has a name inscribed on it and the name seems to be for me. The name comes to me intuitively but seems too wondrous and strange to be for me. I cannot accept it.*

More than 20 years later, I dreamed of the white stone yet again in the following dream:

> *I go back and forth between two buildings, feeling irritated and confused, not sure of my purpose. On the path between them, I pass by a small white stone and a falcon's feather. These objects catch my eye, but I am in a hurry and so walk by them. As I do so, I become aware that, being caught up with my thoughts and passing by these two small objects, so small and out of*

place, I have somehow missed the point of the dream.
Unfortunately, at this moment, I awake.

When I re-entered this dream by undertaking the waking dream process with my guide, I visualised picking up the white stone. The stone felt very secret and mysterious, as if it contained all of space. It communicated purity and forgiveness. The stone said to me, 'A rose knows no shame'; for me, this was an important message – that shame is not a natural state, but something impressed on us, a social conditioning we acquire in childhood and carry into later life.

While we may be familiar with the evolutionary forces at work in stone, it may be surprising to know that certain minerals found in rock produce another form of energy: light. Under ultraviolet light, against a backdrop of darkness, clusters of humble, nondescript minerals such as fluorite, opalite and calcite transform into incandescent stained-glass colours of deep blue, emerald green and crimson. I remember being mesmerised by such beauty when my teenage brother would show me his mineral samples, bathing the stones in ultraviolet light to transport us into a mysterious, beautiful world of dark luminescence.

The colours left their tincture on our hearts, colours we conjured up to lift our spirits. My brother explained how ultraviolet caused the electrons in these minerals to jump to a higher state and then to emit the excess energy as photons of light at different wavelengths, one that we perceived as bright colour. The science was good to know, but even better was the magic of discovering how something perceived as rather ordinary can seize us with its hidden beauty when seen in a different light.

Rocks and stones in dreams put us in touch with time, place and eternity. It is no accident that, according to the biblical account, Jacob's dream of a stairway to heaven began when he stopped for the night, took a stone, put it under his head and slept. He dreamed of a luminous ladder on which angels descended to earth and ascended to God. When Jacob woke up from his dream, he said, 'How awesome is this place! This is none other than the house of God; this is the gate of heaven.'[23] He felt God would watch over him and was empowered to face the unknown. To mark his dream, Jacob took the stone he had slept on, stood it upright, and poured tree oil over it to sanctify it. The tree oil signified blessing and sacrifice because of the time and effort required to grow the tree and produce the oil. Jacob's stone pillow reminds us of how ancient myths depicted both humans and gods as born from stone.[24] Indeed, we live out our lives on the 'speeding stone' that we call Earth.[25]

I keep a collection of stones that remind me of my dreams: a white limestone, pink quartz, a polished sphere of obsidian. A piece of granite could serve to remind Mark of the sheer rock face of his own dream and his underlying desire for a relationship, just as in ancient Rome a block of dark stone stood next to the statue of Eros, the god of love.[26] Find a rock or stone that calls to mind one of your dreams. Touch it and hear what it has to say to you.

Chapter Five

Light Revisioned Through the Prism of Dreams

O Light eternal, alone in Being,
Alone with your Aloneness, you know,
And in knowing, smile with love![1]

– Dante Alighieri

What kind of light illuminates our dreams? Imagine a dream as a prism through which shines the light of consciousness. Through dreams you observe 'the colours of your mind', expressed in images that convey thoughts and feelings. Exploring the properties of natural light, colours and shadows, the physicist Arthur Zajonc observes: 'Light falling on the eye provokes sight. Until that moment, light lives in a universe of its own.'[2] Drawing on more poetic language, the German writer Goethe reflects on the properties of natural light and the 'inner light', concluding that 'the eye is formed by the light, for the light, so that the inner light may meet the outer.'[3] The 'inner light' illuminates our dreams and our path in life.

To understand better the nature of light in dreams, we must first grasp a key attribute of light – that pure light appears invisible, or 'black' like space. If you were to take part in a physics experiment in which a researcher asks you to peer through a peephole into a box full of light in a vacuum, what would you see?

The light contained in the box would appear as black emptiness, because to human eyes light in a vacuum is invisible. However, if a metal wand was inserted into one side of the box and spun around, flashes of the metal would become visible. Yet the light itself remains unseen. We see only the illuminated wand.[4] Thus, to the naked eye the apparently empty reaches of outer space appear black. Light fills interstellar space, but we only see the light when an object like the moon occupies space and so reflects it back to us. To be seen, the so-called 'visible light spectrum' requires the interpenetration of light with matter, the reflected light then being received by our eyes.

What we call 'light' consists only of a small fraction of the full electromagnetic spectrum, which encompasses a wide range of wavelengths, invisible to our perception – radio waves, microwaves, infrared radiation and ultraviolet rays, X-rays and gamma rays.

Various technologies, both natural and created, enable us to harvest the wavelengths of the electromagnetic field to different ends. For example, cells in our bodies and in plants use light to enact processes requisite for life; solar panels absorb sunlight to generate electricity; laser light allows surgeons to perform finely tuned operations; fibre-optics transmit wavelengths as a form of communication; X-rays allow us to see deep into matter; radar uses radio waves to track objects at a distance; infrared telescopes enable physicists to peer through galactic dust, revealing previously unseen galaxies. Astrophysicists use colour as a code for matter, assisting them to identify properties of distant stars and planets that may contain life.

Yet even with all the scientific instruments available, only 5 per cent of the 'matter' comprising the universe can be observed, 95 per cent being invisible 'dark matter' and 'dark energy'. This has led NASA to point out that the matter we can perceive 'shouldn't be called normal "matter" at all since it makes up such a small fraction of the universe'.[5]

Comparably, the inner light of dreams spans the *visible* and *invisible* wavelengths that comprise the electromagnetic spectrum. Much as the spectral properties of visible light arise from within a continuum of wavelengths possessing differing scope and function, so the inner light of our dreams can also enable us to extend the 'wavelength' of our perceptual faculties by revealing the capacities of what has been called the 'extended mind',[6] unbounded by the normal limitations of time and space.[7]

In this sense, 'the stuff that dreams are made on'[8] is composed of not only the light and colours 'seen' in dream imagery, but also the extended mind that encompasses the mysteries of the cosmos. Pure light in a dream can leave an indelible impression, as in this report from the archive of the Alister Hardy Religious Experience Research Centre. An English man in his sixties, who described himself as reckless in his youth, recounted an experience he had in his twenties when he crashed his car while driving under the influence of alcohol. After being diagnosed with a mild concussion, he was sent home to rest. There he fell asleep and had a moving experience, the account of which follows:

> ... *I was one with eternally pulsing light, not a dazzling but a peaceful light, 'such as never was on sea or land'; a light which was also love and safety. Yet I was not conscious of being safe so much as of there being no longer anything to fear. There seemed to be a completeness about everything and everything went on for ever: there was no birth or death, beginning or end. There was no need to be, because in that moment was eternity, it always had been and always would be. Nor was I by any means alone: I was communicating with infinite wisdom, not as an individual but as an entity; this wisdom was in me and flowed through me and yet was also outside me. I had no need for companionship because I was, in a sense, companionship. I seemed to be part of some mighty essence, some ultimate, unknowable reality, to describe which I knew would be impossible, because no earthly analogy could be applied to it. This was the ultimate truth of which all other realities were poor reflections.*[9]

Describing what happened, he insisted that it was more than a dream, and that 'all waking life, in comparison with it, was mere illusion'. He added that the experience helped to strengthen his faith in 'the reality of the unseen world of spiritual values.'

Such a spiritual revelation would not have surprised medieval alchemists, who understood this inner light to be comprised of *scintillae* or sparks from the animating principle of the 'world soul', which they viewed as being akin to the Holy Spirit. They called this light the *lumen naturae*, the inner light of nature – one that imparts wisdom and serves as the guiding 'star' in each of us.[10] The great alchemist Paracelsus tells us that we learn of the light of nature through dreams.[11]

As the moon reflects the light of the sun, so light of our dreams mirrors our inner states of consciousness, revealing how these influence our lives. The following dream of my own, from my early forties, illuminates how I was blocking my 'light':

> *I find myself in a meeting room distracted by an*
> *intense circular beam of round white light about*
> *four inches in diameter that appears on the walls and*
> *bookshelves wherever I look. The light disturbs me.*
> *I think, 'My boss will notice that I'm too sensitive*
> *to the light.' This concerns me, so I get up to turn*
> *the dimmer switch down. I move back to my seat,*
> *thinking the 'problem' has been solved, but notice that*
> *my boss has a chagrined look on his face. Suddenly,*
> *I realise that's what I do in waking life: dim the light*
> *that comes from myself. Then, I wake up.*

When I understood the significance of this dream, I resolved in future to speak out or take action – a resolve that lit up my world in unexpected ways!

Through our dreams and dreamwork, we may learn to recognise self-defeating thought processes or negative life patterns that can literally clutter our dreams. A dream that parallels this idea was had by a woman named Angela, with whom I had been working for a few months. She longed to declutter and simplify her life in order to free up her unrealised creativity. As she relates:

> *I am in a room that is cluttered with all sorts of objects and debris. Things are piled up in untidy, dusty and rusty heaps sprawling all over so that moving around is extremely hard. It looks like one of those rooms builders use to throw things in while they work next door.*

> *Then the scene changes, and I find myself in another room. There's a female friend with me. I turn to my friend, telling her that my project is to get the ceiling of the Sistine Chapel painted right here on this ceiling, but I wonder if it wouldn't look too garish. What does she think? My friend assures me that it would look beautiful. At that precise moment we both look up and there it is … the ceiling of the Sistine Chapel in all its glory and splendour. It takes our breath away; we look at it, ecstatic.*

Working with me on the dream, Angela saw the cluttered room as representing familiar and unhelpful patterns of thought that blocked her creativity. It felt important for her to 'look up' to gain a broader perspective on her situation. Overcoming her fears that the painting might look 'garish' or stand out in an unpleasant way, she discovered that the artwork radiates splendour. Psychologically, this dream illuminates how Angela's creative energy was entangled in her negative, cluttered thinking and fear of standing out. However, as she came to realise, when she 'looked up' from negative thought patterns, she could then move out of the stasis in her life.

Such dreams share characteristics with waking life, blurring the distinction between our dreams and the waking world. For instance, in the summer of 1992, I was working in Riga, Latvia. During that time, most of the Russian Orthodox churches that the Soviets had previously turned into museums, offices or gymnasiums were undergoing restoration. Throughout the summer, workers painstakingly replaced the golden skin of the onion domes gracing the Russian Orthodox Cathedral of the Nativity of Christ (the golden covering had been peeled off and pillaged during the Second World War). Walking past this church, a friend and I noticed that the workers had left the door ajar, so we took the chance to enter. We expected to see the Cathedral's ornate orthodox design. Instead of a richly decorated sanctuary, we found ourselves encased in a Soviet-style concrete office!

I felt physically sick when, instead of looking up to see what should have been an expansive dome, I could only see the office's low ceiling. I could hear workers dismantling the office but couldn't see them. Suddenly, a terrible wrenching noise resounded through the building as a crane dislodged a heavy panel from the ceiling. Jumping back, I watched as the ceiling panel was lifted away, clearing a space through which I could see into the dome of the church. Peering through the dusty light, I could make out the abstract-patterned and gold-flecked dome as its hidden beauty shone forth.

For me, what happened that day provides a waking-world analogy for what can happen in a dream when we learn to recognise the constructs of the conditioned mind that block our essential nature. When this occurs, the constructs fall away, dissolve, lift or are torn asunder, so that a fundamental realisation of our true nature can be revealed and more fully actualised in life.

Working therapeutically with dreams, I have found that negative or nightmarish dreams veil the clear light of the inner world and our capacity for deeply felt, positive emotions such as joy and serenity. Often in such dreams, depictions of darkness fill the dreamer with a sense of dread at what they perceive as a threat, whether known or unknown. Yet an understanding of the relationship between absolute light and, apparently, absolute darkness suggests that what we perceive as darkness invariably contains light.[12]

This is important to remember when our everyday sense of who we are is challenged by the loss of a loved one. At such times, our human capacity to find light in the midst of darkness often comes to the fore in dreams that feature extra-sensory perception (ESP), including pre-cognition and telepathic communication with those who have died[13] – faculties of the extended mind. A study of three archives of ESP accounts found that a significant number take place when we dream.[14] Of these, the majority relate to a close friend or family member who has died or who, shortly after the dream, becomes injured or dies in waking life.

In my own dream life, I have had many 'visitation' dreams of my mother who died many years ago. I had been able to spend her last three months with her before she died. The following dream, which I had a few months after her death, initiated my delayed grieving process by enabling me to cry for the first time since her passing:

> *I dream that I am back near the street where I grew up. A woman invites me into one of the houses. Her skin appears a luminescent sky-blue. This seems strange and lovely at the same time. The house is white, but when we open the door, everything inside has a sky-blue hue, the walls, the objects, etc.*

> *We enter another room where my mother rests, sitting up on a blue bed with the bedspread over her legs. She looks radiant and joyful, surrounded by family members and friends who have died. They stand to either side of the bed and extend in great numbers behind it. I am aware that I see her in a world beyond this one. I run up to her and place my head in her lap, crying out how much I love her and how sorry I am for whatever I may have done to hurt her. She pats*

me lovingly and patiently. For the first time since her
death, I begin to cry, and then I awake. I mourn for
many hours.

This dream gave me the chance to tell my mother what I had
wanted to say before her death but hadn't done so, initiating
my grieving process. The visitation felt more real than real,
taking place in a radiant, non-temporal, non-spatial, tran-
scendent dimension. This reassured me greatly.

In contrast, my father's death happened suddenly. When
the family first heard he had become unwell, the doctors
didn't know he had cancer. At the time, I worked in London,
and so I wasn't sure when to leave for the US, as I had many
responsibilities at work. Then I had a dream that prompted
me to leave as soon as possible. On the night of the dream, I
had spent time in prayer for my father:

In the dream, I am climbing down a steep rocky
slope on a bright, sunny day in the Sierra Nevadas of
California. An unseen man takes my hand to help me
down. With surprise, I realise it is my father's hand.
Suddenly, the reality of his presence strikes me deeply.
I feel it as his hand touches mine – the familiarity of
his way of being, his character. He sits down silently
next to me. It all feels so vivid and real that I become
lucid. I say to him, 'I know this is a dream, but I do
not want to leave your side.' It feels as if I am really
with him, so I stay with him and tell him how much I
love him, how he must know that, and how I know he

loves me. He remains silent, looking at me with deep
concentration and love. As I speak, I begin to cry and
awake from the dream in tears.

Upon awakening, I felt certain that my father was near death
or may even have died and that I had to get to the US straight
away. I left early the next day. Luckily, I managed to arrive a
few days before he died. He could not speak or open his eyes,
but when I sat with him that first night and told him I loved
him, a large tear fell down his cheek. I was the first time my
father and I had ever cried together. I was grateful to be with
him when he died two nights later.

In each of these dreams, the light manifests differently. In
the dream of my deceased mother, the light appeared in the
brightness of the blue environs and in the radiance. In the
dream of my father, the light had a sharp clarity and intensity
that brought lucidity.

Dreams of the deceased and of pre-cognition can help us
to comprehend how the thoughts and feelings had in dreams
may reach beyond the everyday world of sense perception to
the infinite reach of the extended mind, potentially bringing
healing to events of the past and future. In such dreams, the
inner light appears to contain information for the recipient.
An Australian woman, who contributed to the Alister Hardy
Archive, shared her own thoughts on the revelation of what
she called 'Cosmic Light' as follows:

If you have experienced it, you never forget, and it
changes your life. But if you talk about it, people

would think one insane. I have seen it and would have to say that it smiles! And how can light smile?! I think it is a symbol from the deep unconscious that Jung writes about, one of those that integrate and change people's lives. And if, as the Quakers say, there 'is that of God in everyman', then that's probably where it originates. Perhaps the little spark of divinity we each hold is like a transformer power station for electricity and steps down the divine power until it is something we can understand and use.[15]

This woman was understandably hesitant to share what had happened to her with others. Nevertheless, similar accounts of light phenomena have been reported throughout history and are well documented. A study published in 2013 by Annekatrin Puhle analyses over 800 such cases of what she describes as 'transforming light'.[16] Of these, 71 occur in dreams and 22 in lucid dreams. Thirty-five take place 'at night' and 31 'in bed'.[17] According to this research, the light encounters brought people 'comfort' and 'meaningfulness'.[18]

The English writer J.B. Priestley gives a poetic evocation of how a dream revealed to him light's 'flame of life', one he shares in his autobiography. He had the dream at the age of 42, during a time when he felt life had lost all sense. In the dream, he watches from a tower as countless birds of all kinds fill the sky. But then their wings break, they become ill, and suddenly die. He begins to despair that the endless repetition of life and death seems meaningless. As he looks upon 'an enormous plain sown with feathers', the dream begins to shift:

> ... *But along this plan, flickering through the*
> *bodies themselves, there now passed a sort of white*
> *flame, trembling, dancing, then hurrying on; and*
> *as soon as I saw it I knew that this white flame*
> *was life itself, the very quintessence of being, and*
> *then it came to me in a rocket-burst of ecstasy,*
> *that nothing mattered, nothing could ever matter,*
> *because nothing else was real, but this quivering and*
> *hurrying lambency of being. Birds, men or creatures*
> *not yet shaped and coloured, all were of no account*
> *except so far as this flame of life travelled through*
> *them. It left nothing to mourn over behind it; what*
> *I had thought was tragedy was mere emptiness or*
> *a shadow show; for now all real feeling was caught*
> *and purified and danced on ecstatically with the*
> *white flame of life...*[19]

Of his dream, Priestley remarked that he had never felt such deep happiness as he knew at the end of it, and noted that he had not been 'quite the same man since.'[20] The dream broke through his scepticism, giving him an abiding sense of life's meaningfulness.

In our dreams, we can know *ourselves* not only as dependent upon light for our existence but also sharing in light's qualities, as I was moved to realise one night in this lucid dream:

*... I find myself carried a long way down a tunnel
illuminated with black light. Finally, the movement
stops, and it feels as if my 'body' rests on holy
ground in a foetal position on my right side, curled
up on the floor. The black lays heavy over me like a
thick blanket. The position has the feel of total and
complete surrender. A part of me thinks, 'I guess life
knows I need this.'*

*Then a morning light surrounds me. It feels like pure
light but somehow full of life's forms and contains
the sky, trees, birds, the earth and my being. The
light has the musicality of water and air. I think for
a brief moment I've awakened to a bright spring
day and that I must be hearing sounds from outside.
But then I understand the experience to be an
actual awakening to what light truly is, and all that
it contains. I feel like an apple on a grassy field, a
creation of light. I rest like this in the lucid space
until the alarm wakes me up.*

In the following chapters, as we explore the prismatic effects
between light, colour and darkness in dreams, we will
continue to discover that when we work through the psychological complexes that confuse our lives, both our dream life
and waking life become more lucid.

As we become aware of how the inner light of dreams
provides us with deeper intuition and insight, we can more

fully appreciate the healing power of our dreams. We can be heartened by the words of the Persian poet Hafiz:

'I wish I could show you,
When you are lonely or in darkness,
The Astonishing Light
Of your own Being!'[21]

Chapter Six

The Mystery and Magic
of Colour: A Study in Blue

*'There it is!' she cried. 'I have found it at last. This is
the true blue. Oh, how light it makes one. Oh, it is as
fresh as a breeze, as deep as a deep secret, as full as I
say not what.'* [1]

– Isaak Dinesen

On 24 December 1968, people on Earth received a beautiful gift
– the first colour, high-resolution image of an earthrise over the
moon. The final version of the photo creates the impression that
we, the viewers, stand on the moon watching Earth rise over the
moon's empty horizon line. Through the photo, 'Earthrise', our
planet's blue orb set against the barren whiteness of the moon
and the blackness of space, became imprinted on our collective
consciousness. The image brought home the emotive realisation that the blue sky, so seemingly limitless and infinite when
seen from Earth, turns out to be a delicate, diaphanous ring of
biosphere protecting and nurturing life on our planet.

The *Apollo 8* crew had their aim fixed on their goal to
be the first astronauts to complete a lunar orbit, so taking
photos of Earth did not appear on the official protocol for

the mission (astronauts had previously nearly died when distracted by the stellar views from space). But as the *Apollo 8* completed its fourth orbit around the moon, the astronauts, on a spacewalk outside the spacecraft, couldn't help noticing the striking earthrise.

One of them, Bill Anders, hastily loaded his camera with colour film. His commander jokingly pointed out that taking pictures of Earth wasn't scheduled. Even so, Anders, a self-described hardened fighter-pilot with no expertise in photography, took dozens of photos, figuring that one would turn out. Among them, he snapped the photo that took our understanding of Earth to a higher level, giving us a new *gestalt* picture of the planet as a holistic yet fragile, dynamic system, complex in its diversity, singular in its unity, unique in its beauty – a living, colourful presence in the cosmos.

Seen from space, as if in a dream, Earth itself becomes a living, breathing 'symbol', an archetype in the most fundamental sense of the word, impressing itself upon us with its strong presence and imparting a profound quality of Being.[2] We can understand why Anders, when first viewing the earthrise, exclaimed, 'Oh my God! Look at that picture over there! There's the Earth coming up. Wow, that's pretty.' Our response to the reality of 'Earthrise' gives us a more visceral understanding of what Jung meant when he defined archetypal images as those that 'point to realities that transcend consciousness'.[3] Importantly, Jung believed that archetypes 'possess spontaneity and purposiveness, or a kind of consciousness and free will'.[4] Thus, contact with the powerful energy of archetypes can transform us.

An example of such a healing archetypal encounter with Earth is found in the Alister Hardy Archive. A woman who had been contemplating suicide shares how, before falling asleep, she had called out to God for help. She continues:

*I then dreamt that I was travelling through space –
the earth rotating on its axis before me – the stars all
around me. I experienced within the dream a feeling
of most wonderful peace, and when I awakened, I
was both mentally and physically refreshed and my
problems were given a different perspective.*[5]

The vision of Earth from space gave her a meta-perspective, a more serene, life-saving vantage point, that helped her to see her problems in a new light.

Science tells us that gravity has shaped Earth into a sphere that rotates suspended (or nestled) in space-time. Faced with this awe-inspiring 'fact', we can still wonder at Earth's dream-like mysterious beauty. The writer Richard Bach, in his book *Illusions: The Adventures of a Reluctant Messiah*, speaks of this mystery: 'The world is a dream, you say, and it's lovely, sometimes. Sunset. Clouds. Sky. No. The image is a dream. The beauty is real. Can you see the difference?'[6]

I once had a dream that pictures something of the same:

*I find myself in space looking at Earth, surrounded
by a vast dark expanse and then a ring of stars. Earth
has the quality of a bright, blue jewel, and I can see
how its gravity bends space-time. But then Earth*

dislodges itself and floats up towards me like some
great inflatable ball. I feel concern for the planet, yet
also aware of how playful the scene feels. As I lift my
hands to 'catch' Earth I become aware that I dream...

When I wake, I comprehend that the beautiful natural landscapes so dear to me – the deserts, countryside, mountains
and seascapes – all lovingly give birth to life. From a cosmo-
logical perspective, the dream also graphically shows me that
the apparent solidity of Earth is as ephemeral as dreams – the
life the Earth sustains, fragile. This awareness made me weep,
as it felt both a tremendous gain and loss.

Sharing that dream now reminds me of a scene from
Charlie Chaplain's political satire *The Great Dictator*, which
was screened in 1940 during the Second World War. In the
film, a dictator, played by Chaplin, fantasises of world domi-
nance while he dances with an oversized inflatable globe of
the world. The scene ends with a loud 'bang' as the globe
unexpectedly pops and deflates, leaving the 'great' dictator
in tears. The juxtaposition of the two scenes highlights the
difference between the power of love and the love of power.
The former creates the world, the latter destroys it.

Viewed from space, 'Spaceship Earth'[7] shines with a translucent blue, radiating six times more brightly than the moon's
silvery light. The opalescent hue that reflects from Earth gives
us a sense of how colour, itself made of light wavelengths, can
serve as an archetype alive with Being. As one dream teacher
of mine explained, 'It's not what we make of the colours that
is important, but what the colours make of us.'[8] Unlike the

unmissable blue of the Earth, colours in dreams (and life) often appear 'disguised' in the imagery they clothe and so tend to go unnoticed.

During dreamwork, I have often found that people weep when they re-encounter a colour as if for the first time. For example, I worked with a young man, Adam, who had what he considered an unremarkable dream. When Adam re-imagined the dream scene, a bedroom, a detail that he had previously dismissed – a pair of blue socks – caught his attention. As his dream guide, I invited him to imagine putting the socks on and to focus on the blue. In doing so, he associated the socks with Earth and their blue colour to Spirit. Instantly, he sensed a burst of energy at the base of his spine. To calm this powerful energy, I asked Adam to imagine the blue moving into the region of his sacrum, on down to his feet, and then moving upwards again. With the balancing effect of the blue, he felt his spine reinforced with a newfound strength and a sense of purpose that touched him deeply. As Adam discovered, when a colour in a dream appears in clothing, the colour may reflect a quality in us that needs to be recognised and 'worn' like an outer garment in waking life. On a similar note, the poet John J. Brugaletta, imagining a day in which everyone in the world wore different shades of blue – cerulean, sapphire, cornflower, denim and baby blue – writes of how, the day after, a sudden transformation took place. Instead of beginning sentences with 'I', people started them with 'You', now infused with a new spirit of wonder and empathy.[9]

Many people say they do not dream in colour. Yet when researchers awaken participants in a sleep lab during the

REM state, people recall both their dreams and the colours appearing in them more readily and more clearly.[10] Even so, when people retell a dream, they often don't mention colours unless asked. Perhaps we fail to take note of colours because, as Ludwig Wittgenstein pointed out in his *Philosophical Investigations*, 'The aspects of things that are most important for us are hidden because of their simplicity and familiarity.'[11]

Wittgenstein attends to the nature of colour in his treatise *Remarks on Colour*. He asks, 'Can we imagine someone who has a different geometry of colour than we do?'[12] How, Wittgenstein wonders, does a person with colour blindness see and experience colour? Normally, the three colour-sensing cones in our eyes process light wavelengths of red, green and blue to create a palette of crisp distinct colours. When these photoreceptors interfere with one another, colour blindness results. Most people with colour blindness do, in fact, see some colour. However, depending on the type of colour blindness, certain colours look washed out. For instance, people who have red-green colour blindness may see these colours dimmed by a film of pinkish-grey.

Imagine a child who wears toy glasses with coloured red lenses. Perhaps, like me, you were once that child! If so, you would have noticed that the red tint dimmed other colours and gave objects a spectral pinkish-grey tinge. Colours burst back to life once the glasses come off. Now imagine the reverse: How would it be to have had red-green colour blindness from birth and then to put on glasses that enabled you to see colours in their correct wavelengths? Such corrective glasses do exist.[13] When a colour-blind person puts on such new glasses for the first time, they respond with deep emotion: a man in his fifties who received such a gift wept at the bright clarity of the colours. Another stood in amazement staring at the trees and sky, crying with disbelief at the beautiful contrast between the green and the blue. Witnessing such powerful expressions of feeling reminds us of the wonder of colour.[14]

Wittgenstein's investigations into colour, which included conversations with colour-blind people, caused him to conclude: 'Whatever *looks* luminous does not look grey. Everything grey *looks* as though it is being illumined.'[15] Bright colours appear to be illuminated from within, greyish tones (as at dusk) seem to lack an inner illumination. The blue sky of a spring day radiates vitality in contrast to the more melancholic tone of grey-blue. A similar contrast can be seen in images taken by orbiting satellites: the vivid blue of Earth's healthy biosphere is sullied by murky grey blotches over cities with heavily polluted air. When we (and the Earth) are physically and emotionally healthy, we shine with the light of Intelligence and Imagination that radiates from within us.

Dreams not only reveal the emotional tonalities of colour, but also unveil colours in their 'pure' state, unconstrained by form. In your mind's eye, you can visualise an infinite expanse of blue and intuit the impression this colour makes upon you.[16] In daily life, the colour blue appears in the form that contains it – a flower, a pool of water or even the vast expanse of the sea. Yet in dreams, we may directly apprehend how our supra-sensory perception of pure colour touches our very souls, as in the following dream of mine:

I ride a bicycle down a familiar London street in the
dark, early-morning hours. A recent, light snow is
melting. The deep night gives way to a blue dawn so
beautiful I want to get off my bike, kneel, and cry with
joy at the sheer beauty of it. With the beauty and the
feeling, I become lucid in the dream...

A few years on, I had a dream in which blue took on an added
brilliance and intensity, reflecting the pure light of unbounded
Being without reference to a form or object outside itself, not
even the sky:

I am arguing with someone over which of us is more
alone in this world. I say, 'I have left my country, my
family; my mother and dear aunt have died, and my
father hardly knows me [with his dementia].' Then I
see my mother, who shakes her head side to side as if
to say, 'You are not alone.' With the realisation that
she is actually dead in waking life, I become lucid.

I feel as if my soul is carried a long way in a shining
darkness. I repeat a sacred name until a dazzling azure
blue space opens up as a vast field of light before me.
The blue expanse feels like it contains all of creation.
The blue overwhelms me and I 'prostrate' my being
and cry out, 'Forgive me, God, for every time I have
forgotten your blue on the breath.' I say this moved
by a sense of profound gratitude for all the beauty
and wonder I have failed to appreciate fully. Then

I see what appear to be brilliant white clouds lining the circumference above me. This gives way to the blackness again, through which I am carried on the wind until I wake up, thinking about a line from a Sufi teacher: 'The only sin is to forget God on the breath.'

In both dreams, the colour blue radiates a joy and beauty that abides at the core of life. I feel the reality of all-encompassing love unbounded and without judgement. The blue answers a deep longing within me, a desire to feel fully present to life itself. At the time of this dream, I felt I was losing my innocence of heart. My immersion in the blue assured me of the soul's essential purity. The challenge for me would be to trust in, and live by, the soulful quality of that intense blue. In the words of William Blake:

… And we are put on earth a little space,
That we may learn to bear the beams of love…'[17]

Speaking of colours in dreams, the 12th-century Sufi mystic Ibn al-'Arabī discerns that when 'the man of knowledge' is lost in nothingness, 'God grants him an existence from His own existence and paints him with the Divine Color.'[18] Alchemists referred to such 'dyeing' as the 'heavenly tincture'.[19]

From a spiritual perspective, luminous colours in dreams signal the presence of the spirit, which filters through the dream material rather as though the dream were a stained-glass window animated by light. We know that light spreads out as distinct colours when it shines through a stained-glass window because of properties in the coloured glass, but the light itself remains uncoloured, pure in its essence.[20] 'Thus,' as the Sufi scholar William Chittick explains, 'dream images are perceived in sensory forms, yet they are animated by formless awareness.'[21] At the same time, the coloured light of our dreams infuses us so that we may then bring the attributes of the colours we have experienced into our waking life. This infusion kindles a light, helping us to remain hopeful and alive to possibilities even during periods of loss. To convey this renewal of hope, the psychiatrist Elisabeth Kübler-Ross, well known for her description of the stages of grief, draws on the analogy of a stained-glass window illumined from within on a dark night.[22]

Concerning the numinosity of the shining blue, the Tibetan Buddhist tradition teaches, 'At this stage, thou must not be awed by the divine blue light which will appear shining, dazzling, and glorious; and be not startled by it. That is the light of the Tathagata called the Light of the Wisdom of the Dharma-Dhatu [Absolute reality].'[23] Comfortingly, the Tibetan Buddhists also call this blue 'the light of grace'.[24] Instead of feeling daunted, terrified or awed when we meet fields of intense, coloured light in a dream, their teaching tells us, 'That is the radiance of thine own true nature. Recognise it.'[25]

In a modern context, we can compare dreams in which we feel impressed upon by a colour with immersion in a colour therapy pool. Such pools have been used in waking life to enhance the emotional wellbeing of many people, including children. For example, autistic children may have difficulty being aware of their bodies, so when immersed in a pool illuminated by coloured light, they are able, perhaps for the first time, to have a sense of bodily awareness. Writing about such therapeutic 'colour baths', the physicist Arthur Zajonc describes how coloured light, emitted from lamps installed on the edge of a colour therapy pool just below the waterline, only becomes visible when the child enters the water and is bathed in colour.[26] In a parallel way, when a dream swathes us in a 'colour bath', we are invited to know ourselves as bodies of light in a more fluid state of being.

Photographs of Earth from space remind us that no matter how celestial blue may appear, it also heralds life on Earth. Indeed, paint pigments originate in the earth, their colours extracted from stones, minerals, clay, seashells, plants and herbs. The brilliant pigments used in medieval illuminated manuscripts all have their origins in earth-bound substances involving such humble ingredients as pine resin, wax, urine and even dung, as well as caustic lye and deadly materials such as lead and mercury.

Lapis lazuli blue, extracted from the rare mineral lazurite deep in the Himalayas of Afghanistan, requires painstakingly slow grinding into blue powder before it can be mixed with agents to draw out the pigment. The resulting colour, also called ultramarine blue (which means 'the blue from over the sea'), was once the most expensive pigment in medieval Europe. Given the preciousness of lapis lazuli blue, we can understand why Europeans in the Middle Ages believed that the mere sight of its hue dispelled melancholy. Holding a polished sphere of lapis lazuli stone that I bought as a memento of the shimmering blue in my dreams, I feel more serene and secure.

Modern research has shown that light and colour have such psycho-physiological functions.[27] Blue light, for example, inhibits the production of the melatonin that causes us to fall asleep, while at the same time relaxing us so that we feel both bright and at ease, like a calm ultramarine sea. When we understand the properties of colour and their effects, we can appreciate that much as light and colours in the waking world can help us physiologically and emotionally, so can the light and colours of our dreams.

The soul-longing I associate with bright blue also has a literary counterpart in the 'blue flower' yearning of romantic love. This image flourished in German Romanticism of the late 18th and early 19th centuries. The German Romantic writer Novalis, a lucid dreamer, wrote a novel in which the lead protagonist, Henry, longs to find a blue flower that he had seen in a dream within a dream (possibly based on one of Novalis' own lucid dreams):

He dreamed that he was sitting on the soft turf by the margin of a fountain, whose waters flowed into the air, and seemed to vanish in it. Dark blue rocks with various coloured veins rose in the distance. The daylight around him was milder and clearer than usual; the sky was of a sombre blue, and free from clouds. But what most attracted his notice was a tall, light-blue flower, which stood nearest the fountain, and touched it with its broad, glossy leaves. Around it grew numberless flowers of varied hue, filling the air with the richest perfume. But he saw the blue flower

alone and gazed long upon it with inexpressible
tenderness. He at length was about to approach it,
when it began to move and change its form. The
leaves increased their beauty, adorning the growing
stem. The flower bent towards him and revealed
among its leaves a blue, within which hovered
a tender face. His delightful astonishment was
increasing with this singular change, when suddenly
his mother's voice awoke him, and he found himself
in his parents' room.[28]

Although Henry never actually finds the idealised blue flower, his search leads him to find his true love, Mathilde. Ultimately, colours lead us to a direct apprehension of the profound qualities that they reveal.

Henry's intoxication with the flower's blue incandescence is echoed in Aldous Huxley's poetic description of the spring flowers as they appeared to him after he had taken four tenths of a gram of the psychedelic substance mescaline. An hour and a half after taking mescaline, Huxley became mesmerised by flowers 'shining with their own inner light and all but quivering under the pressure of the significance with which they were charged', alive with 'naked existence.'[29] He writes:

I continued to look at the flowers, and in their living light I seemed to detect the qualitative equivalent of breathing – but of a breathing without returns to a starting point, with no recurrent ebbs but only a repeated flow from beauty to heightened beauty, from

deeper to ever deeper meaning. Words like 'grace' and
'transfiguration' came to my mind, and this, of course,
was what, among other things, they stood for.[30]

Huxley understood mescaline to have affected his brain chemistry in such a way that 'things' became free of the concepts
and categories we ordinarily use to delimit them in time and
space and so quivered with extraordinary Beingness. Because
of this, he proposed that careful use of mescaline could potentially give the user an introduction to a mystical experience
of colour perceived in both the inner and outer worlds –
colours becoming primary, more central than any definition
or denotation.

In order to determine the nature of hallucinogen-
occasioned spiritual experience,[31] researchers studied reports
from people who had taken psilocybin, a compound with
similar effects to mescaline. Using a questionnaire designed
to analyse the characteristics of mystical experience, the
researchers identified four salient features of drug-induced
visions: a singular noetic or sacred quality, positive mood,
transcendence of space-time, and ineffability.

Dreams can naturally give us a mystical perception of
colour without the need to use chemical agents. Consider this
homely dream shared by a recently bereaved widow who had
lost her husband of many years:

*[In my dream] I came down in the morning and went
straight to the front door ... Through the glass top of
the door I could see grey foggy mist outside, blotting*

out the oak trees across the road and even the rose
bushes with their last buds in the front garden. It
was not a tempting world to look out upon – bleak
and wintry and dark – but I opened the door. And
there, to my complete amazement, lay on the front
doorstep, covering its entire length, the most beautiful
bouquet of garden flowers that I had ever seen. At the
heart of it were the deepest of velvety red roses, the
flowers I most love, and all around were flame, cream
and golden roses, delicate ferns, and every variety of
Michaelmas daisies, from the deep blue and purple
varieties to the tiniest of white fairy-like clusters.
A profound joy and thankfulness filled my being and
I bent down and picked up the flowers and carried
them into the house.[32]

As a postscript, she adds that this dream 'had such an extraordinary vividness that I felt impelled to go downstairs and to
open the door just as I had done in the dream and to look at
the doorstep where the flowers had been lying.' We can sense
how the coloured light held in the flowers, set against the
grey backdrop, has healing properties for the dreamer. If this
were your dream, I would invite you to paint or buy a similar
bouquet or to plant flowers that remind you of the encouragement the dream imparted.

Another woman, who happens to be a minister of a
church, related to me how she often dreams of being envel-
oped in luminous, pastel flowers that revive her and refuel
her with the energy she needs for her ministry. The colours

in her dream-flowers – soft lavender, yellow, pink and blue – touched her in a very literal and purposeful way. Such dream experiences call to mind a teaching from the 18th-century writer and minister George MacDonald: 'The idea of God *is* the flower.'[33] In even more essential terms, 'The idea of God *is* the colour.' Colours highlight the extraordinariness of the 'everyday' if we could but notice them.

Blue takes its rightful place in the rainbow, where colours exist in harmony and balance. No colour or quality dominates, yet we intuitively sense the distinct qualities and the relationships they share. Similarly, colours displayed in the round on the artist's 'colour wheel' intimate an underlying organisation and imaginative power in their harmonious inter-relationships.

In the colour wheel, blue has a primary relationship to red and yellow. From mixing these three, we get the so-called secondary colours of violet, green and orange. The mixing of two colours reconciles opposites into a new synthesis: out of two colours a new one arises. Contemplating the interplay of chromatic energy of the colour wheel, the artist Paul Klee describes 'motion' as unnecessary because 'there is no question "to move there" but to be "everywhere" and consequently, also "there".'[34] The colour wheel illuminates unity in multiplicity as the varying colours emerge out of one source: light.

Keeping in mind the development of colours on the colour wheel, we can reflect upon the composition of the colours that appear in our dreams, the qualities they bring to us and how these speak to our needs and nature. I recall a dream of mine in which a group of workers load up boxes of what appear to be coloured markers or crayons in preparation for a conference. One of the men sees me and says to his co-workers jokingly, 'You won't be able to hold onto your crayons with all the colours she has in her dreams!' Although the sky-blue crayon has been especially meaningful to me since childhood, each of the colours in a box of crayons holds its own magic and meaning.

As we continue to explore the world of dreams, we will revisit the nature of colours, light and darkness. But before we move on, take a moment to let a colour from one of your own dreams – your own 'box of crayons' – reappear in your mind's eye. Allow yourself to engage with the colour and notice its qualities, where you sense the colour in your body, how it moves you emotionally or inspires you intellectually, and how it touches your heart. Think of the colour as the language of your soul.[35]

Find an object, like my lapis lazuli stone, that mirrors this dream-colour and display it in your home as a reminder of what the colour means to you. Through colours, we witness the 'Presence of the Imagination'[36] coming alive in the world, just as in our dreams. As Goethe's Faust proclaims, we find life in the 'many-hued reflected splendour' of light.[37] Illuminated by the light of the imagination, colours truly become 'acts of light',[38] as they imbue us with their wonderous hues and mysterious qualities of Being.

Chapter Seven

The Geometry of Dreams and the Dimensions of Consciousness

*It is never literally true that any form is meaningless
    and 'says nothing'.
Every form in the world says something. But its
    message often fails to reach us,
and, even if it does, full understanding is often
    withheld from us.*[1]

– Wassily Kandinsky

What does a sphere the size of a marble or hazelnut have in common with the origins of the universe? Perhaps as a child you played with marbles? Like me, you may have had one that you prized above the others. I favoured a large transparent marble with rainbow-coloured swirling strands entwined within it. I used to hold the treasured marble in my hand and roll it around, feeling soothed by its smooth cool surface. Sometimes, I would extend my hand, rest the marble on my open palm, hold it up to the light and wonder admiringly at the colours its form contained. The marble's inaccessible beauty within spoke to me of different worlds. Imagining it now, I can feel its solidity in the centre of my hand.

Little did I know then that one day a physicist, describing the origins of the universe, known as the 'Big Bang', would take every child's imagination to a new level by using a marble about one inch in diameter to show the size of the universe at 10^{-34} seconds![2] This theory purports that all the 'stuff' in the universe exploded out of 'nothing', albeit a particular kind of nothing, namely a quantum void filled with masses of subatomic particles that fluctuate into forms.[3]

In 1373, a time when Ptolemy's flat-Earth perception yet prevailed in Europe, an English woman in her thirties had a series of 16 deathbed visions in the early-morning hours, in which she met Jesus. One of these visions prefigures the something-from-nothing cosmology of the Big Bang:

> *In this Revelation he showed me something else, a tiny thing, no bigger than a hazelnut, lying in the palm of the hand, and as round as a ball. I looked at it, puzzled, and thought, 'What is this?'*

> *Then the answer came: 'It is everything that is made.'*

> *I wondered how it could survive. It was so small that I expect it to shrivel up and disappear.*

> *Then I was answered, 'It exists now and always because God loves it.' Thus, I understood that everything exists through the love of God.[4]*

Inspired, this woman recovered and wrote down what she called her 'shewings'. The book she wrote about her visions, *Revelations of Divine Love*, has become a classic of Christian mysticism. She became known as Mother Julian of Norwich and, inspired by her visions, she withdrew from the world into seclusion in order to contemplate the Divine, living in a small cell that was attached to a church in Norwich, England.[5] Through the narrow window facing outwards, she gave spiritual guidance to all who sought it. Paradoxically, within the confines of her narrow cell, the more Julian turned inward, the greater her outreach in the wider world.

We might wonder how someone from the 14th century had a dream-like vision of a 'little thing the quantity of a hazelnut' that would contain the seed of a scientific theory yet to be conceived. Six hundred years later, the physicist Louis de Broglie postulated an analogy of structure between our minds and our physical world; otherwise, he argued, humanity could not have survived.[6] De Broglie cites Albert Einstein's visual way of thinking as an example of how the mind can reach conclusions that differ from the everyday sense of perception of space and time.[7] According to Einstein's biographer, Einstein credited his capacity to think visually and intuitively in his thought-experiments as leading to his Theory of Relativity.[8]

We see a similar principle at work in a dream that inspired the 19th-century chemist Friedrich August Kekulé to conceive of the structure of the benzene molecule. Kekulé, weary from his researches, had turned his chair towards the fireplace and dozed. He later recounted:

.... Again, the atoms were flitting before my eyes.
Smaller groups now kept modestly in the background.
My mind's eye, sharpened by repeated visions of a
similar sort, now distinguished larger structures of
varying forms. Long rows frequently close together,
all, in movement, winding and turning like serpents.
And see! What was that? One of the serpents seized its
own tail and the form whirled mockingly before my
eyes. I came awake like a flash of lightning. This time
also I spent the remainder of the night working out
the consequences of the hypothesis.

He adds: 'If we learn to dream, gentlemen, then we shall perhaps find truth ... We must take care, however, not to publish our dreams before submitting them to proof by the waking mind.'[9]

Kekulé serpent shares a lineage with the alchemical image of the ouroboros, a snake eternally eating its own tail – a symbol for life's constant regeneration (see figure 7-1).

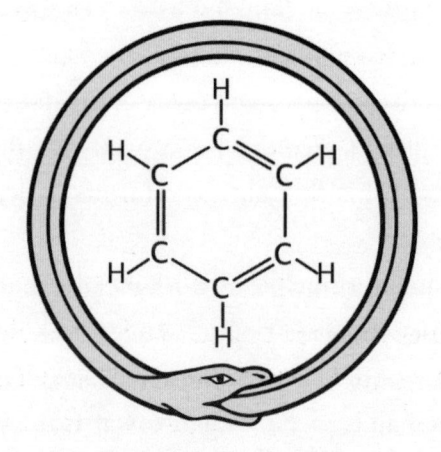

Figure 7-1: The Ouroboros and Carbon Ring

Jung pointed out that Kekulé's practical application of his inner vision accomplished what the lengthy experiments of the alchemists had striven for in vain.[10]

Current research into dreams investigates the correspondences between our dream life and how our minds construct waking reality. Allan Hobson, psychiatrist and dream researcher, has argued that the REM dream state lays down the foundations of a 'protoconsciousness' upon which waking consciousness depends.[11] According to this theory, during sleep, the brain optimises its conceptual model of the world by creating a virtual reality.[12]

The dreamscape is 'fictive' in the sense that it does not correspond exactly to waking life, yet it nonetheless reveals underlying principles of how form and movement evolve in the natural world. One basic principle at work in Nature is *symmetry*. The word *symmetry*, made up of the prefix *sym*, meaning 'the same', and the root *metre* or *measure*, gives us an insight into a key property of symmetry. Every time we look into a mirror, we see one of the most common forms of symmetry: 'bilateral symmetry'. An object possessing bilateral symmetry, such as the human face and form, is composed of two 'mirroring' halves that form a whole. Butterflies, trees and flowers, for example, share this symmetrical property. In Nature, the arts, sciences and dreams, symmetrical proportions, like those inherent to the circle, convey qualities of beauty, harmony, balance and completeness. Dream researcher and physicist Nigel Hamilton has identified symmetrical development as part of a natural and organic process whereby, through the evolution of symmetrical forms in our dreams, '*something is actually being constructed* in the psyche'.[13]

To give an illustrative example of this principle at work, we can visualise the symmetries that form part of a circle's construction. A circle forms from an infinite series of two-dimensional polygons. as follows (see figure 7-2):

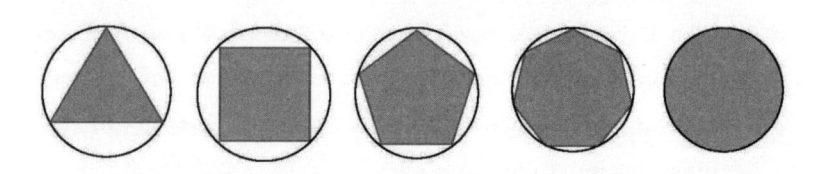

Figure 7-2: Creation of a Circle from Polygons

Starting with the three-sided equilateral triangle, adding a fourth edge to form a square, followed by a pentagon, hexagon and thereby to an infinite series, the straight edges of the polygons eventually round out to create a circle. In this way, a circular shape can be said to contain all the preceding polygons within it, much as the 'ball' held in Mother Julian's hand contained all that exists.

Let us focus on two fundamental geometric forms, the circle and the square, in order to explore how the appearance and evolution of their symmetries can encourage and express a dreamer's progress towards emotional balance.

First, consider the circle. Carl Jung, through his analysis of dreams, understood a circular or spherical shape to be a numinous archetype of the innermost self; forms such as a round stone, table, full moon or pearl all having the capacity to evoke an inner movement towards wholeness. Jung saw this archetype of the self as expressed in the universal symbol of the mandala, which, as he explains, 'portrays the self as a concentric structure ... invariably felt as the representation of a central state or of a centre of personality essentially different from the ego'.[14] In the 13th century, the mystic Meister Eckhart expressed a similar idea as 'Being is God's circle'.[15]

When we lose our sense of direction, a sense of what centres us in life, we can feel fragmented and lost rather than whole. At such times, the geometry of dreams can provide us with an internal compass, guiding us 'home' to our innermost self. For example, a circular shape appears in a dream that I had in my late twenties when teaching at a school in the Swiss Alps. I was feeling rather lonely and unsure about whether to continue teaching or to return to my homeland:

A circle of elders from the church where I grew up appear in an empty white room full of light. One of the dear ladies who had been my Sunday school teacher approaches me and asks what seems wrong. When I tell her of my worries, she takes out a piece of paper with a list on it. Glancing down at the list, she places her finger midway on it and says, 'But Switzerland is on the list!'

I woke up grateful for the dream and affirmed in my choice to move to Switzerland and in my decision to stay a while longer.

We find a circular form elaborated in a visionary dream had by one of the great holy men of the Oglala Lakota tribe, Heȟáka Sápa, more widely known as Black Elk. As an adult, he recollected the vision he had at the age of nine when severely ill, in which, as he relates,

> *I understood more than I saw; for I was seeing in a*
> *sacred manner the shape of all things in the spirit, and*
> *the shape of all shapes they must live together like one*
> *being. And I saw that the sacred hoop of my people*
> *was like many hoops that made one circle, wide as*
> *daylight and starlight, and in the center grew one*
> *mighty flowering tree to shelter all the children of one*
> *another and one father. And I saw that it was holy.*[16]

In Black Elk's vision the 'hoops' overlap, creating increasingly complex symmetries. The multiple symmetries enhance the powerful unifying effect of his vision.

On the medicine wheel of Native American indigenous cultures, the circle is divided into four quadrants, giving the compass of the four directions: north, south, east and west (see figure 7-3).

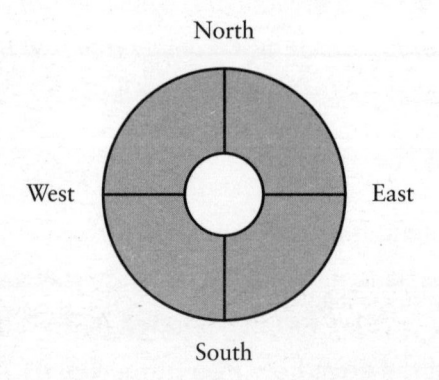

Figure 7-3: The Four Directions

The quadrants also depict the cyclic movements of life on Earth, from day to night, season to season, year to year – the Wheel of Life. On a cosmic scale, this extends to the orbits of planets and galaxies and, beyond that, to the birth and death of universes.

A dream's healing movement towards inner balance is embodied in the sandpainting ritual of the Navajo tradition. The medicine man creates a large medicine wheel of coloured sands on the ground. The mandala's symmetrical imagery portrays the internal balance that the ill person needs in order to achieve physical and psychological wholeness, while the wheel's centre symbolises a three-dimensional portal to the spirit world. The supplicant sits in the centre, facing east, so

Figure 7-4: Navajo Sandpainting

that the spirits can bring healing agents while taking away the causes of the illness and imbalance. Singing holy chants, the medicine man paints the sands from the mandala on the participant's body as a 'visual prayer' (see figure 7-4).[17]

The rebalancing accomplished by the quadrants of the Navajo sand-painting ritual find a parallel in Jung's four-functions model of the human psyche: thinking, feeling, intuition and sensation (see figure 7-5).[18]

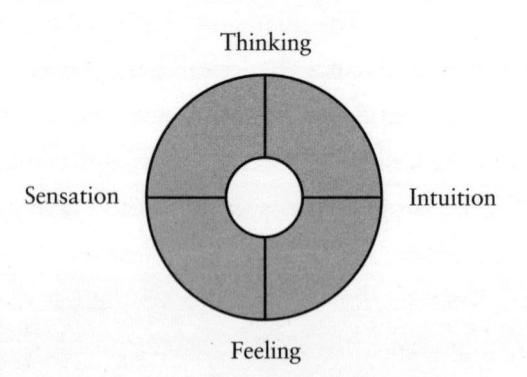

Figure 7-5: The Four Functions

According to Jung, one function frequently tends to dominate in each of us while another remains undeveloped, the effect being to cause an imbalance in the psyche. For example, if we fail to employ our thinking function to help us make discerning, even-handed judgements, we may become too emotionally unstable and liable to act impulsively. Conversely, relying solely on our thinking function, we may become too driven and lose touch with our humanity. Similarly, someone who relies too heavily on sense perception risks neglecting their inner intuitive guidance, while intuition needs to be 'grounded' in everyday life.

A dream had by a man in his forties, Paul, mirrors an imbalance in his feeling function. Paul had lost his parents some years before. He felt his own sense of purpose had died with their deaths, and he had not regained it since. The theme is one I see often in therapeutic dreamwork:

A little boy is lost, and I am looking for him.
The child has no name.

When I asked Paul how he felt when he woke up from the dream, he replied adamantly that he did not know. But, after some time, he suddenly said, 'I know how I felt when I woke up from the dream: lost!' I responded by saying that if something was lost, that meant it could be found. This dream marked the point from which Paul began to make a new start in life by re-engaging with the 'lost child' in himself. Paul's dream experience reminds us that when we feel lost in life, it is important for us to acknowledge our own feeling of lostness before we can move forward.

As we work with our dreams, gaining better insights into ourselves and others, this new understanding may be expressed in the shift from two-dimensional to three-dimensional forms, such as from the circle to the sphere. In dreams, this development entails an increasing gravitas, a further centring of the personality that imparts a healing sense of wholeness and balance.

The inner expansion of consciousness is mirrored in the sphere's flawless internal symmetry – no matter how we cut a sphere in two, both halves remain identical. Nicolaus

Copernicus described the sphere as 'most perfect' and 'best able to contain and circumscribe all else'.[19] Lacking vertices or edges, the sphere provides the smallest surface area for any given volume.

Gravity produces spherical forms at different orders of magnitude, from water droplets to planets and stars. Nurtured by light, out of Earth's spherical unity, myriad forms evolve – mineral, plant, animal and human. On a macroscale, some astrophysicists these days propound a sphere-shaped universe.[20] What may lie beyond that sphere, we do not know!

The appearance of three-dimensional symmetrical forms in dreams indicates a growing capacity to face life's challenges with equanimity, creativity and a more expansive consciousness. For instance, a woman named Rachel shared two dreams with me in which sphericity began to evolve. Prior to having met me, she had been working to free herself from a childhood blighted by harsh and punitive religious dogma, but she had yet to create what she beautifully described as her own 'gospel of the soul'. In the first dream, Rachel watches a female artist who demonstrates a painting technique. She recounts:

I watch in awe as her brush moves with multiple speed over the canvas. Using her imagination, she is creating an image of nature but the brilliance of her stroke and brush techniques is enhanced by a further magical ingredient. So, what's being produced by her is mingled with an independent force that is co-creating the image on the page. 'This is God!' she exclaims to me.

On waking, Rachel aligned the mysterious act of creation with what she called 'the god-element' in herself.

Over the ensuing two years, Rachel also underwent training with me in the psychotherapeutic application of dreams, during which she further developed what Jung would describe as her own 'symbolic life'.[21] Towards the end of her training, the theme of painting returned. In this second dream, both the painter and the shape of the painting surface take a different form from the earlier dream:

> *I'm painting, creating some artwork with rich colours,*
> *in a large shallow round bowl. My brush is whizzing*
> *at top speed, making spirals and circles that merge.*
> *Then I add some water to the bowl – I'm thinking the*
> *patterns will be washed away, but I'm on a sort of*
> *automatic pilot, so swish the water around. As I tip*
> *it out an amazingly beautiful, detailed and complete*
> *picture emerges. It's colourful with reds and yellow*
> *and in three parts. The central panel depicts a biblical*
> *or alchemical figure who fills the space. On either side*
> *are two panels of faces and figures, some serene and*
> *holy and others tortured and stressed... There's an*
> *implication that the characters are aspects of Self that*
> *I need to integrate to attain the central image. I am*
> *filled with a sense of magnitude of what's magically*
> *produced itself to me.*

Comparing these two dreams, Rachel observed that in the second she moves from watching the female artist to becoming the woman who creates – in other words, from observing a two-dimensional picture of the artist to participating in a three-dimensional embodiment of her own creativity. As Rachel herself explained: 'In the first, God produces art; in the second, art produces God. It's as if two parts of a whole have been joined.'

Importantly, the painting surfaces in the first and second dream differ. In the first dream, the artwork arises on a two-dimensional plane. In the second, it manifests in a three-dimensional bowl. The appearance of the bowl parallels a sense of growing spaciousness in Rachel's personality, a balancing of her feeling and intuitive functions in relationships to her previously dominant functions of thinking and sensation. The appearance of three panels indicates an opening to a spiritual dimension within Rachel's psyche, three being a number traditionally associated with divinity. As Rachel senses, the two dreams fit together as part of an ongoing integration of her spirituality and creativity.

Similar to the evolution of the circle to a sphere, dreams can signal a movement from the square to the three-dimensional cube (see Figure 7-6).

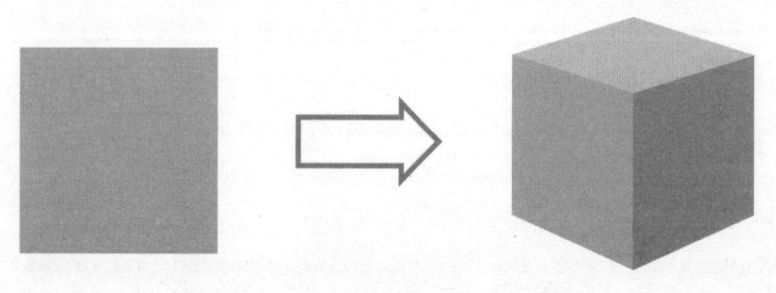

Figure 7-6: Expanding Dimensions

Inwardly, this shift from two to three dimensions represents the realisation of a lived space in which the dreamer is developing the capacity to engage fully with life. Interestingly, the Zen tradition teaches that it is the empty space within a house that makes it habitable, just as the hollow of a cup makes it fillable.

To return to Paul's 'lost child', as Paul continued with his inner work, he had a dream that reflected this same dimensional shift. He found himself standing in an unfamiliar, unfurnished room with three unknown people. He noticed two odd things about the room – there were no windows, and the floor was covered by a few inches of water. Although this dream initially frightened Paul, I could see it as holding promise: the four people (in total) suggested something being 'squared' or more fully structured and contained within Paul's psyche. The as yet unfurnished room, a three-dimensional space, revealed potential for his self-development, while the water implied the healing emergence of life-giving feelings.

Paul said that the windowless room made him feel claustrophobic. 'What,' I wondered, 'does "claustrophobic" mean to you?' He sat up in his chair: 'That's exactly what the man in the dream asked me! It must be important!' After that, he related the claustrophobic feeling of 'having no choices' to how he felt about his life. In this example, reflecting on his dream enabled Paul to 'see' how he was feeling and why. He could then explore whether or not it was absolutely true that he had no choices and how he might make choices more possible for himself, opening new windows on his life.

As we focus on the movement from the square to the cube, I will briefly share the significance of a sequence of four dreams from my own life over an 18-year period.

The first dream occurred when I was 27, two years after I had moved from the United States to Poland, where I set up an English department in a teacher-training college for foreign language teachers. At the time of this dream, I was in love!

> *My partner and I stand on the beach in California looking out at the sea. On the horizon, a large wave rises up, the black immensity of it increasing to skyscraper heights. The surface looks like obsidian, smooth and shiny. As the tidal wave approaches, it sucks up the water in front of it. Taking a hold of my partner's hand, I say, 'We can survive this if we run out to meet the wave and dive low under it.' We run out into the water to meet the wave. Then I shout, 'Dive!' I am aware of the wave's awesome power and pressure as it passes endlessly over us. Finally, we float up to the surface. The water floods the shore for miles. On the surface of the black seawater float photographs from our childhoods, in the old Kodak style – square with a white border. Strangely, a wooden pier sticks out of the water, and we swim for it.*

In this dream, two-dimensional squares appear in the form of photographs from my childhood. But at the time of dream, my focus was externalised, so I was not aware of how the emotions of my past were shaping my life choices.

Between this dream and the next in this series, some 16 years passed. Over those years, although I had any number of life experiences, living, studying, writing and working in different countries, my conditioned responses and unconscious patterns had not changed much. Longing for real change in myself and my life, I undertook trainings in psychotherapy and yoga, gaining both theory and practice as I learned ways to work with the psyche and body, and entering a more introspective phase in my life. These new ways of thinking and being gave me deepening insight into myself and others. My dreams became increasingly lucid, with imagery indicative of a movement towards a more conscious understanding of my own conditioned worldview.

One night, I had a dream in which the imagery reminded me of the earlier dream of photographs floating on the sea, but with a difference:

> ... *I notice a wall on which hundreds of key chains*
> *hang on hooks. Squares of glass, half an inch*
> *in thickness, dangle from each key chain. Small*
> *photographs from my childhood have been embedded*
> *in each. Fingering one of the key chains, I see that*
> *the glass gives a life-like dimensionality to the photo*
> *within, making it look as if I could step into the*
> *scene. The glass key chains reflect the light, bringing*
> *out the vitality in each image. I suddenly realise that*
> *I am looking upon key moments from my childhood*

and the early events that had shaped my life. I feel
tenderness towards my child self. Then I awake.

The dream reflected my growing awareness of the conditioning of thought and behaviour that I had learned as I child, but
rather than judging myself dismissively or critically, I could now
look upon the child in me with understanding and compassion.

After completing the training in psychotherapy, I became
the director of a charitable counselling centre – a very
demanding job, particularly as the main funding source
for the charity was soon to be withdrawn! The task ahead
felt daunting, and only my belief in the value of the service
outweighed my fears. I decided I would take each day one
step at a time. Then I had this dream:

I am at the centre where I work, which has three
counselling rooms in a row. Entering the middle room,
I am surprised it opens into a kind of massive airplane
hangar. There, many workers carry large shining black
cylinders, each with gold writing on the top. They go
about their tasks reverently and silently. I now see that
cubic receptacles line the hangar's left wall – at least
6 million, I think to myself! It strikes me as odd that
white ash covers everything. I suddenly realise that
these workers have a sacred task: they are sorting out
all the ashes from the Jewish victims of the Holocaust
and placing the ashes of each individual into a cylinder,
the writing in gold leaf on the top recording the
person's name in Hebrew. The workers have nearly

completed their work. I feel profoundly moved by the
preciousness of every individual life lost, the weight of
their suffering, and the terrible price that has been paid.
I fall to my knees with the power of this awareness.
Then I awake, deeply moved.

On a universal level, the dream addresses a collective awareness of what the tragedy of the Holocaust has meant for
humanity. On a personal level, the three-dimensional cubical
boxes both foretell and prepare me for the capacities that I will
need for the work ahead. The many workers who appeared
in the dream suggest to me that I will have help from many
others in supporting the centre, which, thankfully, I did. The
dream also heralded the transformative work of the counselling centre, where so many people would undertake the
life-changing task of sifting through the ashes of their lives to
reconstitute a new sense of self.

The final dream came at the end of a challenging first year
as director of the charity:

I am walking with my mentor. He cups his hands
saying, 'This is how it can always be.' I am swept
into the interior of an immense cube composed of
luminous blackness. The winds in that space carry me
across the various diagonal, vertical and horizontal
axes that meet at the cube's mid-point. The winds
refresh and invigorate me, and my consciousness feels
light and full of spirit, like a child on a swing. Then I
awake feeling refreshed.

In this lucid dream, the abstract shape of the cube becomes the primary structure. In the event, I went on to direct the centre for another seven years. Throughout my time there, I had a number of dreams such as this one, supporting me and giving me inspiration and strength.[22]

Our efforts to realise the truths our dreams hold can be likened to the endeavour to solve the problem posed by geometers of antiquity to square the circle. The challenge was to find a way to show how the surface area of a circle could be made equal to the surface area of a square. This mathematical conundrum has no perfect solution – the result is always an approximation, no matter how the size of circle and square are adjusted. There is, however, a symbolic solution for the alchemists' attempts to square the circle which, although not mathematically precise, created what Jung viewed as a profound image of the inner self,[23] one that can be illustrated as follows (see Figure 7-7):

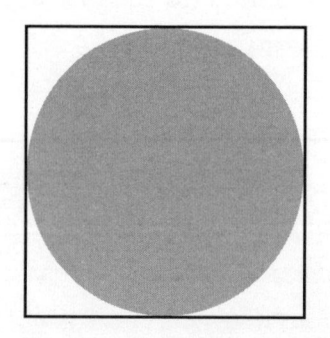

Figure 7-7: The Squaring of the Circle

In a dream, the squaring of the circle may appear in imagery such as the full moon reflected in a square mirror.

By envisioning the squaring of the circle as a sphere contained within a cube, there comes a further enhanced sense of expanding possibilities, a widening and deepening of consciousness. This could be revealed by the presence of a round table within the four walls of a room.

When we understand the ways in which a dream's internal geometry gives form to our state of being, we grasp more fully how each dream, like a sphere no bigger than a marble, or the hazelnut-sized ball remarked upon by Julian of Norwich, holds 'everything that is made'.

Chapter Eight

The Power of Healing Presence in Dreams

All real living is meeting.[1]

– Martin Buber

If I asked you to describe a loved one to me, a dear family member or friend, you could no doubt readily give me a snapshot description of them, what they look like, how you know them and what you love about them – the many ways you know them by heart. Yet, if I asked you to describe qualities of their *presence*, how it feels to look into their eyes or to be with them, words may prove more elusive.

The nature of presence shares the ineffability and evocativeness of dreams, conveying a quality of feeling rather than something readily defined. In the Middle Ages, alchemists, intrigued to discover that it takes 800lb of rose petals to create 1lb of rose-scented concentrate, concluded that a person's soul could likewise be distilled into an essence suggestive of their essential nature – the fragrance of the soul.[2]

Dictionaries give the derivation of 'presence' from the prefix *prae*, meaning 'in front of', and from the Latin verb *esse*, 'to be', and *praesentia*, 'a being before'.[3] 'Presence' impresses itself upon us, touches our souls and draws out previously unrealised qualities from within us. Like a fragrance, the longer a person's presence stays in our heart and mind, the stronger that sense of presence.

To get in touch with the healing power of presence in a dream, rather than simply describing what happened, we first need to consider how we *feel* in response to the dream. Just as in human relationships, the *feeling* nature of presence holds the key. For instance, one woman I worked with told me she'd had a dream in which she was sitting with her younger sister. She hadn't seen her sister much over the years but had always admired her for her strength and intelligence. When telling me about the dream, she pointed out that she didn't recall what they had said to each other, rather that, 'It was more a feeling. Like our souls were touching. That's what happens in dreams sometimes, our souls touch each other.' She added, 'It was a lot like sitting here with you now.'

When two souls touch, something new comes into being in the space between them, a special healing quality of presence that feels different from the more usual exchanges with others we have in everyday life. The psychologist Carl Rogers, exploring the relational quality between client and therapist, said of his own work, 'Over time, I think that I have become more aware of the fact that in therapy I do use my *self*. I recognize that when I am intensely focused on a client, just my *presence* seems to be healing, and I think this is probably true of any good therapist [italics added].'[4] In the Rogerian approach to psychotherapy, a therapist embodies healing presence by being genuine, accepting and empathetic – in other words, unconditionally 'present' – towards their client.

Drawing on Buddhist teachings, the psychotherapist John Welwood asks, 'What is *unconditional presence*?', and responds simply, 'Being present to our experience as it is.'[5] While this might sound as if it would be easy to do, for most of us that feels hard because we constantly want to avoid situations that cause us anxiety, discomfort or pain. Rather than being curious about uncomfortable feelings, we tend to reject them, building up protective defences against them. In contrast, when we respond to our life experiences, including our dreams, with openness and equanimity rather than fear, we enter into a more compassionate understanding of ourselves and others.

The medieval tradition of icon painting provides an interesting parallel here. Icons imaginatively serve to link the world of the senses and a deeper, more subtle dimension, imbued with qualities of true presence. It has been said that the icon gives us 'a sacred window onto the invisible world.'[6] One icon painted in the early 15th century, attributed to the Russian icon painter Andrei Rublev and prefacing this chapter, conveys this sense of soul-touching presence.

In the icon, we see three figures gathered round a table to share a meal, their heads bent in quiet communion. You may already have noticed that these figures have wings that merge with the landscape and halos that indicate an illumined intelligence, signs that we have entered the supra-sensory realm of angelic presences. Before you begin to analyse, interpret or judge this artwork, take a moment to be truly *present* to the qualities it emanates, feelings such as serenity, intimacy, harmony, balance, peacefulness and completeness.

Let us approach this icon as if it were a dreamscape. From left to right, the beings sitting round the table wear luminous outer garments of red, blue and green in the original painting, of a richly textured, diaphanous quality. Their unnaturally long arms and necks give them a larger-than-life appearance, foregrounding their importance, whereas the background has less significance. Their wings encircle them. A dynamic energy circulates in a harmonious flow among these elegant yet humble beings as they gaze at one another around the table.

When viewed in colour, the icon's backdrop shines in gold leaf, illumined as if from within.[7] In icons, no external light source is depicted, so no shadows appear. This is generally the case with dreams too. In both, illumination comes from the inner light.

Looking closely at Rublev's icon, we can see that the inverse perspective used in icon painting – narrow at the front and broader at the back – places the viewer at the centre of image, along the axis of symmetry. The empty space at the table beckons each of us to sit and partake of the meal and share in the angels' intimate gathering and quiet power, one alive with feeling.

Now imagine joining these celestial strangers at their table. Take a moment to consider how it feels to do so. Does the invitation cause you to feel sceptical, unsure, embarrassed, unworthy, unprepared, timid, impatient, disinterested, curious, confident, joyful, grateful, or something else altogether? Are you open to the possibility or do you contract and withdraw?

It doesn't always feel straightforward to accept an invitation like this and to relate to it in a responsive, friendly way. Our reaction tells us much about our emotional response to the opportunities that dreams, just as life, offer us.

Tradition has it that this icon depicts a biblical teaching in which the Old Testament patriarch Abraham receives strangers hospitably, serving them a meal, only to realise after the unknown guests had left that he had hosted angels.[8] As onlookers, we too can see the guests through Abraham's eyes, making these strangers guests at our own table. While portraying a particular time and place, the icon asks us to enter into the universality of the teaching: 'Do not neglect to show hospitality to strangers, for thereby some have entertained angels unawares.'[9] Abraham finds that the 'strangers' bring him good news: his wife, Rachel, although well past her childbearing years, will give birth to a child.

Similarly, in our dreams, when we are able to receive the 'stranger' with kindness, we find new life born into our daily living in unexpected ways. A dream reported by a woman interned at the time in Auschwitz during the Second World War powerfully demonstrates this:

I dreamt that I was walking towards a small river with very turbid waters. On the other bank, my eldest brother, Stachu,[10] was coming towards me (he had already died when I had this dream). Both of us stepped into the water at the same time. My feet sank into the mud. When we met in the middle of the deep river, my brother handed me a huge, fiery fish. I scream, terrified:

> '*Stachu, I can't carry it, I can't carry it.*' *And he calmly replied:* '*You'll carry it, you'll carry it.*'

She continues: 'When [later] I was down with typhus ... his words consoled me in my illness, [and] gave me hope that I would survive typhus. And indeed, I did.'[11]

Although the fiery fish frightens the dreamer, we know from alchemy that fire also serves as a powerful agent of transformation and purification. That a water creature, a fish, is aflame, causes fear. Nevertheless, we can also notice that this strange blending of the two images has a mysterious quality, like the burning bush of the Old Testament out of which Yahweh spoke to Moses. The fiery fish arises between the figure of the brother and his sister, bearing the numinous quality of an overpowering mysterious presence that inspires both awe and terror – the *mysterium tremendum*.[12] When we perceive the *mysterium tremendum* as originating from a power outside of us, felt to be 'wholly other',[13] it can become unbearable, as in this dream. However, although the dreamer feels terrified by the strange quality of the fish, the brother's reassurance acts as an antidote to her terror, his love helping her to overcome her fear.[14]

Exactly what the fish signified for the dreamer, she does not say, but she later credits her brother's words heard in the dream – 'You'll carry it' – with helping her to survive potentially fatal typhus. This Auschwitz survivor reports the dream as being about her physical survival, yet, viewed from a transpersonal perspective, she has also been given spiritual fortitude to 'carry' the burden of the camp's horrors and to survive.

A creature like a dream-fish emanates presence all the more when the dreamer can fully engage with it. As an example, we can turn to a dream had by Angela, whose earlier dream of the Sistine Chapel was included Chapter Five on light. Angela had this next dream during a difficult time in her personal life, when her need to carve out a creative space for herself came to the fore. Only when she shared the dream in waking life did the sense of presence within truly come alive:

I am resting on a bed with my father ... The bed is unusual insofar as it is a water tank! Suddenly a huge goldfish slips out of it and starts circling the room obsessively. My father and I are baffled and startled; 'Where does that come from?' shouts my father. 'Who's put it here? Small fish are fine but not this monster!' I jump out of bed and survey the scene. At first, I find the fish kind of alien and scary, but then I realise that, despite its size, it is harmless. The poor creature is simply distressed. It is compelled to come out because it is too big for the bed and can no longer bear such a confined space. On the other hand, it cannot stay out of the bed because it needs the water to breathe, so the fish is condemned to move in and out of its prison in an inescapable, frantic vicious circle. I watch it quietly, thinking with increasing compassion that I will have to capture it and take it to the sea.

After Angela told me this dream, we explored it as a waking dream. In the process, she imaginatively engaged directly with the fish, taking the creature up in her arms. In doing so, she felt compassion towards the fish and an appreciation of its powerful energy. This moved her profoundly. She felt able to contain the energy the fish held and stood absorbed in doing so for a few moments. When I suggested she go ahead and let the experience unfold, she carried the fish to the sea where she let it go, enacting this movement as she narrated the unfolding dream. When Angela released the fish into water, she felt reassured that the large goldfish now had a place expansive enough to swim in unencumbered.

Reflecting upon the dream and dreamwork, she viewed the fish as both herself and as a spiritual symbol.[15] Angela added, 'So, for me the dream is not just a re-enactment of the pain and claustrophobia that made me leave home when I was in my twenties, but it also tells me that the needed leap, right now, is at a spiritual level.' She understood the movement from the 'waterbed to the seabed' as moving towards her transpersonal Higher Self, explaining that 'this road passes through the heart, with compassion that doesn't reject the fish as the odd one out, as the wrong thing in the wrong place, but embraces it and makes the effort of the journey to freedom.' In so saying, she spoke for a more positive masculine archetype, a fatherly quality in herself that could provide her with guidance and forceful energy.

In both dreams reported here, a fish has associations with healing presence: the first with life-saving emotional reassurance and the second with direct awareness of empowerment to take action. The psychological and spiritual elements within each dream overlap and inform one another, a dual psycho-spiritual perspective, in which personal and transpersonal elements combine.

A being in a dream may also bring physical healing, as I personally experienced when a severe sinus infection incapacitated me for weeks. I had recently moved to London from Switzerland during a troubled time in my life, and I felt despondent. Then, I had this dream:

I stand in the afternoon light. A being who reminds me of the angel Gabriel from a dream I had many years before approaches me and says, 'I hear you haven't been feeling well.' As he speaks, he lifts his right forefinger and touches my sinus areas under each eye. In the dream, I instantly feel better, and I realise that when I wake up, I will begin to get well. As he turns and walks away, I cry out to him, 'Can you heal my spirit?' He turns and comes up to me again. He looks at me with a great deal of love as he raises his finger to the point between my eyebrows. His fingertip seems just a hair's breadth away from me, and I can feel its heat and power. Then suddenly he looks at me very tenderly and with deep regret slowly lowers his hand. It feels as if he suddenly got a message not to heal me this way. We look long at each other, and I realise with disappointment and resignation that whereas the healing of my body would be rapid, the healing of my spirit would take years – at least another seven years, if not longer. And then I wake up.

Although my meeting with a healing presence in this dream felt timeless, the dream itself held a very earthy sense of time. Specific intervals of time given in dreams often turn out to have a literal application. In this case, seven years after this dream, I started training in the psychotherapy programme that would lead to my working more closely with dreams. It was then that my inner healing truly began.[16]

Dreams, like icons, also reveal time as existing on two levels – *chronos* and *kairos*. The former denotes chronological time, the continuum of past, present and future, named after the Greek god Chronos, 'the father of time'. The latter, named after the Greek god Kairos, describes the quality of time experienced, for example, when we come into real presence. In such moments, time becomes fluid, and may even seem to stop altogether, as when we are fully in the 'now'.

To return to Rublev's icon, both *chronos* and *kairos* are in evidence. The icon's background locates the historical event in time (Abraham's house, the oak tree standing next to it and a nearby mountain), yet the emphasis is on the participation of three figures in communion together – the sharing of *kairos* over a humble meal also expresses the Christian understanding of Divine presence as a trinity of Father, Son and Holy Ghost. (In this icon, coming from the Eastern Orthodox tradition which Rublev followed, the Trinity is sometimes pictured with female representations.) *Kairos* infuses everyday actions, such as breaking bread together, with a sacred quality.

Thus, a sacred encounter can leave a lasting impression of a deep communion with healing presence, as in the following dream, had by the dreamer at a time of great personal distress.

He describes the dream as the shortest but most powerful he'd ever had, adding that, even many years on, it remains as vivid and heartfelt as when it first took place. He relates:

> *I am walking along a path or track when I suddenly become aware of a person beside me on my right. I turn to look and there is a man of around 30 years. His face and eyes shine with love and he smiles, a smile that seemed to go right inside me and fills me with joy! Then I awake and know instantly that my companion was Jesus.*

Sacred encounters in dreams and icons convey a sense of presence that transcends religious dogma, restoring the original meaning found at the heart of the word 'religious': 'To heal, to bond, to join, to bridge, to put back together again' – capacities that the Jungian analyst Robert Johnson calls 'our sacred faculties'.[17]

Most people today are more familiar with icons as graphic images on their computers than with religious icons. Yet computer icons share certain attributes with their medieval counterparts. For example, to access the internet, we click on the image of the chosen 'icon', initiating software that extends the reach and capacity of our minds, revealing previously unseen worlds to us. By means of a simulated world, effectively a virtual reality, we enter into the technological cathedral of the mind, an architectural space 'housing' an intelligence that seems vastly greater than that of the individual mind.

In so far as the internet connects us in positive ways, bridging the distance between individuals and widening our field of consciousness, it has the potential to nourish our sacred faculties and emotions in our waking and dreaming lives. However, it is essential that our hearts also be engaged and for us to be mindful enough for thoughtful reflection, or else the constant flow of images entices us into the world of sensation rather than the Imaginal World within.

In 2017, the film director Werner Herzog made a documentary about the internet entitled *Lo and Behold, Reveries of the Connected World*.[18] Herzog's opening expression 'Lo and Behold' alludes to both *chronos* and *kairos*. The word 'Lo' in the title comes from the first two letters ever transmitted using the internet, briefly linking the University of California at Los Angeles with Stanford University near San Francisco (before the computer system crashed). 'Lo and behold' are words traditionally reserved for angelic messengers who herald a Divine presence. In this context, the title ironically refers to the almost worshipful esteem with which the public views the internet and the power it holds.

Herzog speculates, 'Can the internet dream of itself?' In one sense, the internet has fast become a new field of dreams, a global platform for what the visionary Teilhard de Chardin called the 'noosphere', 'the thinking layer' of an evolving planetary consciousness.[19] On the negative side, Herzog uncovers an internet used for nightmarish purposes: sexual harassment, cyber bullying, political propaganda and unbridled consumerism, devoid of empathy or compassion.

Most of us now spend more than a full day a week online,[20] *far more than we spend in dreaming*, looking outside for 'information' rather than seeking it within. Around 75 per cent of teenagers in the United States check their messages on social media as soon as they wake up, before doing anything else.[21] How differently might they feel if, upon waking, they first spent time checking in with their nightly dreams! The 'online world' stimulates the imagination and can also create a superficial sense of presence and intimacy. Yet without physical connection and emotional support – the human touch – spending long periods of time online may deepen a feeling of disconnection, isolation and loneliness.[22]

Computer programs like Google's DeepDream use algorithms and layered networks to turn familiar objects into fantastical creations. In one instance, when asked to distinguish patterns in photographs of clouds, the computer's layered network, attempting to mimic basic patterning structures of the human brain, produced a bizarre hybrid creature floating in the sky with the head of a dog and the body of a fish.[23]

Such computer-generated images, although they may stimulate new ways of seeing patterns in everyday objects, do not arise from an individual's life and so fail to enrich meaningfully our subjective sense of being. The CGI dog-fish does not emanate the living presence of a 'dream being'. Derived from a compilation of web-based imagery, it belongs to everyone and no one! In contrast, dream imagery comes tailored from the fabric of our own lived experiences and personality, fitting our nature and our need, and cultivating empathy towards ourselves and others.

While reflecting on the CGI dog-fish, the image of a dream-fish I had first met in my teens surfaced from the depths of my memory. The marvels of CGI pale into insignificance when I recall the numinosity of my dream-fish:

I stand alone in the empty playground where I went to school between the ages of eight and eleven. I feel unhappy about being back in a place that I do not remember with much fondness. The playground's emptiness reminds me of how I long for a different way of life. When I look up, I am amazed to see an unusually large angelfish – a few inches thick and about five feet long – swimming in the air at eye level, peering into my eyes intently with its bulbous, dark eyes. The fish moves its full lips silently as its beautiful, translucent body shimmers with ever-changing colours. I gape in surprise at the fish as it looks at me intently. Initially, I feel frightened, but then I realise it means me no harm. On the contrary, it appears to be speaking to me. Then I awake.

Throughout the challenges of my teens, the dream memory of that 'air-fish' stayed with me, offering encouragement. Looking back, I wish there had been a dream guide to help me use my imagination to speak with the fish or to touch it. Closing my eyes today, I still feel the air-fish's creativity and magical spirit.

In my early twenties, the air-fish took on added significance when I studied English literature. As part of my studies, I came across a fairy tale called 'The Golden Key', written by the Scottish writer George MacDonald. In this story, a similar air-fish appears to a little girl named Tangle when she becomes lost in a forest. MacDonald paints an enchanting picture of this air-fish: 'It was a curious creature, made like a fish, but covered, instead of scales, with feathers of all colours, sparkling like those of a humming-bird. It had fins, not wings, and swam through the air as a fish does through the water. Its head was like the head of a small owl.'[24]

Numerous air-fish accompany Tangle on her journey, helping to nourish her by allowing themselves to be cooked in a pot and eaten. A kindly woman reassures Tangle that 'they are not ... destroyed. Out of that pot comes something more than the dead fish, you will see.'[25] When Tangle eats the delicious meat, she is able to understand the sounds of the forest creatures as speech, and the chatter of insects too. Afterwards, a little fairy flies out of the pot – the air-fish has transformed!

The air-fish of my own dream similarly fed my soul with the sustenance I particularly needed then – a taste of magic and beauty that spoke of unrealised possibilities. The air-fish brings to life what George MacDonald himself said of dreams: 'I believe that, if there be a living, conscious love at the heart of the universe, the mind, in the quiescence of its consciousness in sleep, comes into a less disturbed contact with its origin, in the heart of the creation...'[26]

The magnificent presence of the air-fish in my dream also reminds me of John Welwood's teaching on 'unconditioned awareness':

> Pure awareness is direct, unfabricated, knowing, clear and fluid like water. Although we swim in this sea of pure awareness, our busy mind is constantly hopping from island to island, from thought to thought, jumping over and through this awareness which is its ground, without ever coming to rest there. Meanwhile,

our unconditioned awareness operates silently in the background, no matter what our busy mind is doing. Everyone has access to this. It is our most intimate reality, so close that it is often hard to see.[27]

Our dreams give us a natural means of waking up to this awareness more directly, never more important than in today's world, where an array of technologies immerse us in an impersonal digital reality and so easily distract us from knowing ourselves.[28]

To reconnect with a healing presence from one of your own dreams, find pen and paper and a quiet spot, close your eyes, take a few deep breaths, and then bring the presence-bearing image to mind. Spend a minute or two silently sensing the qualities that the healing presence evokes in you. Perhaps, like my dream air-fish, it puts you in touch with a magical quality of wonder and offers calm reassurance or, as Angela felt when she held her goldfish, you may sense a powerful creative force. Alternatively, you may feel tremendous awe, even fear, like the woman who dreamed of a fiery fish in Auschwitz, yet somehow better able to carry life's burdens. Whatever you feel, stay with the feeling for a few moments. Then, with your next out-breath, release that feeling into the world. Now take up your pen and give yourself a few minutes to write down what the dream presence has to tell you.

This is what my dream fish recently 'said' to me:

From whence have I come? From within you and from without. Find the magic in me. You are not alone, you are loved. Learn to see my beauty in each moment, even amidst what feels hard and ugly in yourself and life. Like me, you swim in the air of Earth and Spirit, immersed in an invisible world that gives life to all you see. Remember me when the world feels colourless and grey and I will bring new colours to your life.

When we re-engage with the power of real presence in our dreams, a healing touch becomes available to us, no matter if the dream occurred many years before!

Consider the words of the Taoist master Lao Tzu, written over 2,500 years ago:

The Way itself is like something
Seen in a dream, elusive, evading one.
In it are images, elusive, evading one.
In it are things like shadows in twilight.
In it are essences, subtle but real,
Embedded in truth.[29]

'Subtle but real', the images and essences in our dreams may take many forms, ranging from inanimate objects to living creatures – plants, fish, birds and animals – from personifications of human or ideal beings to abstract light and colour-based imagery.[30] All invite us to leave the glare of blue-lit technologies, to slow our frenzied pace of life, and open ourselves to the healing power of true presence illumined within our dreams.

Chapter Nine

Nightmares: From Fear to Freedom

When you lie down, you will not be afraid;
when you lie down, your sleep will be sweet[1]

– Proverbs 3:24

Have you ever had a nightmarish dream of falling from a great height or being chased by a threatening stranger or fearsome creature? If so, you are not alone in your experience; many people across cultures commonly report having such dreams.[2] But while knowing that others have similar nightmares may offer some comfort, it is more comforting still to know that in a frightening dream, instead of fleeing, each of us has the power to make peace with what we fear.

A wide-ranging study on the effectiveness of therapy for dealing with nightmares suggests that changes to the *beliefs* we hold about nightmares and the ways we respond to fear play a key role.[3] This chapter will explore how, by making such changes, we discover that we can acquire power over our fears, that we have within us more light than darkness. In this process, as we gain a sense of mastery over *our response* to frightening dream content, we learn to trust that we can move from fear to freedom, not only in our dreams but in life too.

The origins of the word 'nightmare' are to be found in Anglo Saxon and Old Norse folk traditions. Legend has it that a Swedish king and renowned warrior, Vanlandi, was unknowingly put under a spell cast by a sorceresses whom he had angered. That night while sleeping, he called out that a 'mare was treading on him'.[4] His guards could see the apparition smothering his head, but when they moved to his head to fight the mare off, the mare then trod on his legs and feet, causing his death.[5] King Vanlandi lacked a counter-spell, a charm, that could protect him, and so could not throw off the mare, which suffocated and crushed him.[6] Metaphorically, this story reminds us that nightmares catch us off guard, and that when they 'tread on us', we may find our breathing constricted or our limbs paralysed. We may even fear for our life.

On the other hand, it may have been that the king was suffering from a medical condition called sleep apnoea, in which the airway periodically becomes obstructed during the night. This condition can be life-threatening, and frequent nightmares of suffocation or drowning may alert us to this physiological disorder. It is important also to be aware that nightmares, when they occur repeatedly, even several times in the same night, causing insomnia and distress, may be associated with a chronic sleep disorder known as parasomnia. Such disorders are physiologically driven and may require medical intervention.[7] If you think you have a parasomnia, it is best to contact your doctor. Also, if you have been diagnosed with a mental illness or are feeling emotionally unstable, the type of dreamwork described in this chapter may be unsuitable and should only be considered with the guidance of a mental health professional.

According to a study in 2019, not all 'bad' dreams should be regarded as pathological. Having identified the neural correlates of fear in both REM dreaming and the waking state, researchers recruited 89 participants to keep records of their dreams for a week. Then, while awake, the subjects were placed in a magnetic resonance imaging (MRI) chamber and shown distressing pictures in order to see how their brains reacted to the negative stimuli. The researchers found that the more fear people had experienced in their dreams during the preceding week, the less their brain scans showed evidence of a fear response.[8] However, the study also confirmed that if the dreamer felt overwhelmed by fear in their dream – so terrifying was the nightmare – far from potentially conferring any benefit in waking life, the effect was negative. This preliminary study on the neural correlates of fear in dreams and in wakefulness supports the theory that dreams can have an adaptive role in moderating our fears and could pave the way for further research on clinical outcomes. To quote Lampros Perogamvros, one of the researchers involved in the study, 'Dreams may be considered as a real training for our future reactions and may potentially prepare us to face real life dangers.'[9]

The existential fear of threat to life underlies many frightening dreams, and this foreshadows how we might respond when faced with the actuality of death – either our own or that of a loved one. Yet, paradoxically, to face the fact that death is part of life has long been recognised as a spur to appreciating the full gift of life. Throughout history, philosophers, poets and spiritual teachers have given this paradox deep thought. Plato in his *Phaedrus* quotes Socrates as saying, 'True philosophers make dying their profession.'[10]

Although we may attempt to evade or deny thoughts of death, nightmares forcibly make us aware of our existential vulnerability, shattering the illusion of control we like to think we have over our lives. Yet nightmares also compel us to consider afresh the great questions of life: What matters most to us? What blocks our will to act? How do we remain composed when under duress? How might we feel, live and love more fully, less fearfully? Nightmare scenarios urgently call upon us to develop the courage needed to overcome our fears. Every night, as we surrender to sleeping and dreaming, we have a renewed chance to become aware of the limited view that we hold about ourselves and the world around us, opening the way to a more empathetic and expansive under-standing of the natural cycle of birth, life and death.

Some years back, I worked for two years as a volunteer on a hospice ward where terminally ill patients received care during the weeks before their death. There, I found that many people in end-of-life care, who are approaching the mystery of death, welcome companionship, no matter how briefly, while they await the inevitable. From these individuals, I learned much about how even a few moments of attentiveness can create a soulful space, helping to relieve fear and bring about a new sense of calm that enhances both living and dying.

One morning on the ward, the nurses asked me to spend some time with John, a young man who had a brain tumour, describing him as 'agitated' and 'confused'. When I entered John's room, I found him lying in his bed, eyes closed, tossing from side to side and shouting incomprehensibly as if in torment. I sat down by his bedside and tried to make out his words. Eventually, I realised what he was saying: 'I've got to get off, get off!' I leaned over, took his hand and asked, 'Get off what?' He answered, 'Off of this life.' Then he cried out, 'I'm dying, I'm dying, but that's okay, isn't it?' 'Yes,' I said, 'that's okay.' He told me that trains kept going by and he couldn't get on. Treating the situation as if it were a waking dream, I replied, 'Don't worry. You've got a ticket, and when your train comes, you'll have no problem getting on.' John calmed down and said, 'Yeah, yeah, I've got a ticket.'[11] He seemed greatly relieved and fell back to sleep peacefully. Assured that he had his 'ticket', he remained calm until he died a few days later.

In reframing our understanding of death, it is also of note that a trailblazing analysis of over 300 near-death experiences (NDEs) by Peter and Elizabeth Fenwick found that 82 per cent of those taking part in the study reported that their NDE lessened or even removed their fear of death.[12] When I was volunteering at the hospice, I met an elderly man in the patient lounge who shared a similar experience with me. He asked me, 'Do you believe there's an afterlife?' As soon as I answered 'Yes', he raised his fist in the air and exclaimed, 'Well, I tell you, I don't believe; I *know*.' He continued:

I had surgery for a brain tumour. I wanted to die. I had so much pain. And I did die on the operating table. I saw the other side, I did, and I'm not afraid at all now. I know there's something there. Saw my grandchild who'd died and my old friends. Some people here are afraid of death, but I tell them they don't have to be afraid. It's like going out to the pub to meet your friends. That's all it is.

He paused and asked if I believed him. I assured him I did. He explained, 'I don't talk about it with the folks back home. They'd think I'm touched.' I told him a dream I'd had about seeing my own mother 'on the other side'. 'That's it!' he exclaimed. 'It's all real!' His declaration 'I don't believe; I know' reminded me of the words of Carl Jung, who, when asked in his later years if he believed in God, replied, 'I don't need to believe; I know.'[13]

Strange as it may seem, every breath we take reflects the cycle of life and death, because the very air we depend on brings us a little closer to death each day. Without oxygen we die, yet the transformation of oxygen into energy leaves by-products of oxidation in our bodies that eventually lead to cell death.[14] As every living thing possesses mitochondria dependent on oxygen, death is hardwired into the system. Yet since death has a dreadful finality about it for so many, few of us make peace with it before it arrives and instead fight off 'letting go' until the last moment.

There is another kind of death that needs facing in the midst of life, which is 'dying' to an old way of being, whether an old attitude of mind or pattern of behaviour. Symbolically, we 'lose' our life to find it. When we are able to do this, the energy released transforms both our dreams and life for the good. If we think of death as a transformation of energy, then when something 'dies', a good deal of life energy gets freed up in the process, much as fallen leaves in autumn provide nutrients in the soil for the trees to grow the following spring.

I will now give two examples of working therapeutically with nightmares to help transform the emotional energy blocked by fear into making positive life changes. The first concerns Angela, whom we have met in previous chapters. At the time of the following dream, she had been moving towards making time for her creativity, but still felt frustrated by a busy schedule and a lack of real time and space for herself:

> *I am going on holiday to France on a narrowboat.*
> *My sister gives me a map of the area. I know I will*
> *be navigating a river but now, looking at it on the*
> *map, I realise that pretty soon the river comes to*
> *a waterfall, a huge plunge of exactly one million*
> *centimetres,*[15] *the size of a skyscraper! I am horrified*
> *and decide it's not safe, it's not something I want to*
> *do … yet the map is three-dimensional and alive.*
> *It shows me that all the boats that have taken the*
> *plunge are unharmed. I can see them in one piece*
> *continuing their navigation along a peaceful river.*

Angela awoke deeply frightened, for although the scene displayed on the magical 3D map had made her curious about the journey, she felt certain that the waterfall would destroy her. Nevertheless, the numinous power of the waterfall could indicate the potential for powerful healing. Subsequently, we agreed to undertake the waking dream process together.

As Angela re-entered the dream, I could see from her face that being on the boat itself gave her pleasure, and so, to help her feel safe, I suggested that she focus on those feelings. In doing so, she felt in touch with a sense of freedom and mystery, aware of these emotions as sensations in her throat and neck. To enhance the feeling of safety, I asked her to choose a sacred word to repeat to herself. Whenever Angela's fear made her body tense up, we paused so she could breathe deeply and repeat the sacred word until her body relaxed again. Each time this happened, I reminded her that this was a dream and she did not need to be afraid.

As we continued with this dream narrative, the boat drew closer to the edge of the waterfall. At the waterfall's edge, I asked her to freeze-frame this picture in her mind's eye and to notice the feelings that arose. 'Very treacherous,' she replied. When I asked her if she recalled ever feeling this way in waking life, she described the time some years before when her partner was unexpectedly diagnosed with cancer, dying soon after.

Once Angela had made this connection and could acknowledge her grief, she felt ready to let herself be carried over the waterfall, along with deep feelings and tears. As she did so, she felt a powerful release of energy in the pit of her stomach, her solar plexus. We stayed present to this feeling for some time, allowing it to suffuse her. The tension left her body and Angela sat peacefully for some minutes, until she said that she felt ready to come out of the experience.

I asked her how she would apply the waking dream to her life. She replied that from the New Year, she would keep one day a week free, explaining, 'The idea is to devote one day to *being* instead of *doing*. Nothing allowed – no work, no bureaucracy, not even emails. A small step but difficult to take.'

Angela's realisation speaks for many of us. In her case, the dreamwork had given her confidence to take decisive action – she had, after all, met the fear that her grief would overwhelm her. Not only did she survive the descent down the immense waterfall, she also tapped into its power, moving through her conditioned limitations to a realisation about how she wanted to change her life.

Figuratively speaking, Angela had descended into the innermost part of her being. The alchemical descent into the 'innermost part of the earth' involves what the medieval alchemists called a *mortificatio*, a breaking down or 'death' of a basic substance that was pictorially displayed in images of disintegration and destruction.[16] This process of mortification had to occur before the chemistry of a new element could arise. Similarly, in the alchemy of dreams, such imagery often speaks to the 'mortification' of a *way of thinking about ourselves or others*, an attitude we hold in waking life that no longer does us good.

Angela's waking dream process tracked the associated feelings in her physical body, giving her an embodied sense of her feelings. Later, she also drew a picture of her waterfall 'dive'. 'Whenever I look at it,' she said, 'I feel enormously energised, especially in the solar plexus. I feel a sense of freedom, my life force awakening.' The movement from fear to freedom within Angela's waking dream process illustrates not only a transformation of her fear but also the renewal of her confidence and, importantly, the development of her will.

Although we cannot perceive Angela's will directly, we sense it through the life-changing decisions she makes as a result of working with her dream. A fully developed will harnesses the power we need to achieve our aims. For this we need to align our own personal will with what Roberto Assagioli, the founder of psychosynthesis, calls the 'transpersonal' or 'highest' will, giving us the capacity to act with compassion towards ourselves, others and all of creation.[17]

As the psychologist Mark Thurston has pointed out, we can apply transpersonal will to overcoming our fears in our dream life just as well as in our waking life.[18] We can do this, as Angela did, through dreamwork or, as we shall see, *in the course of the dream itself*. As we learn to move beyond our initial fear, this awareness empowers us to take decisive action and to access with the Higher Wisdom needed to move from fear to freedom.

Once aligned with transpersonal will, we release ourselves from the limitations of the ego and open ourselves instead to beauty, compassion and love. This is the Power of Will – very different to the ego's 'will to power'! This will comes as a natural expression of a person's authentic self. Then, like a bird, we each intuitively know how to take wing.

The second illustration of dreamwork comes from a sequence of three dreams had by Rachel, prior to her having the dream of the painted bowl shared with us in Chapter Five. These dreams took place during a period of terrorist attacks in the United Kingdom:

*A terrorist is coming. I'm quite calmly planning my
protection and arrange with a woman that I'll lie
down and hide on the floor beneath her seat. I'm
satisfied with my plan but realise she's very small and
may move her legs, at which point I'll be exposed. I
decide it's a risk I have to take.*

As Rachel thoughtfully reflected, 'Here's a force from within
the ego, one of fear and the need for protection. Hiding behind
the legs of another suggests a very small child experiencing
terror and attack. However, there is a degree of acceptance
and surrender to the situation – sufficient protection is available
and a resignation to the risk.'

In this dream, we see the awakening of Rachel's will in her
acceptance of risk and in her decision to take evasive action.
At the same time, in her waking life, the dream prompts her
to explore how a traumatic episode from her childhood influences
her reactions whenever she feels vulnerable as an adult.

In Rachel's second dream, the perceived level of threat
has increased:

*A man comes to my door – it is glass and ajar. I see
him with a knife and gun in one hand and a container
of water in the other. He's here to attack but he's
taking his time in preparation, not barging through
the open door but first using the water in some way
to prepare the firing of his gun. I make my escape in
dread of what is to come.*

In this second dream, Rachel again took evasive action, but awoke feeling she would need to face this unknown intruder. Accordingly, with me she later undertook the waking dream process. This time, when she tried to get away, she found herself in water up to her knees, making it difficult to run. She determined to wait rather than running away, choosing instead to focus, with my guidance, on calming her breath. I reassured Rachel that she was safe; she didn't need to be afraid and could always choose to stop the process. Choosing to continue, after a pause, she suddenly burst out laughing. 'What's happened?' I asked. She explained that the man had dipped his gun in the water and filled it! In a flash she realised that the 'gun' was actually a water pistol and so could not harm her.

Rachel's re-engagement with the dream required her to face the gunman and activate her will to resist running away. As a result, she gained an empowering sense of freedom that changed her experience of the original dream entirely.

Reflecting further on the dream, Rachel likened the watery aspect to her feelings, her unwept tears. She recognised that her actual fear was of the impact of her own feelings – the bullet from the gun – and that she would need to acknowledge those feelings to disarm them.

Rachel then recalled a childhood experience, aged eleven, at her Catholic boarding school, when a nun publicly and cruelly accused her of being 'evil' in a school assembly. She described this as a traumatic 'character assassination'. She thoughtfully shared,

From this I learned to hone the art of containing my emotional response, and it brought a sense of great power, protection and wellbeing that cut through the grief ... Now it's time to allow a connection to a vulnerable self and surrender to the threat that is posed because that threat no longer applies to me as it did to my eleven-year-old self.

From this dream and subsequent dreamwork, Rachel concluded, 'I don't need to protect my wounds. Imperfection and vulnerability are a part of life and being human.'

Not long after, Rachel had the following dream:

I find myself in a darkened room. The door opens and there's a sense of inevitability. The shadow of a man with a machine gun enters. I raise my hands in surrender and walk towards the window with my back to him. I see the shadowed outline of myself against the half light of the window.

The man is there to assassinate me. He's from ISIS. I say, 'I can worship Allah.' This is to try and save myself but also to let him know that I'm a spiritual person. The execution is delayed for a day. I notice I'm calm in the circumstances.

Rachel saw this dream as an 'embrace' of both the spiritual and masculine aspects of herself, as well as connecting with current waking-world events.

Notably, in this dream, she remains calm. In turning her back to the terrorist and telling him that she too can worship Allah, Rachel expresses an openness unfettered by dogmatism while noticing her own calmness in speaking to the 'terrorist' – *a movement towards a conscious act of will within the dream.*

Following this dream, Rachel felt less fearful not only about the actual terrorist threats around that time but also in terms of revealing her own vulnerabilities. The sequence of dreams had allowed for the expression of fear and the facing of it both in sleep and in waking life through the safe environment of the therapeutic setting.

Themes from a living-world nightmare frequently cross into our dreams, challenging us to rise above individual fears and to take action in response. Dreams had by people living under the coercive pressure of the Nazi regime in Germany in the 1930s and 1940s powerfully illustrate both the fearfulness of the times and the power of the will.

During the rise of Nazism in Germany, the journalist Charlotte Beradt, of Jewish descent, would awake drenched in sweat from a repeated nightmare in which she had run breathlessly across fields, hiding at the top of towers and in graveyards as she fled from Stormtroopers (*Stoßtruppen*) intent on torturing and killing her. Upon waking, she wondered if others shared her fears. In response to her dream, she began to collect dreams from people living under the Nazi regime.[19]

At great risk to her own life, Beradt managed to smuggle the dreams she had collected out of Nazi Germany by using a code to disguise their content and hiding the dreams separately in books that she then sent to friends abroad. In 1939, she fled to the United States, where she eventually gathered the dreams into a volume, first published in German in 1966, and two years later in English, entitled: *The Third Reich of Dreams: The Nightmares of a Nation, 1933–1939.*[20]

Beradt explores how the atmosphere of fear created by the brutal totalitarianism of the outer world entered into the nation's dream life, and how these dream 'diaries of the night' were seemingly 'dictated to them by the dictatorship'.[21] She reports numerous dreams in which people wanted to take action against the regime but failed in their attempt. One man dreamed of having decided to write a formal complaint to the government but ended up enclosing a blank piece of paper in an envelope. He recalled feeling both proud and ashamed for doing so. Another woman dreamed that she attempted to call the police to make a similar complaint but found she could not say a word when the phone was answered. Beradt offers these as examples of how the will atrophies 'under constant compromising'.[22]

The nightmare quality of these dreams arises from the tension between the dreamer's desire to act according to their conscience and their fear of doing so. The conflict can be extreme, as in one man's dream that he broke his spine while unsuccessfully resisting raising his right arm to make the required Nazi salute to Goebbels.

Beradt also cites dreams of people whose strength of will overcame their fears. For example, one woman who was active in the Resistance dreamed of being pursued by

Nazis. Eventually she lost them by jumping across balconies and leaping down to the street near a café. There she noticed two men speaking in low tones. One said, 'We must protest the transaction', using the word 'transaction' as a code for the regime's actions. The other replied, 'Can't be done.' Undaunted, the dreamer decided she would enlist both of these men in her cause, whereupon she placed her hands on their shoulders and pulled them along with her. They all shouted, 'We've got to protest!'[23] dozens of times in unison while others looked on, nodding in agreement but not joining in. Upon awaking, the dreamer felt the need to continue chanting these words to strengthen her resolve. This dream shows strength of will overcoming ambivalence, expressed in the dream by the earlier exchange between the two men.

People who challenged the Nazi regime faced imprisonment, torture and death. Yet those who could not heed the call of their dreams to action suffered too, for they underwent a 'living death', as the Nazi regime invaded both the dreamer's waking life and their sleep. Commenting on the dreams in Beradt's collection, the psychologist Bruno Bettelheim observed:

> Those who could at least (or particularly) in their dreams say 'yes' or 'no' clearly could not be rent in their inner life by external reality. But as long as the majority has no unequivocal 'yes' or an equally definite 'no' to say, the risk of another Third Reich overwhelming our inner and outer life is still with us.[24]

Rather than viewing nightmares as something to be feared, we can understand frightening dreams as eliciting qualities that challenge us to develop the Highest Will. Dreamwork then facilitates the emergence of these qualities. To encourage this development, we can also undertake practices that calm the mind and put us in touch with our inner, spiritual strength; for example, meditation, repetition of a sacred word, breath practices and prayer – yogas of body and mind that 'still' what the yogis call 'the movements in consciousness'.[25] If further help is needed, we can seek additional support by undertaking therapy to explore not only the source of our fear but also to develop the qualities we need to move forward.

Developing our will and a growing capacity to become more lucid in our dreams go hand in hand, as this nightmare of my own reveals:

> As I walk down a residential street on a sunny day, a man I do not know approaches me, appearing out of nowhere, startling me. He carries a wide, unsheathed sword and has raised it to strike me. I am terrified and freeze with fear, certain this man will kill me. Unexpectedly, as I look up at the sword, poised before it falls, I feel moved by the sword's shining strength and beauty and by its unusual appearance in a suburban setting ... Struck by its beauty, I become aware that I am dreaming. I kneel and say, 'I'm not afraid', bowing my head.

In that moment, when I became attentive to beauty, I also became lucid and no longer feared 'death'. My emotional response to beauty overcame my thinking mind's assessment of the sword as an instrument of destruction, allowing me to move beyond my instinctive fear and to stay attuned to the qualities inherent in beauty – balance, harmony and proportion.[26] As a result, my *way of being* rather than my *way of thinking* shaped how I related to the man and his sword. Kneeling before Beauty, I bowed my head, free from fear. As a result, the dream then unfolded in ways I could not have expected:

> *To my surprise, the man then turns the sword on its side and, slowly lowering it, rests it on the crown of my head. I receive its gentle touch as a blessing, an opening...*[27]

Recognising goodness and beauty in times of adversity remains a lesson I continue to relearn in dreams and in daily life.

The lucid dream given here serves to introduce the next chapter, devoted to the practice of lucid dreaming. But, importantly, while lucid dreaming can be a powerful tool for treating nightmares,[28] even if we just *believe* that we don't have to suffer from our nightmares,[29] or if we simply write them down, the frequency of nightmares and their intensity reduces.[30]

As we develop the capacity to face our fears in our dreams, we are better able to face them in waking life, both individually and collectively. Humanity will need to call upon this capacity in confronting the nightmare scenarios plaguing our world today. We are being challenged to exert and express our Highest Will to live not in fear and antipathy but with trust and love.

We can then become more curious about our own fears and wonder in a more welcoming way what we might like to ask of them and what they might be asking so urgently of us. If after reading this chapter you now feel ready to recall a dream in which you felt pursued by fear – in whatever nightmarish form it may have taken – take a moment to pause and ask, 'Why are you pursing me? What do you want of me?' and see what response arises. Simply voicing these words can release fear's tight grip and begin the movement towards freedom. If the fearfulness persists, you can also tell your fear, 'You have no power over me.'

When we assert the Highest Will within us, rather than feeling that a sword looms dangerously over us, we can meet what we fear and realise, 'This is a dream. I don't have to be afraid.'

Chapter Ten

Journeys into the Deep: Lucid Dreaming and Lucid Surrender

...for often, when one is asleep, there is something in consciousness which declares that what then presents itself is but a dream.[1]

– Aristotle

To prepare for our journey into lucid dreaming, I invite you once more to search your memory for a dream, any dream that has felt important to you. We began the first chapter looking for a shell on the seashore. Just as you held the mystery of that shell in your hand, now, with this dream, turn it over in your mind's eye, exploring it with the lens of new insights gained from reading this book. Consider the dream in all its aspects – forms, colours, light, sensations, thoughts, actions, emotions and essence.[2] How might this dream add to your understanding about yourself and your life? For now, keep your dream close at hand, like a small shell tucked in your pocket, as we shall be returning to it later in the light of our journey into dream lucidity.

Each empty shell you find on the beach once housed a living creature. Similarly, energy, movement and meaning enliven your dreams. We tap into this life force when we revisit our dreams through dreamwork. But there is another, more direct, way of engaging consciously with our dreams, through the practice of lucid dreaming – becoming aware of dreaming while the dream is taking place.

During a lucid dream, we may appear 'asleep' to the outer world, but within, we have 'awakened', sometimes in surprising ways, as happened to me in this dream:

> *I suddenly 'wake up' in my bed, where I have been*
> *sleeping, surprised to notice that the sloping attic*
> *ceiling, painted a soft blue, is now aglow with light.*
> *I feel confused as a bright morning light fills the*
> *room even though the curtains are drawn, and I*
> *know it is deep in the night. Then, I realise that I*
> *am actually dreaming. In that moment, I see that the*
> *light emanates from a figure at the foot of my bed.*
> *Instantly, I recognise Jesus. He stands quietly in a*
> *radiant white robe, illuminated from within, holding*
> *his palms open towards me. Both his humanity and his*
> *divinity are fully present. The power of his presence*
> *overwhelms me, and I awaken from the dream.*

This dream marked the beginning of a 12-year period in my life during which I had vivid and increasingly lengthy lucid dreams, often many times in a night or week. My subsequent reflections on lucid dreaming derive firstly from my own ongoing experience as a lucid dreamer; secondly as a dream guide helping others to develop their dream awareness; and thirdly from scientific research in the field of lucid dreaming.

In this short account of lucid dreaming, we start on the 'surface', beginning with a brief overview of how the lucid brain state has been evidenced by neuroscience, conceptualised and popularised. We then explore increasing degrees of lucidity, diving into the depths of conscious dreaming towards full lucidity – a relatively unchartered zone of human experience.

Our 'descent' will take us from the more commonly recognised features of lucid dreams into imageless lucid dreams, a place where, as mystics describe it, only light exists. Here, we find what the great Tibetan Buddhist 'dream yoga' master Chögyal Namkhai Norbu advises: 'The final goal of dream practice is to make dreams become awareness, and, there, at the ultimate point, dreams actually cease. You use your practice so that your dreams influence daily life.'[3] But first let us begin with the science of lucid dreaming that has sought to track the neural activity suggestive of conscious awareness during dreams.

Although we can only truly know consciousness through our subjective experience, different states of consciousness can be objectively identified by the electrophysiological measurement of brainwaves by the electroencephalogram (EEG). In 2009, for the first time, electrical fluctuations in brain activity during a lucid dream confirmed that lucid dreaming was a hybrid neurological state, having characteristics of both waking and sleeping consciousness.[4] Further research has also suggested that lucid dreaming can be associated with a gamma brainwave frequency of 40Hz, more commonly associated with highly focused waking states rather than typical dreaming.[5]

In normal REM dreaming, brain activity associated with emotional arousal and hallucinatory imagery increases, while the activity of the frontal cortex, normally associated with the capacity for reflective awareness and reasoning, decreases. In contrast, as the dreamer acquires lucidity, these areas of the brain 'wake up'. In lucidity, our capacity for meta-awareness – the awareness that we are aware – makes our thinking more finely tuned and reflective.[6] The presence of a 40Hz brainwave frequency is also found in the practice of meditation, leading the distinguished sleep and dream researcher James Pagel to call lucid dreaming 'a trainable, meditative-like state developed while in sleep'.[7] We can see this shift in consciousness beginning to take place in one of my early lucid dreams:

I walk waist-deep in a creek at the base of the Eastern Sierras. Sunlight filters through the leafy covering, glimmering on the water's surface and the creek's golden sands. A few feet in front of me, a massive rainbow trout swims to the surface and then remains still. The trout looks too large to be a creek fish. I decide to catch the fish with my hands the way my father and I used to do when I was young, but then I realise that the fish represents the Spirit and stop myself. I notice that the trout has turned on its side, revealing a rainbow. The fish looks exhausted. 'How,' I wonder, 'can the Spirit be weary?' Then it occurs to me that the fish also represents me. I now realise that

if I were awake and entering the dream through the
waking dream process, then my dream guide would
invite me to touch the fish. At that point, just as my
finger comes to within a hair's breadth, the trout darts
down into the water. Feeling disappointed, I awake.

This dream illustrates a key feature of the lucid dream: the lucid dreamer's insight into their experience during the dream itself.[8] In my case, I realised that rather than attempting to possess the fish, I needed to interact with the rainbow trout in a more relational way. This dream also shows what the pioneering lucid dream researchers Ursula Voss and Allan Hobson have described as the sense of having 'two selves', the result of a dynamic integration of waking and dreaming states.[9]

Advances in computer technologies have led some neuroscientists to conceptualise the dreaming brain as creating a three-dimensional 'virtual reality' – an immersive, simulated world.[10] While this is a useful analogy, it risks treating consciousness as a by-product of physics, excluding the possibility that dreaming may possess its own intelligence and qualities of being. It further precludes the idea now being advanced in some quarters that rather than consciousness being produced by the brain, the brain may be acting as a conduit for our connection to a 'conscious universe'.[11] Either way, our understanding of lucid dreaming will deepen as new technologies give us a window into a more refined and nuanced understanding of the spectrum of consciousness possible *within* lucidity.[12]

The lucid state allows the lucid dreamer to create and enact scenes of their choosing, with all the hyper-realism of waking life but without the normal constraints, e.g. flying weightlessly, changing physical form, and even having dream sex at will. More recently, studies have also indicated that lucid dreaming can improve waking activities; for example, giving inspiration for creative writing[13] and music-making,[14] as well as improving motor skills, including throwing darts![15]

Since the mid-1970s, when lucid dreamers first used pre-planned eye movements during REM sleep to signal their lucid state to researchers,[16] the literature on the phenomenology of lucid dreaming has burgeoned.[17] Over half the population will recall having had a lucid dream at least once in their life; however, the percentage drops off dramatically in terms of frequency.[18] Accordingly, finding ways to induce lucid dreams 'on demand' has become a growing enterprise, with many 'how-to' publications available. Technologies include using light, sound, electrical[19] or chemical stimulation. However, a meta-analysis of 35 research studies on induction techniques suggested that no single technique showed a consistent result.[20] Even so, the practice of mindfulness meditation in waking life, which encourages a reflective and attentive focus on 'mindful presence', appears to enhance the dreamer's ability to become lucid more frequently.[21]

The popular Western definition of lucid dreaming describes a state in which the dreamer becomes aware that they are dreaming *while asleep* and *can control the dream narrative*. The idea that we become lucid in order to 'control' the dream unfortunately mirrors the Western worldview that the natural world must be 'controlled' rather than treated with reverence and drawn upon as a source of wisdom.

Indeed, humanity's ambition to 'control' Nature is having dire consequences. As the reality of climate change looms large, Nature's long-term fine-tuning makes human exploitation of the Earth look sadly short-sighted. Ultimately, for life on Earth to survive and flourish, we must work *with* Nature rather trying to dominate it. We must let Nature be our guide.[22]

We find a powerful parallel in lucidity, when we become receptive to what the interior landscape of the dream can teach us. By working *with* our dreams in lucidity, we also learn how to work *with* the outer world in a more cooperative and balanced way, mindful that we simply cannot, and should not, attempt to control everything.

In lucid dreams, as in life, it is tempting to be distracted by what in the Hindu faith is called 'the veil of Maya' – the continually changing surface layer of experience, so that we become caught up in the thrill of the 'virtual' world offered by lucidity, be it flying, eating our favourite food or having dream sex. In the process, we may, just as happens in waking life, be susceptible to re-enacting unhelpful life patterns as we seek to fulfil unmet emotional needs. Even so, when people spend time in the lucid dream simply having fun,[23] such 'play' can give a person a heightened sense of consciousness that may help contribute to their personal growth.[24]

It follows that just as in life, the 'surface layer' of the lucid dream can be employed for good or ill. Yet, beyond the desires that captivate us, spiritual practices across the world teach that within the dreaming state there resides a more serene experience of pure consciousness, one that brings serenity, joy and a deep sense of Beingness. Very different from the turbulent emotions of the ego, this is the original nature of the soul.

The Sufi tradition, which has a long history of cultivating visionary dreaming, identifies this spiritual quest in the Islamic teaching, 'I was a hidden treasure and I longed, I yearned, I desired to be known,'[25] referring to our longing to know ourselves, and to be known, both as individual souls and as the limitless and universal Soul at the heart of creation and dreams. The more heartfelt this yearning, and the more it springs from compassion and love, the more it energises and transforms the lucid dream experience.

To initiate lucidity that reveals soul yearning, we do not need to draw on external props and inducements. A lucid dream of my own brought home this realisation to me:

I attend a lecture where a man is teaching about the phenomena of various dream experiences that are possible when a person is connected to a large black box that sits on the table before him. As he continues, I realise he is actually talking about deep lucid dreaming. I become lucid and feel moved to say aloud, 'You don't need this machine. All you need is your body, mind and heart.' I feel tremendously excited by this understanding, and then I wake up.

One way to help develop the capacity for lucid awareness is by entering a non-lucid dream in the waking state with the help of a dream guide. We can then relive the dream *as if* in real time with the benefit of meta-awareness, while exploring the dream scenario and emotions in a safe setting. Working this way with non-lucid dreams offers the opportunity to become more patiently attentive. As an example of this process, I recall working with Louise, a woman approaching her sixties. Louise wanted to reflect on what her dreams might have to tell her about the next stage of her life. She decided to re-enter a dream in which she drifted in a small rowboat down a wide river. At first the sensation felt quite pleasant, but then she became visibly anxious about where she was heading and worried that she would tip the boat over.

To calm her, I invited her to be curious about what she had previously mentioned only in passing: the feeling of the cool breeze on her face. As she imagined the wind, she gently ran her fingertips over her cheeks. This sensation opened up a profound awareness of what Louise called the 'fertile void', putting her in touch with a deep feeling of joy. She realised that in her fear she had missed the comforting touch of the breeze. Reconnecting with this sensation infused her with new confidence and energised her for dealing with the changes in her life that lay ahead.

In a further dream, Louise swam underwater quite happily until she became afraid that she would not be able to breathe and abruptly woke up. In her waking dream sequence, when she re-entered the water and became concerned about her breathing, I encouraged her to breathe deeply in through her nose and out through her mouth until the tension in her body relaxed. This settled her to the point where she recognised that by using her faculty of creative imagination, she actually could picture herself breathing underwater – a liberating feeling!

Louise reported that she began to have dreams during which she could decide how she was going to respond to a situation, even to 'rewind' the dream scenario and re-experience the dream sequence more consciously a second time. With the development of her dream awareness, Louise recognised that far from being powerless, she could make positive choices of her own. In Louise's own words,

> It was difficult learning not to rush, but rather to stay with the 'tiny moments' that held such richness when I stopped long enough to be with them. Becoming aware of the air, like water caressing my face, was significant in starting to recognise 'keys' [to lucid awareness], as was the realisation that I could breathe and feel in my element underwater. I realised there was a lot of richness in parts of dreams I had overlooked because they had less emotional charge to them. I also realised that there were positive aspects in me and an ability to explore myself more deeply in ways I had not known before, becoming more trusting of my own process, of its wisdom and being able to surrender to that.

While we can learn to feel more able to 'breathe' in our dreams, it can be a further challenge to engage feelingly with what arises as we move towards lucidity. The following dream illustrates this challenge. I had worked with the dreamer, Vera, as her dream guide for a year. We begin with her dream, followed by an excerpt from the waking dream process that followed:

> *I was on an imposing bridge, ornate with piers and arches in black wrought iron. It felt as though it was dawn, the shimmering light, pure and peaceful. Ahead of me was a man, and for some reason he had to get further onto the bridge. There was something blocking his way. It looked something like a stile, but elaborate, so not impossible to climb over. He was having incredible difficulty trying to lift his legs and couldn't seem to find a way over it. As I looked down, I saw the most amazing sight: hundreds and hundreds of Manta rays, absolutely enormous, the size of a large room. I was astounded by the sight, the colours of the Manta rays, the myriad shades of the palest pinks and greens, diaphanous, blending into each other as they moved, a silvery foam bubbling between them, and yet I felt this was a London bridge – this was the Thames! I was trying to attract the man's attention to this wondrous sight: 'Don't worry about what you are doing, look at this!' I cried.*

When Vera re-entered the dream, I asked her what she would wish for the man on the bridge to see. She replied.

> The beauty. Something magical. The power. He wasn't interested, just fixated on getting over the barrier. I was drawn to looking the other way, and there was the most

unbelievable sight: a solitary black Manta, colossal, at least the size of a five-storey building. Unlike the other Manta rays, this Manta ray was on his side, half out of the water, and going in the other direction!

'What,' I asked, 'did the Manta's gesture communicate to you?'

'It feels how my life is at the moment filled with black-ness,' Vera responded, 'and yet there was a majesty about this...' As she spoke, she made a sweeping movement with her right arm along the side of her chair, as if she were leaning over the bridge into the water.

'Keep doing that movement,' I prompted. 'What does it put you in touch with?

'It makes me want to touch something,' she replied, 'to be in connection with something.'

'How would it be to touch the black Manta?' I asked her. 'Can you imagine that? Just let yourself breathe. How does it respond to your touch?'

She paused a long while, swinging her arm gracefully by her side before replying, 'It allows my touch, neither likes nor dislikes it. I can feel the undulations of its body, graceful, pulsing, conveying something to me, exquisite, like an alien!' She puzzled: 'Something so mysterious, and yet there is this solid harsh bridge!'

'What,' I asked her, 'does the bridge mean for you?'

She paused again, and then said, 'The bridge is probably reality, grounding.'

I reflected: 'Giving perspective, and somehow bridging dimensions.'

Vera continued: 'The Manta came to me so that I could touch it, and because it was on its side half out of the water, and so immense, I could easily reach it.'

'Yes,' I noted, 'the darkness of difficult things going on but also the transpersonal within, the darkness, black light, the mystery, all coming together.'

'If he hadn't been on his side,' Vera added, 'he would have obliterated everything.'

In response, I quoted from the Kabbalah, which teaches that 'the Absolute withdrew itself to allow Being to exist.'

Vera continued:

When I think of the dream, it feels like my life, so fixated on the struggle, the bleak overwhelming darkness, and yet auspicious. It reminded me of the quality of the black light, the magic, the dimensions beyond, the transpersonal. Am I that man on the bridge who can see nothing but the struggle? Is there beauty, grace and delicacy within me crying to be freed? Do I have the power and majesty to survive this journey?

To begin with, it was hard for Vera to see that even when her thoughts make her anxious, her heart is nonetheless in touch with the Manta ray's power. In this dream, Vera's appreciation of the Manta ray's majestic beauty increased her dream awareness. By re-engaging with the dream, she was able to interact with the Manta ray *more consciously and less fearfully*, enabling her to draw on the creature's power to find strength for the challenges that lay ahead, crossing over the 'bridge' into a new phase of life.

In the dreamwork of Louise and Vera, we can see the beginnings of ego-surrender to transpersonal presence. Stephen LaBerge, renowned for his work at the forefront of lucid dream research since the 1980s, has observed: 'To go beyond the ego's model of the world, the lucid dreamer must relinquish control of the dream – surrender – to something beyond the ego.'[26] As we shall see, when surrender can be maintained and even deepened within lucidity, then the imagery in the dream gives way to more 'imageless' or 'dreamless' dreaming, in which clear light, abstract forms, and an awareness of love on a cosmic level suffuses the dream. Yet, at present in the West, exploration of this kind of experience within the lucid state has only been explored by a handful of researchers and lucid dreamers, myself included.[27]

Interestingly, seemingly minor elements in lucid dreams can, as it turns out, play a key role. For Louise, it was the cool touch of the breeze that caressed her cheek. For Vera, it was the expansive darkness of the Manta ray. As we continue our descent into imageless lucid dreaming, I now want to explore the importance of 'darkness' more deeply.

Generally, darkness is thought of as the absence of light, but as shown in Chapter Five, light appears as darkness if there is no object on which the light falls. In the depths of lucid awareness, a luminous darkness that I refer to as 'Black' or 'Dark Light' prevails. Out of this luminescent expanse of darkness, shining forms emerge, emitting their own light, much as bioluminescent creatures shine in the ocean's darkness.

To help convey such dazzling darkness and what it can teach us, I will relate three of my own dreams that took place over a 15-year period. In this series, the imagery moves from forms to 'imageless' dreams. The first dream, which briefly initiated me into the presence of 'Black Light', came shortly before I left the United States for Poland, when I was 25.

I walk directly into the sea and realise that I can breathe in water. Far out from the shore, I come upon an immense black waterspout, spinning so fast it looks like it moves in slow motion. The water, the colour of black obsidian, shines. Numbers in bright, solid colours whirl on the darkness. I long to touch the bright blackness, but when I raise my hand to do so, fear overwhelms me, as I'm convinced that if I touch the waterspout the entire universe will fall apart. Then I awake.

In this initial dream, the shining darkness appears in the form of the waterspout, which both attracts and frightens me. My thinking mind overrides my heart-longing to touch the waterspout. Although I am aware that I can breathe in water and that I am drawn to the waterspout's magnetism, childhood memories bring up my conditioned reaction of fearfulness in response to a powerful force, which, in the dream, is projected onto the waterspout.

As a child, I learned to believe that when I expressed something deeply meaningful, it would often be angrily dismissed. Hence, my 'world' would collapse. This conditioned response continued into adulthood. Nonetheless, when I awoke from this dream, I could recognise that a creative power, larger than my own, moved through the mysterious waterspout and the coloured numbers that swirled upon the darkly shining water. This recognition helped me to withdraw my projections of fears from the dream imagery. After that, whenever I recalled the dream, I felt encouraged rather than frightened, and was able to express what felt important to me more fearlessly.

The next lucid dream in this series occurred 12 years later, soon after the dream of Jesus that opened this chapter. By this time, I had started training in psychotherapy, and had discovered that the frightening dreams I'd been having since childhood were in fact 'lucid'. Because of my training, I now had the confidence to allow myself to become fully lucid. As a result, I had an entirely different type of lucid dream, something I had never experienced before and which I hadn't realised was even possible:

Driving through the California foothills on a summer's day, I lose control of the car. It veers off the side of the road at high speed. After a number of futile attempts to keep the car on the road, I become aware I am dreaming and calmly make the decision to give up trying to control the car.

The car goes faster and faster until it feels as if it has become a particle of light. At what seems the speed of light, the car hurtles towards a golden hillside and

*everything blurs together. When the car slams into
the hillside, my body and the dreamscape disappear.
Everywhere becomes an expansive luminous
blackness. An incredible pressure and noise centres
between my 'brows'. Then all goes very silent and still.
I know I have been dreaming, and I wonder if I have
actually died during the dream. Although I am drawn
to this infinite space, with this thought, I wake up.*

Prior to this dream, I had decided that whenever I became lucid, I would trust my dreams and seek to learn from them, keeping in mind the teaching of Kahlil Gibran: 'Trust your dreams, for in them you find the gate to eternity.'[28] When I let the 'car' take over, I knowingly put this to the test. In this way, I felt able to overcome my instinctive fear of death. The subsequent disappearance of the dreamscape and the appearance of the mysterious darkness left me feeling more curious than frightened. By this time, I had learned for myself that a dream, as Ibn al-ʿArabī had taught in the 12th century, 'may be interpreted within sleep itself'.[29] However, I lacked an understanding of how best to maintain lucidity, especially in imageless dreaming.

Later, seeking to find the best way to extend and deepen my dream lucidity, I asked one of my dream teachers what to do when I became lucid. He simply replied, 'When you become lucid in a dream, meditate.' Following his advice, the next time I became lucid, I bowed my head in an attitude of surrender.

I have found that this attitude encompasses thankfulness, supplication, praise, worship and wonder. Such 'surrender' includes prayerfully meditating in lucidity, as well as meditatively singing and chanting sacred songs or verses, or simply waiting quietly and breathing deeply to still my mind. This attitude of heart and mind allows me to maintain a receptive stance while letting the dream unfold without attempting to exert 'control' over the dream. Based on many such lucid dream experiences, I decided to call this way of being in lucidity 'Lucid Surrender' – a subject about which I have reflected upon extensively.[30]

At the moment of Lucid Surrender, the original dreamscape immediately falls away, as if swept off by a mighty windstorm, unveiling an 'imageless' infinite space, a void of Black Light filled with emotive and even ecstatic 'winds'. In such instances, my dream body also disappears, sometimes reappearing either as luminous darkness or else brightly coloured light. Yet in such experiences, I do not feel 'disembodied'. On the contrary; all my physical senses intensify along with my feelings and thoughts as they align in a subtle body of light.

Gradually, I have learned how to deepen lucidity, both by stilling my thoughts and overcoming my fear of the darkness, truly a fear of the unknown. Learning to withdraw my negative projections from the darkness freed me to be more trusting and to engage with the luminous blackness and the light forms that emerged.

By the time of the lucid dream that comes next, I had already learned from numerous Black Light encounters how to maintain the attitude of Lucid Surrender. In turn, the dreams have revealed new vistas to me, as shown in the third dream in the series:

*After falling asleep, I 'awake' to find my being lifted
onto the dark winds and moved by an intense feeling
of bliss. To keep my focus, I can only manage to
repeat 'Oh Holy One'. I continue to concentrate on
repeating this invocation while a small pinprick of my
consciousness remains curious about where the winds
will take me this time.*

*I end up deposited, on my side, in a still, boundless
place where the winds cease. There, I am surrounded
on all sides by an endless black shining sea in which
delicate, laser white and gold patterns form. They
remind me of seafoam on a moonlit night, but infinitely
more beautiful. Standing up, I notice that my limbs
appear as black silhouettes against the background.*

*When I enter this 'sea', the light moves through me
like breath and weaves me into its soothing power.
My exhaustion and separateness melt away. I am
aware that I am being knowingly held and supported.
It seems, too, that the sea of light also relishes this
moment. The thought comes that this exchange is to
enable me to complete tasks in life and to share this
sea of light with others. After some while my being is
lifted back onto winds that return me to sleep, until
the morning alarm wakes me.*

In Lucid Surrender, I receive profound spiritual nourishment
from the light forms that I encounter on the Black Light.

Such dreams call to mind an Islamic teaching inspired by the visions of the Prophet Mohammed: 'My heart has seen the Lord in the most beautiful of Forms.'[31] Another Sufi teaching describes the human heart as possessing two eyes: one that sees the realm of forms in manifestation revealed by the outer light; and one that sees 'only that which is rendered visible by the light of unity and oneness'.[32] The same dual perspective of the lucid dream, in which the dreamer is both the observer and the observed, can be profoundly transformative. What begins as a feeling of fear becomes empowerment. What we think of as a crisis transforms into a mystery. What we experience as a living death brings us to a realisation of the eternal within.

If you will now return your thoughts to the dream that you recalled at the beginning of our descent into the depths of lucid dreaming, take a moment to reflect on the dream from a more 'lucid' perspective. For instance, consider moments in the dream to which you might have given more attention. Was there a small detail that had escaped your notice? Had you missed the opportunity to pause and look at a 'dream being' directly in the eyes or to ask their name? Use your active imagination to engage with the being, or even with an object that catches your attention. In retrospect, were there times in the dream when, having noticed an inconsistency within the dream or an unusual feature, you might have become more fully aware? Were their instances when you wish you had acted differently within the dream? If so, how would you have wished to act? This kind of enquiry encourages us to develop lucid insight into our dream experiences.

When responding to such questions, it is important that we do so with compassion towards ourselves, understanding that dreams invite us to participate in our dream life in a new way. Remember that if we miss the chance to act as we might wish in one dream, we will have the opportunity to do so in another! Recognise, too, that if you find it difficult to 'surrender' in a dream by allowing the dream to unfold, you are, nevertheless, becoming conscious of a new dimension that you are being invited to experience. But if lucidity eludes us, we can recall an insight Louise shared following on from her dreamwork with me: 'My attitude towards dreams and the waking dreamwork has changed in that I have learned that the ability to dream lucidly wasn't an end in itself, but that it provided another context in which one can deepen awareness.'

In learning to develop lucidity, we become able to 'see in the dark' and become more at ease with the unknown and the mystery of life. In recognising that much of our existence is beyond our control, we can rest assured in the knowledge that we 'belong to more than ourselves'.[33] Returning to waking life after being immersed in a lucid dream, we bring with us a consciousness of the magic of each moment and the miracle of the everyday.

Epilogue

For a World in Need of Dreams

Dreams: tonight's answers for tomorrow's questions.[1]

– Mark Thurston

Alone, circling the dark side of the moon and cut off from radio contact, the astronaut Michael Collins reflected on his unique perspective as he peered through the window of the *Apollo 11* command module. Looking out at the moon, where his fellow *Apollo* astronauts had landed, and beyond to Earth, blue and white against the black backdrop of space, Collins reflected, 'I am alone now, truly alone, and absolutely isolated from any known life. I am it. If a count were taken, the score would be three billion plus two over on the other side of the moon, and one plus God knows what on this side.'[2]

Similarly, it can feel this way when we look upon the dreamscape, aware that we dream, and yet recalling our earthly life beyond the dream. From the perspective of a lucid dream, we may think, like Collins, that no one stands behind us looking on. Yet an entire universe awaits, vibrant with life about which we know next to nothing.

Collins returned to Earth with deep insight into the planet's fragile, silent beauty, one that eradicates borders and silences arguments. We can extend this insight to our dreams, for when we explore and share our dreams, we realise the nature of our common humanity – earthlings inhabiting a wondrous planet.

Fifty years on from the moon landing, the human population has nearly tripled.[3] As the needs and desires of humanity exhaust Earth's resources, the wounds upon the planet have become more visible from space. Satellite images display the dull grey smears of air pollution by day over cities, and the unnatural glare of electric lights by night. Time-lapse imagery compiled from footage over the past 20 years dramatically highlights the loss of coral reefs, forests and glaciers.[4]

Only radical changes in human attitudes and behaviours can give hope for the future.[5] Technological and economic restructuring will not happen without insight, intuition and imagination, guided by empathy, courage and compassion. Dream awareness can help us to draw on the inspiration needed to overcome limited worldviews, empowering us to transform ourselves and the world in which live.

To help us to contain our fears so that we can respond with grace even as we face the threat of the extinction of life on Earth, we need the vision and emotional depth that dream awareness can impart. In becoming attentive to the world within, we become attentive to the world without, in reciprocity.

Sometimes a dream gives us a down-to-earth insight. Consider, for instance, a dream of a creature of the earth, the humble beetle. The man who shared the following dream with me had been undergoing many life changes that involved him in worldly concerns he could never have foreseen:

I was in a house where horrible things kept
happening. Black beetles crawling, unpleasant scenes
everywhere, like a haunting. I realised I was creating
this disturbance with my mind and decided to stop.
Then everything soon came right ... I was the one
generating the 'hauntings', not the others who were
present. But they were happy to find me back to
normal. I think there was another dream earlier in the
night when, in despair, I called on God for help.

When relating the dream to me, the dreamer expressed surprise at how distressed he felt by the beetles. Naming the cause of his haunted feeling was the challenge the dream left him to ponder. Yet, the dream holds great promise not only for the dreamer but for all of us, for when we recognise that *we* ourselves create the disturbances with our thoughts, we can instead direct our will towards ways of being that serve us better.

Although the dreamer associated the 'hauntings' with the beetles, at the same time the beetles can be considered as living creatures in their own right. Beetles are necessary for life on the planet. Some half a million known species of beetles go about moving waste, aerating soil and pollinating flowers. Their presence in nature indicates the freshness of the water and soil that supports life. Beetles have their place in the natural world, and we need them to help sustain life on Earth.

This man shared how, around the time of this dream, beetles had been overrunning his home in spite of his efforts to catch them and put them back outside. The dream weaves a waking-world preoccupation into this dreamer's personal psychology. But such a dream becomes the opportunity for all of us to consider our relationship to the 'hauntings' that plague the Earth as a consequence of our thoughts and actions. Our dreams remind us that we too are born of the Earth and cannot live apart from it.

We can take heart in knowing that at times of great crisis, dreams often throw us a lifeline. As this book started by the seashore, I now invite you to return there, this time with a dream set near the sea. The dreamer, a woman whose husband of many years had recently died, had the dream during her bereavement, when she felt especially low:

> *I was being swept along in a broad, swirling river towards the open sea. It was a wild, stormy day, with dark rain clouds racing along overhead. The trees on the banks of the river were being tossed hither and thither in the wind which blew over the face of the waters. I must perish in such turbulence! As I was being swept along, I heard a quiet voice saying, 'Take hold of the rope', and lying beside me in the water I saw the end of a strong rope. 'Hold it firmly, but easily,' said the voice. I took hold of it in the way I had been told, and imperceptibly the raging waters became calm – or I quiet in their midst. I looked again at the rope and saw that it was no longer an end that I held; it stretched before me and behind me and I knew that I only needed to hold it in this way to be taken to the sea. I knew too that it had been there all the time. I was no longer afraid, and the waters that had before*

seemed so hostile, sweeping me to the sea against my
will, now seemed friendly.[6]

This woman adds: 'I awoke from this dream to feel that I had discovered the key to all life – the whole secret of being.' She recounts how, after the dream, she bought an old piece of rope, like the one in the dream, and, holding it, lay on her bed in the same position as when she lay in the water. Doing so helped her to accept her loss and to reconnect her with the will to live.

The dream tells all who will listen to 'take the rope and to hold it firmly but easily', to go forward in life not in fear but with trust, and so to live the dream of the awakened heart.

Notes

1 Richard Bach, *Illusions: The Adventures of a Reluctant Messiah* (New York, NY: Dell Publishing Co. Inc., 1977), 26.

Foreword
1 www.ccpe.org.uk and www.driccpe.org.uk
2 www.helpcounselling.com

Author's Introduction
1 Adapted from the text accompanying 'Emblem XLII' in H. M. E. de Jong, *Michael Maier's Atalanta Fugiens: Sources of an Alchemical Book of Emblems* (York Beach, ME: Nicolas-Hays Inc., 2002), 266.
2 This question was inspired by one asked by Greta Thunberg from Sweden, who, at the age of 15, started what became a global school strike movement to stop climate change. In her words, 'What is the point of learning facts when the most important facts given by the finest scientists are ignored by our politicians?' See her article, 'I'm striking from school to protest inaction on climate change – you should too', *The Guardian*, 26 November 2018, https://www.theguardian.com/commentisfree/2018/nov/26/im-striking-from-school-for-climate-change-too-save-the-world-australians-students-should-too
3 I would like to acknowledge the inspiration of Joseph Campbell, a preeminent scholar of mythology, who in an interview observed that 'we are the consciousness of the earth' and that 'the only myth worth talking about in the future is going to be one that is talking about the planet … and everybody on it.' See Joseph Campbell, *The Power of Myth* (with Bill Moyers), ed. Betty Sue Flowers (New York, NY: Doubleday, 1988), 32.
4 Matthew Walker, a neuroscientist and sleep specialist, makes this point in his thought-provoking *Why We Sleep: The New Science of Sleep and Dreams* (UK: Penguin Random House, 2019), 280.
5 Researchers teaming up with Google Earth have used colour graphics in time-lapse imagery to depict the rate of deforestation on Earth from 2000 to 2012. From this film, we get a visceral understanding of how human activity profoundly changes the Earth. The 650,000 images from a NASA satellite allowed researchers to track the rapid deforestation, powerfully revealing the loss of 900,000 square miles (2.3 million square kilometres) of forest. Refer

to M. C. Hansen et al., 'High-Resolution Global Maps of 21st-Century Forest Cover Change', *Science*, 342, No. 6160 (15 November 2013): 850–853, doi: 10.1126/science.1244693

6   See North Carolina State University, College of Agriculture and Life Sciences, Department of Horticulture Science (webpage), 'Tree Facts', accessed 8 August 2010, https://projects.ncsu.edu/project/treesofstrength/treefact.htm

7   Cited in Walker, *Why We Sleep*, 296.

8   Dennis Campbell, 'NHS Prescribed Record Number of Antidepressants Last Year', *The Guardian*, 29 June 2017, https://www.theguardian.com/society/2017/jun/29/nhs-prescribed-record-number-of-antidepressants-last-year

9   These figures are based on data from the University of Oxford's online 'Our World in Data', Global Change Data Lab (webpage), published May 2018 and updated April 2019, https://ourworldindata.org/global-mental-health. I have applied the 1 in 7 statistic to the global population of 7.7 billion as of 2019. The World Health Organization's *Investing in Mental Health* puts mental health disorders at 1 in 4 of the population (Geneva: World Health Organization, 2003), 4, https://www.who.int/mental_health/media/investing_mnh.pdf

10 World Health Organization, World Health Assembly, 'Global Burden of Mental Disorders and the Need for a Comprehensive, Coordinated Response from Health and Social Sectors at the Country Level: Report by the Secretariat', 65 (20 January 2012): 4, https://apps.who.int/iris/handle/10665/78898

11 Independent Mental Health Taskforce to the NHS in England, 'The Five Year Forward View of Mental Health' (February 2016):10, https://www.england.nhs.uk/wp-content/uploads/2016/02/Mental-Health-Taskforce-FYFV-final.pdf

12 Andrew J. Watson and James E. Lovelock, 'Biological Homeostasis of the Global Environment: The Parable of Daisyworld', *Tellus*, 35B (September 1983): 284–289, doi.org/10.1111/j.1600-0889.1983.tb00031.x. Also available at http://www.jameslovelock.org/?s=daisyworld

13 'Amsterdam Declaration on Earth System Science' presented at 'Challenges of a Changing Earth: Global Change Open Science Conference Amsterdam, The Netherlands, July 2001', Global International Geosphere-Biosphere Programme Change (website), http://www.igbp.net/about/history/2001amsterdamdeclarationonearthsystemscience.4.1b8ae20512db692f2a680001312.html. Four international global change research programmes joined to create this declaration: the International Geosphere-Biosphere Programme (IGBP);

the International Human Dimensions Programme on Global Environmental Change (IHDP); the World Climate Research Programme (WCRP); and the International Biodiversity Programme DIVERSITAS.

14 See Chapter Two, 'The Science and Symbols of Sleep and Dreams', for studies on the connections between dreams and wellbeing.

15 See Eugene Aserinsky and Nathaniel Kleitman, 'Regularly Occurring Periods of Eye Motility, and Concomitant Phenomena, During Sleep', *Science*, 118, No. 3062 (1953): 273–274, doi: 10.1126/science.118.3062.273

16 Carl Gustav Jung, 'The Practical Use of Dream Analysis' in Herbert Read, Michael Fordham and Gerhard Adler (eds), *The Practice of Psychotherapy*, Vol. 16, trans. R. F. C. Hull, Bollingen Series XX, Vols 1–20 (Princeton, NJ: Princeton University Press, 1955–1992), para. 330.

17 A prayer attributed to the Lakota people of North America.

18 Robert A. Emmons and Michael E. McCullough, 'Counting Blessings Versus Burdens: An Experimental Investigation of Gratitude and Subjective Well-Being in Daily Life', *Journal of Personality and Social Psychology*, 84, No. 2 (2003): 377–389, doi: 10.1037/0022-3514.84.2.377

19 Quoted in an interview with Joseph Campbell in Joseph Campbell's *The Power of Myth* (with Bill Moyers), ed. Betty Sue Flowers (New York, NY: Doubleday, 1998), 21–22.

20 See Anne Baring's illuminating 'Dreams: Messages of the Soul', Reflections 11 (1999), accessed 8 August 2019, https://www.annebaring.com/anbar16_reflections011_dreams.htm. Baring notes that she has recounted the original version from Heinrich Zimmer's *The King and the Corpse* (Bollingen Foundation, New York: Pantheon Books, 1957), 202. For a profound compilation of her thoughts on dreams and on the challenges facing humanity, see Anne Baring's epic *The Dream of the Cosmos: A Quest for the Soul* (Dorset, UK: Archive Publishing, 2013).

21 For more on dream sharing, see Robin Shohet's *Dream Sharing: A Guide to Understanding Dreams by Sharing and Discussion* (Northamptonshire, England: Crucible, 1985). The book brings to life Shohet's observation that 'Very often the meaning of a dream only emerges when the dream is shared.'

22 Campbell, *The Power of Myth*, 34.

Chapter One – The Sea of Dreams: An Exploration of Hidden Depths

1 Anne Morrow Lindbergh, *Gift from the Sea* (New York, NY: Random House Inc., 1978), 17.

2 Aserinsky and Kleitman, 'Regularly Occurring Periods of Eye Motility', 273–274.

3   See T. Horikawa et al., 'Neural Decoding of Visual Imagery During Sleep', *Science*, 340, No. 6132 (3 May 2013): 639–642, doi: 10.1126/science.1234330

4   John Lesku, Anne Aulsebrook and Erika Zaid, 'Evolutionary Perspectives on Sleep' in Katja Valli and Robert J. Hoss (eds), *Dreams: Understanding Biology, Psychology and Culture*, Vol. 1, 3–26 (Santa Barbara, CA: ABC-CLIO LLC, 2019).

5   Walker, *Why We Sleep*, 72.

6   Robert Stickgold, J. Allan Hobson and R. Fosse, 'Sleep, Learning, and Dreams: Off-line Memory Reprocessing', *Science*, 294, No. 5544 (2 November 2001): 1052–1057, doi: 10.1126/science.1063530

7   See Josie E. Malinowski and Chris Edwards, 'Evidence of Insight from Dreamwork' in Robert J. Hoss and Robert P. Gongloff (eds), *Dreams: Biology, Psychology and Culture*, Vol. 2 (Santa Barbara, CA: ABC-CLIO, 2019): 469–478; and Christopher L. Edwards, Perrine M. Ruby, Josie E. Malinowski et al., 'Dreaming and Insight', *Frontiers in Psychology* (24 December 2013), doi: 10.3389/fpsyg.2013.00979

8   See, for example, Miloslava Kozmová, 'Emotions During Non-Lucid Problem-Solving Dreams as Evidence of Secondary Consciousness', *Comprehensive Psychology* (1 January 2015), doi.org/10.2466/09.CP.4.6; and Tracey L. Kahn and Stephen P. LaBerge, 'Dreaming and Waking: Similarities and Differences Revisited', *Consciousness and Cognition*, 20 (2011): 494–514, doi: 10.1016/j.concog.2010.09.002

9   Consider the abstract of research by Erin J. Wamsley, 'Dreaming and Offline Memory Consolidation', *Current Neurology and Neuroscience Reports*, 14, No. 3 (March 2014): 433, doi.org/10.1007/s11910-013-0433-5

10 For a neurological perspective see, Els van der Helm and Matthew P. Walker, 'Overnight Therapy? The Role of Sleep in Emotional Brain Processing', *Psychological Bulletin*, 135, No. 5 (September 2009): 731–748, doi: 10.1037/a0016570. Rosalind D. Cartwright, in her *The Twenty-Four Hour Mind: The Role of Sleep and Dreaming in Our Emotional Lives* (New York, NY: Oxford University Press, 2010), brings together findings from her academic, clinical and personal experience over a lifetime of research in the field of sleep and dreams. For an extensive analysis of emotional growth through psychological and spiritual development in dreams, see Nigel Hamilton, *Awakening Through Dreams: The Journey Through the Inner Landscape* (London: Karnac Books, 2014).

11 Ninad Gujar et al., 'A Role for REM Sleep in Recalibrating the Sensitivity of the Human Brain to Specific Emotions', *Cerebral Cortex*, 21, No. 1 (January 2011): 115–123, doi.org/10.1093/cercor/bhq064

12 For a wide-ranging discussion of dreams and their role in creativity across the arts, see the section 'Dreams and the Arts' in Robert J. Hoss and Robert P. Gongloff (eds), *Dreams: Understanding Biology, Psychology and Culture*, Vol. 2 (Santa Barbara, CA: ABC-CLIO LLC, 2019), 641–666.

13 See Allen Hobson's November 2009 article, 'REM Sleep and Dreaming: Towards a Theory of Protoconsciousness', *Nature Reviews Neuroscience*, 10, No. 11 (November 2009): 803–813, doi: 10.1038/nrn2716

14 For more on the development of empathy and dreams, see Mark Blagrove, Sioned Hale, Julia Lockheart et al., 'Testing the Empathy Theory of Dreaming: The Relationships Between Dream Sharing and Trait and State Empathy', *Frontiers in Psychology* (20 June 2019), doi.org/10.3389/fpsyg.2019.01351

15 Refer to Keith Hearne, 'Lucid Dreams: An Electro-Physiological and Psychological Study' (Ph.D. thesis, University of Liverpool, England, 1978), https://www.keithhearne.com/phd-download/. Also, Stephen LaBerge, Lynn Nagel, William C. Dement and Vincent Zarcone Jr, 'Lucid Dreaming Verified by Volitional Communication During REM Sleep', *Perceptual and Motor Skills*, 52 (1981): 727–32, doi.org/10.2466/pms.1981.52.3.727

16 See Ursula Voss et al., 'Lucid Dreaming: A State of Consciousness with Features of Both Waking and Non-Lucid Dreaming', *Sleep*, 32, No. 9 (1 September 2009): 1191–1200, https://www.ncbi.nlm.nih.gov/pmc/articles/PMC2737577/; and J. Allan Hobson, 'The Neurobiology of Consciousness: Lucid Dreaming Wakes Up', *The International Journal of Dream Research*, 2, No. 2 (October 2009): 41–44.

17 Chögyal Namkhai Norbu, *Dream Yoga and the Practice of Natural Light* (Ithaca, NY: Snow Lion Publications, 1992).

18 For a review of revelatory dreaming in Christianity, see Morton T. Kelsey's *God, Dreams, and Revelation: A Christian Interpretation of Dreams* (Minneapolis, MN: Augsburg Fortress Publishing, 1991). Henry Corbin provides an inspiring introduction to what he calls 'theophanic' imaginal visions in his *Swedenborg and Esoteric Islam: Comparative Spiritual Hermeneutics*, trans. Leonard Fox (West Chester, PA: Swedenborg Studies, 1999), and Kelly Bulkeley gives a wide-ranging overview in *Dreaming in the World's Religions: A Comparative History* (New York, NY: New York University Press, 2008). Catherine Shainberg's *Kabbalah and the Power of Dreaming: Awakening the Visionary Life* (Rochester, NY: Inner Traditions, 2005) provides a practical guide to the Kabbalistic tradition and revelatory dreams. For a thorough presentation of Jewish mysticism and practices, see *Kabbalah* by Gershom Scholem (New York, NY: Meridian, 1978).

19 For a detailed analysis of the inner landscape of dreams from an alchemical perspective, see Nigel Hamilton's *Awakening Through Dreams*, 2014.

20 Yuval Nir et al., 'Sleep and Consciousness' in A. E. Cavanna et al. (eds), *Neuroimaging of Consciousness* (© Springer-Verlag Berlin Heidelberg, 2013), 170, doi: 10.1007/978-3-642-37580-4_9

21 A quote from Andrew Powell's *The Ways of the Soul: A Psychiatrist Reflects: Essays on Life, Death and Beyond* (London: Muswell Hill Press, 2017), xvii.

22 The scientist Rupert Sheldrake uses this term in his book *Science and Spiritual Practices: Reconnecting Through Direct Experience* (London: Coronet, 2017), 21.

23 See www.driccpe.org.uk. The DRI also offers educational events and courses that are open to the public. Additionally, the DRI hosts an archive of research into dreams and using dreams in research as well as teaching videos on dreams from the spiritual perspective. I also teach courses on lucid dreaming. See http://ccpe.org.uk/?page_id=126

24 Fulvio D'Acquisto, 'Dreaming Autoimmunity: Exploring Dreams in Patients Suffering from Autoimmune Diseases' (Master's thesis, F. D'Acquisto, 2017).

25 Dave Billington, 'Client Experience of the Waking Dream Process' (Master's thesis, D. Billington, 2014), http://www.driccpe.org.uk/?portfolio-view=1575-2

26 Judy Pascoe, 'Drawing Dreams: The Transformation Experience of Expressing Dream Imagery as Art' (Master's thesis, J. Pascoe, 2016), http://www.driccpe.org.uk/?portfolio-view=drawing-dreams-the-transformational-experience-of-expressing-dream-imagery-as-art

27 Nigel Hamilton, 'Psychospiritual Transformation: Light, Colour, and Symmetry' in Robert J. Hoss and Robert P. Gongloff (eds), *Dreams: Understanding Biology, Psychology, and Culture*, Vol. 2 (Santa Barbara, CA: ABC-CLIO, LLC, 2019), 634–640.

28 Marlene Botha, 'The Transformative Effects of Colours in Transpersonal Dreamwork' (Master's thesis, M. Botha, 2010), http://www.driccpe.org.uk/?portfolio-view=the-transformative-effect-of-colours-in-transpersonal-dreamwork-m-botha

29 Nigel Hamilton, 'The Personal and Therapeutic Significance of Directional Movement within the Space of a Lucid Dream' (paper presented at the International Association for the Study of Dreams Conference, June 2017), http://www.driccpe.org.uk/?portfolio-view=the-personal-and-therapeutic-significance-of-moving-and-interacting-within-the-space-of-a-lucid-dream-nigel-hamilton-phd

30 Mary M. Ziemer [Melinda Powell], 'Lucid Surrender and Jung's Alchemical Coniunctio' in Ryan Hurd and Kelly Bulkeley (eds), *Lucid Dreaming: New*

Perspectives on Consciousness in Sleep, Vol. 1 (Santa Barbara, CA: Praeger, 2014), 145–166.

31 For a collection of first-person accounts of life-changing dreams, see Robert J. Hoss and Robert P. Gongloff (eds), *Dreams That Change Our Lives* (Ashville, NC: Chiron Publications, 2016).

32 In London, the Centre for Counselling and Psychotherapy Education, CCPE, offers therapeutic support that includes dream guidance. Contact 0(207) 266-3006. www.ccpe.org.uk.

33 An expression used by Amit Goswámí, 'Quantum Psychology: An Integral Science for the Ecology of the Psyche' (paper presented at the International Transpersonal Conference, Prague, 30 September 2017).

Chapter Two – The Science and Symbols of Sleep and Dreams

1 Quoted in Joseph Campbell's *The Mythic Image*, Bollingen Series C (Princeton, CT: Princeton University Press, 1974), I–1.

2 The Islamic scholar, Henry Corbin, describes the Imaginal World in his '*Mundus Imaginalis*, or the Imaginary and the Imaginal' in *Swedenborg and Esoteric Islam*, 1–33. This theme will be further developed in Chapter Three, 'Dreams, Trees and Their Roots in the Imaginal Mind: Transforming Waking Life'.

3 Cited in Tom Cheetham's beautiful *All the World's an Icon: Henry Corbin and the Angelic Function of Beings* (Berkeley, CA: North Atlantic Books, 2012), 161, from Jung, *The Collected Works*, Vol. 13, para. 207n17.

4 Nick Littlehales, an elite sports sleep coach, provides a helpful and concise recovery programme to get people back into the full benefits of good sleep in his *Sleep: The Myth of 8 Hours, the Power of Naps...and the New Plan to Recharge Your Body and Mind* (UK: Penguin Random House, 2016).

5 Figures from the Sleep Council's 'The Great British Bedtime Report' (Chapel Hill, Skipton: UK, 2017), 2. Statistics based on a survey of over 5,000 individuals in the UK. See https://sleepcouncil.org.uk/wp-content/uploads/2018/04/The-Great-British-Bedtime-Report-2017.pdf

6 Researchers speculate that melatonin may have an as yet unknown role in the absorption of the toxic by-products produced when cells metabolise oxygen, toxins that damage our DNA and cause cancer. Use of artificial light suppresses the production of the melatonin and so, in the long term, may increase the risk of breast and prostate cancer. See Thomas C. Erren et al., 'Shift work and Cancer: The Evidence and the Challenge', *Deutsches Arzteblatt international Deutsches Arzteblatt International*, 107, No. 38 (2010): 657–62, doi: 10.3238/arztebl.2010.0657

7   Cited from Marianna Virtanen et al., 'Long Working Hours and Coronary Heart Disease: A Systematic Review and Meta-Analysis', *American Journal of Epidemiology*, 176, No. 7 (2012): 586–596, doi: 10.1093/aje/kws139 in Claire Caruso, 'Negative Impacts of Shiftwork and Long Work Hours', *Rehabilitation Nursing: The Official Journal of the Association of Rehabilitation Nurses*, 39, No. 1 (January–February 2014): 16–25, doi: 10.1002/rnj.107

8   Caruso, 'Negative Impacts of Shiftwork', 16–25.

9   Cited in the Royal Society for Public Health's 'Waking Up to the Health Benefits of Sleep' (March 2016): 11. See https://www.rsph.org.uk/uploads/assets/uploaded/a565b58a-67d1-4491-ab9112ca414f7ee4.pdf

10 Ibid., 8.

11 Ibid., 9.

12 See the National Health Service, NHS, 'How to get to Sleep: Sleep and Tiredness' (last updated 22 July 2019), https://www.nhs.uk/live-well/sleep-and-tiredness/how-to-get-to-sleep/

13 See *Listen to Your Body: The Wisdom of the Dao* by Bisong Guo and Andrew Powell for a practical Daoist perspective on how best to follow this suggestion (Honolulu, HI: The University of Hawaii Press, 2001).

14 Walker, *Why We Sleep*, 297.

15 Walker, *Why We Sleep*, 275.

16 Janne Grønlie et al., 'Sleep and Protein Synthesis-Dependent Synaptic Plasticity: Impacts of Sleep Loss and Stress', *Frontiers in Behavioral Neuroscience*, 7, Article 224 (21 January 2014), doi: 10.3389/fnbeh.2013.00224

17 Walker, *Why We Sleep*, 48.

18 For more on the science of this process, see Lulu Xie et al., 'Sleep Drives Metabolite Clearance from the Adult Brain', *Science*, 342, No. 6156 (18 October 2013): 373–377, doi: 10.1126/science.1241224

19 Ehsan Shokri-Kojori et al., 'ß-Amyloid Accumulation in the Human Brain after One Night of Sleep Deprivation', *Proceedings of the National Academy of Sciences* USA, PNAS, 115, No. 17 (24 April 2019): 4483–4488, doi: 10.1073/pnas.1721694115

20 Andy R. Eugene and Jolanta Masiak, 'The Neuroprotective Aspects of Sleep', *MEDtube Science*, 3, No. 1 (March 2015): 35–40. PMID: 26594659

21 See early references to this phenomenon in Pier Luigi Parmeggiani, 'Interaction Between Sleep and Thermoregulation: An Aspect of the Control of Behavioral States', *Sleep*, 10, No. 5 (1987): 426–435; and J. Allan Hobson, 'Sleep and Dreaming', *The Journal of Neuroscience*, 10, No. 2

(1 February 1990): 371–372, doi.org/10.1523/JNEUROSCI. These ideas on this are further developed in J. Allan Hobson, Charles C.-H. Hong and Karl J. Friston, 'Virtual Reality and Conscious Inference in Sleep', *Frontiers in Psychology*, 5, No. 1133 (9 October 2014): 9, doi: 10.3389/fpsyg.2014.01133

22 Although dreams have primarily been associated with REM sleep, research shows that dreams do occur in non-rapid eye movement sleep (NREM). However, reported dreams tend to be shorter, less clear and, as a result, less memorable. See Jaakko O. Nieminen et al., 'Consciousness and Cortical Responsiveness: A Within-State Study During Non-Rapid Eye Movement Sleep', *Scientific Reports*, 6, No. 30932, (August 2016): 1–10, doi: 10.1038/srep30932

23 For the full story, see the article by David Cox, 'David Karnazes: The Man Who Can Run Forever', *The Guardian*, 30 August 2013, https://www.theguardian.com/lifeandstyle/the-running-blog/2013/aug/30/dean-karnazes-man-run-forever

24 Grønlie et al., 'Sleep and Protein Synthesis-Dependent Synaptic Plasticity', 3.

25 4D technology takes two-dimensional ultrasound scans, makes them three-dimensional, and adds multimedia effects as an overlay. As an example, see 'Dreaming in the womb – 33 week fetus', *Naked Science*, Science and Technology Documentary Series. Posted on https://www.youtube.com/watch?v=RVlVcsp-ed4, accessed 8 August 2019. A playlist of *Naked Science* videos are available at: https://www.youtube.com/playlist?list=PLpWCFDSTg8dvapwbRd7AVbpNAkFXhqtyo

26 Cited in Madeleine M. Grigg-Damberger and Kathy M. Wolfe, 'Infants Sleep for Brain', *Journal of Clinical Sleep Medicine, Official Publication of the American Academy of Sleep Medicine*, 13, No. 11 (15 November 2017): 1233–1234, doi: 10.5664/jcsm.6786

27 Ibid., 1234.

28 Walker, *Why We Sleep*, 195.

29 Walker, *Why We Sleep*, 208–209. Walker includes a lively account of the research he and his colleague undertook to test his theory in which he showed two randomly chosen groups emotionally charged imagery twice and measured their brains' emotional reactivity to the imagery. Participants viewed the imagery either in the morning and evening of the same day or in the evening of one day and the morning of the next, allowing one group to sleep between viewing the images. Those that slept showed less emotional reactivity and more activation of the pre-frontal cortex associated with logical thought.

30 Walker, *Why We Sleep*, 206–214. See also Walker's original study with Els van der Helm: 'Overnight Therapy? The Role of Sleep in Emotional Brain Processing', *Psychological Bulletin*, 135, No. 5 (September 2009): 731–748, doi: 10.1037/a0016570

31 Walker, *Why We Sleep*, 208.

32 Quoted in Cheetham, *All the World's an Icon*, 162. See also Jung, *Collected Works*, Vol. 14, para. 753.

33 Antonio Zadra, 'Chronic Nightmares' in Robert J. Hoss and Robert P. Gongloff (eds), *Dreams: Understanding Biology, Psychology, and Culture*, Vol. 2 (Santa Barbara, CA: ABC-CLIO LLC, 2019), 480.

34 Barry Krakow et al., 'Imagery Rehearsal Therapy for Chronic Nightmares in Sexual Assault Survivors with Posttraumatic Stress Disorder: A Randomized Controlled Trial', *Journal of the American Medical Association, JAMA*, 286, No. 5 (1 August 2019): 537–545, doi: 10.1001/jama.286.5.537

35 Ibid., 543.

36 Ibid., 544. See also Chapter Nine of this book, 'Nightmares: From Fear to Freedom'.

37 For a vivid and informative account of parasomnias, refer to Guy Leschziner's *The Nocturnal Brain: Nightmares, Neuroscience and the Secret World of Sleep* (London: Simon & Schuster Ltd., 2019). Ryan Hurd gives a detailed account of a specific parasomnia in his *Sleep Paralysis: A Guide to Hypnagogic Visions and Visitors of the Night* (Los Altos, CA: Hyena Press, 2011).

38 See Hans J. Markowitsch and Angelica Staniloiu, 'Amygdala in Action: Relaying Biological and Social Significance to Autobiographical Memory', *Neuropsychologia*, 49, No. 4 (March 2011): 718–733, doi: 10.1016/j. neurophsychologia.2010.10.007

39 Walker, *Why We Sleep*, 203–204. As Walker explains, apparently only 2–3 per cent of dreams actually contain imagery from the preceding day, whereas 30 to 55 per cent of dreams appear thematically related to the day's emotional content.

40 See Rosalind D. Cartwright's early research in this area, 'Dreams that Work: The Relation of Dream Incorporation to Adaptation to Stressful Events', *Dreaming*, 1, No. 1 (1991): 3–9. https://doi.org/10.1037/h0094312, and also her comprehensive *The Twenty-Four Hour Mind: The Role of Sleep and Dreaming in Our Emotional Lives* (London: Oxford University Press, 2010), 162–168.

41 For a systematic study of this condition, see Antonio R. Damasio's *Descartes' Error: Emotion, Reason and the Human Brain* (New York, NY: Avon Books,

2006). Damasio describes how such a condition is found in people who seem perfectly 'normal' and may test high on intelligence tests but who, through brain injury, have lost their capacity to make decisions, especially significant life choices. He suggests that in decision-making, the personal and social domains will be 'compromised' if there is damage to the ventromedial prefrontal cortices where 'reason and emotion "intersect"' (70).

42 Smaranda Leu-Semenescu et al., 'Can we still dream when the mind is blank? Sleep and Dream Mentations in Auto-activation Deficit', *Brain*, 136, No. 10 (1 October 2013): 3076–3084, doi.org/10.1093/brain/awt229

43 For a comprehensive review, see Tracey L. Kahn and Stephen P. LaBerge, 'Dreaming and Waking: Similarities and Differences Revisited', *Consciousness and Cognition*, 20 (2011): 494–514, doi: 10.1016/j. concog.2010.09.002

44 To obtain these statistics, David T. Saunders et al. undertook a meta-analysis of numerous lucid dreaming studies on lucid dreaming prevalence and frequency. Refer to David T. Saunders, Chris Roe, Graham Smith and Helen Clegg, 'Lucid Dreaming Incidence: A Quality Effects Meta-Analysis of 50 Years of Research', *Consciousness and Cognition*, 43 (2016): 210, http:// dx.doi.org/10.1016/j.concog.2016.06.002

45 Jung, *The Collected Works*, Vol. 10, para. 304.

46 Cited in Peter J. Forshaw's illuminating study, 'Curious Knowledge and Wonder-Working Wisdom in the Occult Work of Heinrich Khunrath' in Robert J. W. Evans and Alexander Marr (eds), *Curiosity and Wonder from the Renaissance to the Enlightenment* (New York, NY: Routledge, 2016), 126.

47 Peter J. Forshaw outlines the importance of the oratory to European alchemists, particularly Heinrich Khunrath, in his '"Behold, the dream cometh": Hyperphysical Magic and Deific Visions in an Early-Modern Theosophical Lab-Oratory' in Joad Raymond, *Conversations with Angels: Essays Towards a History of Spiritual Communication, 1100–1700* (UK: Palgrave Macmillan, 2011), 175–200.

48 Corbin presents a summary of Swedenborg's understanding of the 'inner breathing' or 'inner respiration' in his *Swedenborg and Esoteric Islam*, 87. Also, see Wilson Van Dusen's introduction to G. E. Klemming (ed.), *Swedenborg's Journal of Dreams: 1743–1744* (New York, NY: Swedenborg Foundation, 1996), 18, for a summary of Swedenborg's use of the breath.

49 The link between our personal sense of self as human individuals in space and time is thoughtfully developed in *The Development of Autobiographical Memory* by Hans J. Markowitsch and Harold Welzer, trans. David Emmans (New York, NY: Psychology Press, 2010).

Chapter Three – Dreams, Trees and Their Roots in the Imaginal Mind: Transforming Waking Life

1   James Allen, *As a Man Thinketh* (Public Domain, 1903), 54.

2   Ludwig Wittgenstein, *Remarks on Colour*, ed. G. E. M. Anscombe, trans. Linda L. McAlister and Margarete Schättle (Oxford: Blackwell Publishers, Ltd., 1977), No. 165, 39e.

3   If you would like to develop your capacity for working with images, see Dina Glouberman's *Life Choices, Life Changes: Develop Your Personal Vision for the Life You Want* (London: Hodder & Stoughton, 2003).

4   See Martin Buber's *I and Thou*, trans. Ronald Gregor Smith (New York: MacMillan Publishing Group, 1958; originally published 1937), for Buber's development of the I–Thou versus I–It ways of relating.

5   Ibid., 6.

6   See Corbin's foundational essay, '*Mundus Imaginalis*, or the Imaginary and the Imaginal' in *Swedenborg and Esoteric Islam*, 9.

7   Ibid., 18–20.

8   Stephen LaBerge, Benjamin Baird and Philip G. Zimbardo, 'Smooth Tracking of Visual Targets Distinguishes Lucid REM Sleep Dreaming and Waking Perception from Imagination', *Nature Communications*, 9, No. 3298 (2018), doi: 10.1038/s41467-018-05547-0

9   Christopher L. Edwards, Josie E. Malinowski, Shauna L. McGee et. al., 'Comparing Personal Insight Gains Due to Consideration of a Recent Dream and Consideration of a Recent Event Using the Ullman and Schredl Dream Group Methods', *Frontiers in Psychology*, 6, No. 831 (June 2015), doi: 10.3389/fpsyg.2015.00831

10 The study 'Visual Imagery without Visual Perception?' by Helder Bértolo includes the dream illustration; *Psicológica*, 26, (2005): 173–188. The original study in English, 'Visual Dream Content, Graphical Representation and EEG Alpha Activity in Congenitally Blind Subjects', led by Helder Bértolo, can be found at *Cognitive Brain Research*, 15, No. 3 (February 2003): 277–284, doi: 10.1016/s0926-6410(02)00199-4

11 See 'The Sensory Construction of Dreams and Nightmare Frequency in Congenitally Blind and Late Blind Individuals' conducted by Amani Meaidi, Poul Jennum, Maurice Ptito and Ron Kupers in *Sleep Medicine*, 15 (2014): 585–595, doi.org/10.1016/S0926-6410(02)00199-4

12 Bértolo, 'Visual Imagery', 184.

13 Meaidi, 'The Sensory Construction of Dreams', 594.

14 Buber, *I and Thou*, 6.

15 See Iain McGilchrist's remarkable study of the brain's right and left

hemispheres, *The Master and His Emissary: The Divided Brain and the Making of the Western World* (New Haven, CT and London: Yale University Press, 2009), 177.

16 Ibid., 31.

17 McGilchrist notes this right-brain activation in REM sleep, citing research by John Stirling Myer, Yoshiki Ishikawa, Takashi Hata and Ismet Karacan, 'Cerebral Blood Flow in Normal and Abnormal Sleep and Dreaming', *Brain and Cognition*, 6, No. 3 (July 1987): 266–294, doi.org/10.1016/0278-2626(87)90127-8.

18 See Sigmund Freud, *The Interpretation of Dreams* (First Part) in *The Standard Edition of the Complete Psychological Works of Sigmund Freud*, ed. and trans. James Strachey in collaboration with Anna Freud (London: The Hogarth Press and The Institute of Psychoanalysis, 1981; originally published 1900), 49. See also Freud's footnote No. 2 to the revised edition: 'At bottom, dreams are nothing other than a particular *form* of thinking, made possible by the conditions of the state of sleep.' Vol. 6, 506.

19 Joseph Campbell, *The Mythic Image*, i–8.

20 For more on Einstein's thought experiments, see Walter Isaacson, *Einstein: His Life and Universe* (London: Simon & Schuster Ltd., 2007), especially 3–4 and 26–27.

21 Quoted in an interview with Einstein by George Sylvester Viereck, 'What Life Means to Einstein', *Saturday Evening Post*, 26 October 1929, pages 17 and 110, http://www.saturdayeveningpost.com/wpcontent/uploads/satevepost/what_life_means_to_einstein.pdf

22 James Hillman, *Archetypal Psychology Uniform Edition of the Writings of James Hillman*, Vol. 1 (Putnam, CT: Spring Publications, 2013), 18.

23 Robert Steele and Dorothea Waley Singer, 'The Emerald Table', *Proceedings of the Royal Society of Medicine*, 21, No. 3 (January 1928): 485–501, https://www.ncbi.nlm.nih.gov/pmc/articles/PMC2101974/?page=1

24 Henry Corbin, *The Man of Light in Iranian Sufiism*, trans. Nancy Pearson (New Lebanon, NY: Omega Publications Inc.), 6.

25 Quoted in Peter J. Forshaw, 'Behold, the dream cometh', 175. Forshaw points out in an endnote that this quote, used by Khunrath in the 1609 edition of *The Amphitheatre of Eternal Wisdom*, is attributed to Julius Caesar Scaliger. See endnote No. 1, 189.

26 Doc Childre and Howard Martin, *The Heartmath Solution: Proven Techniques for Developing Emotional Intelligence* (London: Judy Piatkus Publishers Limited, 1999), 33.

27 Ibid., 40.

28 Blaise Pascal in *Blaise Pascal's Penseés: Thoughts on God, Religion, and Wagers*, trans. William F. Trotter, Section IV: 'Of the Means of Belief', No. 277 (Greenwood, WI: Suzeteo Enterprises, 2005; originally published 1660), 56.

29 Childre and Martin, *The Heartmath Solution*, 6.

30 Ibid., 10 and 30–31.

31 These figures are cited in Sheldrake's *Science and Spiritual Practices*, 31, from Herbert Benson, *The Relaxation Response* (New York, NY: William Morrow, 2000).

32 The Holy Bible, New International Version, NIV® Daniel 4:9–16.

33 The Holy Bible, American King James Version, AKJV, Daniel 2:30.

34 The Holy Bible, NIV ® Daniel 4:4.

35 This translation of Rilke's untitled poem is my own. The original version in German can be found in *Rainer Maria Rilke, Die Gedichte* (Frankfurt am Main and Leipzig: Insel Verlag, GmbH, 2006), 619.

36 Richard Powers, *The Overstory* (London: Penguin Random House, 2018), 221.

37 Peter Wohlleben, *The Hidden Life of Trees* (Vancouver, BC: Greystone Books Ltd., 2015), 10–11.

38 Ibid., 6–18.

39 See Eetu Puttonen et al., 'Quantification of Overnight Movement of Birch (Betula pendula) Branches and Foliage with Short Interval Terrestrial Laser Scanning', *Frontiers in Plant Science*, 7, Article 222 (29 February 2016), doi: 10.3389/fpls.2016.00222

40 C. G. Jung, *Modern Man in Search of a Soul*, trans. W. S. Dell and Cary F. Baynes (London and New York: Routledge Classics, 2002; originally published 1933), 74. The entire sentence reads, 'In psychic life, as everywhere in our experience, all things that act are actual, regardless of the names man chooses to bestow on them.'

41 Quoted from a letter that Einstein wrote to a father whose son had died in Silvan S. Schweber, *Einstein, Oppenheimer and the Meaning of Genius* (Cambridge, MA: Harvard University Press, 2008), 300.

42 Jung, *The Collected Works*, Vol. 10, para. 304.

43 Edward F. Edinger, *Anatomy of the Psyche: Alchemical Symbolism in Psychotherapy* (Peru, IL: Open Court Publishing, 1994), 178.

44 For more on how this term came into common usage, see the article '"Dreamtime" and "The Dreaming": Who dreamed up these terms?' by Christine Judith Nicholls, The Conversation UK (28 January 2014), http://theconversation.com/dreamtime-and-the-dreaming-who-dreamed-up-these-terms-20835

45 For a scholarly account of the historical roots of the Australian peoples, see Josephine Flood, *Archaeology of the Dreamtime: The Story of Prehistoric Australia and its People* (New Haven, CT: Yale University Press, 1990).

46 Mircea Eliade, *The Quest: History and Meaning in Religion* (Chicago, IL: University of Chicago Press, 1969), 10.

47 Quoted in Joseph Campbell's *The Mythic Image*, I–1.

48 For more on this topic, see Elizabeth and Neil Carman's *The Cosmic Cradle: Spiritual Dimensions of Life Before Birth* (Berkeley, CA: North Atlantic Books, 2013), 225–237.

49 Allen, *As a Man Thinketh*, 54.

50 The physicist David Peat, in his book *Blackfoot Physics: A Journey into the Native American Universe* (London: Fourth Estate Limited, 1996), 287, compares the science of Western and Indigenous cultures, outlining striking parallels.

51 Presented in Roger Cook's beautiful *The Tree of Life: Symbol of the Centre* (London: Thames & Hudson), 18.

52 Ibid.

53 Ibid.

54 For an expansive development of this theme, see Mircea Eliade, *Images and Symbols: Studies in Religious Symbolism*, trans. Philip Mairet (Princeton, NJ: Princeton University Press, 1991).

55 Mircea Eliade, *Shamanism: Archaic Techniques of Ecstasy*, trans. William R. Trask (St. Ives Pls, UK: Arkana, Penguin Books, 1989), 39–40.

56 The physicist Arthur Zajonc gives an enlightening overview of experiments on light involving the 'quantum domain' in his book *Catching the Light: The Entwined History of Light and Mind* (New York and Oxford: Oxford University Press, 1993), 292–329. For a concise introduction to the subject of quantum theory refer to John Polkinghorne's *Quantum Theory: A Very Short Introduction* (London: Oxford University Press, 2002).

57 For the complete poem see W. B. Yeats' 'The Two Trees' in *William Butler Yeats: Selected Poems and Three Plays*, 4th edition, ed. M. L. Rosenthal (New York, NY: Scribner Paperback Poetry Edition, Simon & Schuster Inc., 1996), 17–18.

58 Damasio, *Descartes' Error*, 250.

59 For more on reciprocity from the standpoint of 'co-creative dream theory' see Scott Sparrow's work on 'Imagery Change Analysis: Working with Imagery from the Standpoint of Co-creative Dream Theory' (2013), http://www.driccpe.org.uk/?portfolio-view=imagery-change-analysis-working-with-imagery-from-the-standpoint-of-co-creative-dream-theory-scott-sparrow.

Chapter Four – The Language of Rocks, Stones and Minerals: A Case Illustration

1   From *The Gospel of Thomas*, presented by Hugh McGregor Ross (London: Watkins Publishing Inc., 2002), 77$_N$. This text forms part of what has become known as the Nag Hamâdi Library, a collection of manuscripts written in the 3rd or 4th century AD and hidden away until their discovery in 1945. The collection represents writings of early Christians that were not accepted into the canon of recognised texts.

2   For a detailed presentation of 'The Waking Dream Process' developed by Nigel Hamilton, see his *Awakening Through Dreams*, 2014.

3   When working with dreams, the imagery may also present a metaphor to draw our attention to a potential medical issue. For example, the blockage in this dream could mirror a physical blockage. Because Mark touched his chest area when describing the dream, I asked him if he had any heart issues. Mark reported that he had in the past but had recently been checked and at present had no reason for concern. However, the dream alerted him to be mindful of his condition between annual medical reviews. For an overview of somatic and health issues in dreams, see Robert J. Hoss, 'Somatic and Health-Related Dreams' in *Dreams: Understanding Biology, Psychology, and Culture*, Vol. 1 (Santa Barbara, CA: ABC-CLIO LLC, 2019), 292–301.

4   An alchemical maxim quoted in Mircea Eliade's *The Forge and the Crucible: The Origins and Structures of Alchemy*, 2nd edition, trans. Stephen Corrin (Chicago and London: University of Chicago Press, 1978), 153.

5   Ibid., 42, 121.

6   Taken from excerpts of Sir James Jeans' 1931 book *The Mysterious Universe* cited in Ken Wilber (ed.), *Quantum Questions: Mystical Writings of the World's Greatest Physicists* (Boston, MA: Shambhala Publications Inc.), 151.

7   Quoted by Eliade, *The Forge and the Crucible*, 158.

8   Ibid., 156–157.

9   Jung, *The Collected Works*, Vol. 9, Part II, para. 61.

10 Ibid., paras. 13–15.

11 The Holy Bible, NIV® Ezekiel 36:26.

12 Jung, *The Collected Works*, Vol. 14, para. 778.

13 Hazrat Inayat Khan, *The Sufi Message of Hazrat Inayat Kahn: The Unity of Religious Ideals*, Vol. 9 (Geneva, Switzerland: International Headquarters of the Sufi Movement, 1979), 229.

14 From Barbara Somers' moving question, 'What makes your heart sing – what brings you to your joy?' See her book *Journey in Depth: A Transpersonal Perspective*, written with Ian Gordon Brown, ed. Helen Marshall (Leicestershire, UK: Archive Publishing, 2002), 34–36.

15 C. G. Jung in Aniela Jaffé (ed.), *C. G. Jung: Word and Image*, Bollingen
    Series XCVII, Vol. 2 (Princeton, NJ: Princeton University Press, 1979), 123.
16 *The Gospel of Thomas*, 50_{n2}, 38.
17 Quoted from Kurt Seligman's *The Mirror of Magic* (New York, 1948), 110,
    cited in Jean Chevalier and Alain Gheerbrant (eds), *The Penguin Dictionary
    of Symbols*, trans. John Buchanan-Brown (London: Penguin Books, 1996),
    1072.
18 Jung, *The Collected Works*, Vol. 16, para. 86.
19 The idea of 'greening' derives from Hildegard von Bingen's favourite theme
    of 'O nobilissima viriditas' or 'Oh most noble greenness', a theme she
    celebrated in her 'Responsory for the Virgin'. See Hildegard von Bingen,
    Mystical Visions, translated from *Scivias* by Bruce Hozeski and introduced
    by Matthew Fox (Santa Fe, NM: Bear & Company, 1995), 380. For the
    musical rendition of this piece, see http://www.hildegard-society.org/2017/04/
    o-nobilissima-viriditas-responsory.html or *O nobilissima viriditas: The
    Complete Hildegard von Bingen*, Vol. 3, Peter Wishart Symphony.
20 Robert A. Johnson, *Inner Gold: Understanding Psychological Projection*
    (Kihei, HI: Koa Books, 2008), 58.
21 A quote from Robert Stickgold, Director of the Center for Sleep and
    Cognition at Harvard Medical School, in the *National Geographic Magazine*
    (August 2018) feature article, 'The Science of Sleep' by Michael Finkel,
    40–77.
22 Khalil Gibran, *The Prophet* (New York: Alfred A. Knopf, 1951), 38.
23 The Holy Bible, NIV® Genesis 28:17.
24 Eliade, *The Forge and the Crucible*, 20 and 43.
25 From William Stafford's poem 'Glances' in *Travelling Through the Dark*
    (New York, NY: Harper & Row Publishers, 1962), 69.
26 Eliade, *The Forge and the Crucible*, 20.

Chapter Five – Light Revisioned Through the Prism of Dreams

1   From Dante's *Divine Comedy, The Vision of Hell, Purgatory and Paradise*,
    1321. This passage comes from Paradise, Canto 33, and this my own
    translation of the original Italian. To access a bilingual edition of Dante's
    work, see *The Divine Comedy of Dante Alighieri, Vol. 3, Paradiso*, trans.
    Courtney Langdon (London: Harvard University Press, 1921), last updated
    26 November 2019, https://oll.libertyfund.org/titles/212
2   Arthur Zajonc writes eloquently on this subject in his book *Catching the
    Light: The Entwined History of Light and Mind* (New York and Oxford:
    Oxford University Press, 1993), 316.

3   Ibid., 184. Zajonc himself has translated this passage from Goethe's *Zur Farbenlehre*, or *Theory of Colours*, found in Erich Trunz (ed.), *Goethes Werke, Hamburger Ausgabe*, Vol. 13 (Munich, Germany: C. H. Beck, 1982). For comparison, the translation by Charles Lock Eastlake reads, '…the eye is formed by the light, with reference to light, to be fit for the action of light; the light it contains corresponding with the light without.' (Mineola, NY: Dover Publications Inc., 2016), xxvi.

4   Zajonc, *Catching the Light*, 1–2. Zajonc, along with colleagues, set up a science exhibit, called 'Project Eureka', that invited people to peer into a space filled with light in a vacuum. Then they were asked to look again after a metal rod had been inserted. The presence of light became 'visible' via the illuminated rod.

5   See the NASA article 'Dark Energy, Dark Matter', accessed 8 August 2019, https://science.nasa.gov/astrophysics/focus-areas/what-is-dark-energy

6   The 'extended mind' theory purports that cognition extends beyond the individual mind to environmental structures ranging from objects and symbols to people, and spreads across space and time. This original theory has also been used by scientists to research extra-sensory perception. See Andy Clark and David Chalmers, 'The Extended Mind' in *Analysis*, Oxford Journals, Oxford University Press, 58, No. 1 (January 1998): 7–19, http://www.jstor.org/stable/3328150

7   I have written more on this theme in 'Metaphoric Presence in Spiritual Dreams' in the anthology *Dreams: Understanding Biology, Psychology, and Culture*, Vol. 2, 628– 633.

8   Drawn from Shakespeare's *The Tempest*, Act 4, scene 1, 156–157, originally 'We are such stuff/As dreams are made on…'

9   This dream is from one of over 6,000 reports of a spiritual or religious experience recorded by the Alister Hardy Religious Experience Research Centre archive at the Religious Experience Research Centre (RERC), University of Wales Trinity Saint David, Lampeter, UK. All quotations from the archive are followed by the account number, in this case RERC 000266. I wish to thank the RERC (http://www.uwtsd.ac.uk/library/alister-hardy-religious-experience-research-centre/) and the Alister Hardy Trust (http://www.studyspiritualexperiences.org/) for their permission to access and quote material from the archive.

10 See Carl Jung's summary of the alchemical understanding of the *lumen naturae* in his *The Collected Works*, Vol. 8, paras 388–396.

11 Ibid., para. 391. Jung cites this particular teaching from the *Liber de Caducis* by Paracelsus.

12 See Chapter Nine, 'Nightmares: From Fear to Freedom', for more on this topic. Chapter Ten, 'A Journey into the Deep: Lucid Dreaming and Lucid Surrender', explores the nature of Dark Light.

13 For more about this subject, Stanley Krippner, Fariba Bogzaran and André Percia de Carvalho provide an overview in *Extraordinary Dreams and How to Work with Them* (Albany, NY: State University of New York Press, 2002); Robert L. Van de Castle's chapter on 'Paranormal Dreams: Psychic Contributions to Dreams' in his *Our Dreaming Mind* (New York and Toronto: Ballantine Books, 1994) gives many accounts and examples of research in the field, as does *Dream Telepathy: Experiments in Nocturnal Extrasensory Perception* by Montague Ullman, Stanley Krippner and Alan Vaughan (Charlottesville, VA: Hampton Roads Publishing Company, 2001).

14 These figures are cited from a study on 'Spontaneous cases of psi within accounts submitted to the Alister Hardy Religious Experience Research Centre' by Pauline Linnett and Chris Roe, which compared ESP accounts from three sources: L.E. Rhine (1962), Sannwald (1963) and the Alister Hardy RERC archive (paper presented at the British Psychological Society, BPS, Transpersonal Section, 20th Annual Conference, 16–18 September 2016).

15 The Alister Hardy Religious Experience Religious Centre archive, Account 000166.

16 Annekatrin Puhle has compiled an analysis of 800 cases of transformative experiences involving light in her *Light Changes: Experiences in the Presence of Transforming Light* (Guildford, UK: White Crow Books, 2013), 218.

17 Ibid.

18 Ibid.

19 The dream in its entirety is quoted by Gerhard Adler in his *Studies in Analytical Psychology* (London: Routledge Taylor & Frances Group, 1999), 144, from Priestley's *Rain Upon Godshill*, 301.

20 Ibid., 144.

21 Excerpt of 'You Are With the Friend Now' from *I Heard God Laughing: Poems of Hope and Joy, Renderings of Hafiz* by Daniel Ladinsky (London: Penguin Books Ltd., 2006), 1, used with permission.

Chapter Six – The Mystery and Magic of Colour: A Study in Blue

1   Isak Dinesen (Karen Blixen), 'The Young Man with the Carnation' in *Winter's Tales* (London: Penguin Books, 2001/1942), 29.

2   The noun *arkhē* in Greek means a 'first place or origin' and originates from

the verb *arkhein*, 'to be the first'; *typos* means 'a model, type, mark, or blow' and refers to the 'blow' associated with the act of pressing an authenticating seal into wax or paint. The seal stands for the authority of the person or body who issued it.

3 Jung, *The Collected Works*, Vol. 11, para 557.

4 Ibid.

5 The Alister Hardy Religious Experience Religious Centre archive, Account 786

6 Bach, *Illusions*, 26.

7 Richard Buckminster Fuller coined this expression. Fuller, an architect and inventor, also designed the geodesic dome.

8 Nigel Hamilton made this observation about the nature of colour in dreams in a lecture on 'Alchemical Dreams' during my advanced training in psychotherapy at the Centre for Counselling and Psychotherapy Education, CCPE, London, 2009.

9 For the complete poem, entitled 'Day of Color', see *John J. Brugaletta: Selected Poems* (Athens, GA: Futurecycle Press, 2019), 13. I would like to thank John Brugaletta for encouraging me to write and to dream!

10 Robert J. Hoss, *Dream Language: Self-Understanding Through Imagery and Color* (Ashland, OR: Inner Source, 2005), 97.

11 Ludwig Wittgenstein, *Philosophical Investigations*, 2nd edition, trans. G. E. Anscombe, (Oxford: Basil Blackwell, 1986), No. 129, 48e.

12 Ludwig Wittgenstein, *Remarks on Colour*, No. 154, 36e. By 'geometry of colour' he refers to our concepts of colour that we form in connection to 'three-dimensionality, light and shadow.' See also No. 144, 36e.

13 The company Enchroma first developed these glasses. See https://www. enchroma.com for more information.

14 You can find such scenes posted on www.youtube.com. See, for example, https://www.youtube.com/watch?v=XSD7-TgUmUY

15 Wittgenstein, *Remarks on Colour*, No. 224, 47e.

16 Wassily Kandinsky describes this colour effect further in his study *Concerning the Spiritual in Art*, trans. M.T. H. Sadler (New York, NY: Dover Publications Inc., 1977), 28.

17 From William Blake's poem 'The Little Black Boy' (1789) in *Songs of Innocence and Experience*, v. 13–14, ed. Sir Geoffrey Keynes (Oxford University Press, 1970), 134. Copyright © 1967, Oxford University Press. Reproduced with permission of the Licensor through PLSclear.

18 Andrew Harvey, *The Essential Mystics: Selections from the World's Great Wisdom Traditions* (San Francisco, CA: HarperSanFrancisco, 1997), 147.

19 From the alchemical emblem 'The Secret Symbols of the Rosicrucians'

presented by Adam McLean in his *The Alchemical Mandala: A Survey of the Mandala in the Western Esoteric Traditions* (Grand Rapids, MI: Phanes Press Inc., 2002), 124. See his website (www.levity.com) for an unrivalled database of alchemical treatises and emblems.

20 An analogy drawn by William C. Chittick in his *Imaginal Worlds: Ibn al-'Arabī and the Problem of Religious Diversity* (Albany, NY: State University of New York Press, 1994), 8.

21 Ibid., 58.

22 Quoted in Jim Clemmer, *The Leader's Digest: Timeless Principles for Team and Organization Success* (Toronto, Canada: TCG Press, 2003), 84.

23 W. Y. Evan-Wentz (ed.), *The Tibetan Book of the Dead*, trans. Lama Kazi Dawa-Samdup (New York, New York: Oxford University Press, 1968), 106.

24 Ibid., 107.

25 Ibid., 104.

26 Arthur Zajonc, *Catching the Light*, 199–200.

27 For a more in-depth study of the psychological and physiological effects of natural light, see Jacob Israel Liberman, *Light: Medicine of the Future* (Santa Fe, NM: Bear & Company, 1991).

28 Novalis, *Henry Von Ofterdingen: A Romance*, Dover Thrift Editions (Mineola, NY: Dover Publications Inc., 2015), 3.

29 Aldous Huxley, *The Doors of Perception* (London: Flamingo; originally published 1954), 7.

30 Ibid., 8.

31 Katherine A. Maclean et al., 'Factor Analysis of the Mystical Experience Questionnaire: A Study of Experiences Occasioned by the Hallucinogen,' *Journal for the Scientific Study of Religion*, 51, No. 4 (December 2012): 721–737, doi: 10.1111/j.1468-5906.2012.01685.x

32 The Alister Hardy Religious Experience Religious Centre archive, Account 000128.

33 From 'Truth' quoted in C. S. Lewis (ed.), *George MacDonald: An Anthology 365 Readings* (San Francisco, CA: HarperSanFranscisco, 1973), No. 187, 81.

34 Paul Klee, *Pedagogical Sketchbook*, trans. Moholy-Nagy (London: Faber & Faber, 1977), 61, Figure 87.

35 Henry Corbin, *The Man of Light in Iranian Sufiism*, trans. Nancy Pearson (New Lebanon, NY: Omega Publications Inc., 1994), 142.

36 An expression used by Ibn al-'Arabī quoted by William C. Chittick in his *Imaginal Worlds: Ibn al-'Arabī and the Problem of Religious Diversity*, 26.

37 Johann Wolfgang von Goethe, *Faust*, trans. Albert G. Latham (New York: E. P. Dutton & Co., 1908), 15.

38 Johann Wolfgang von Goethe, *Theory of Colours*, trans. Charles Lock Eastlake (Mineola, New York: Dover Publications Inc., 2006), xvii.

Chapter Seven – The Geometry of Dreams and the Dimensions of Consciousness

1   Kandinsky, *Concerning the Spiritual in Art*, footnote No. 6, 29.

2   See the cover of the April 2002 issue of *Discover* magazine, on which a marble is used to portray the universe in its earliest stages of expansion to illustrate its feature article, 'Where did everything come from?: Guth's Grand Guess', by Brad Lemley, *Discover*, 23, No. 4 (April 2002), 32–39.

3   For a concise explanation of the quantum void, see Frank Close, *NOTHING: A Very Short Introduction* (Oxford: Oxford University Press, 2009).

4   Julian of Norwich, *Revelations of Divine Love: Mother Julian of Norwich*, eds. Halcyon Backhouse and Rhona Pipe (London: Hodder & Stoughton, 1997), 10–11.

5   St John's, Timberhill, Norwich, enshrines St Julian's Church, the cell where she is believed to have lived.

6   See excerpts from Louis de Broglie's writings in 'Aspirations Towards Spirit', *Quantum Questions*, ed., Ken Wilber (Shambala Press: Boston, 2001), 122.

7   Ibid.

8   Isaacson, *Einstein*, 26. According to Isaacson, the preparatory school at Aarau, where Einstein chose to spend a year before attending Zurich Polytechnic, drew on the teaching theory of the Swiss educational reformer Johann Heinrich Pestalozzi, a keen supporter of visualisations to promote learning.

9   Quoted from Kekulé's own report in the *Berichte der deutschen chemischen Gesellschaft*, 1890, pages 1305–1307. The report appears in a lecture entitled 'Kekulé Dreams' by Dr Water Libby, University of Pittsburgh, in the first of a series of papers presented on the 'Psychology and Logic of Research' given at the Mellon Institute of Industrial Research of the University of Pittsburgh, 14 February–2 May 1922. See Walter Libby, 'The Scientific Imagination', *Scientific Monthly*, 15, No. 263 (1922): 269, https://archive.org/details/jstor-6552/page/n7. Although there have been inconsistencies in Kekulé's reports of this dream over time, as Libby's paper documents, Kekulé was known for his use of dream-based intuitions for developing hypotheses.

10 C. G. Jung, *The Collected Works*, Vol. 13, para. 143.

11 See Hobson, 'Sleep and Dreaming: Towards a Theory of Protoconsciousness', 803–813.

12 J. Allan Hobson and Karl J. Friston, 'Waking and Dreaming Consciousness: Neurobiological and Functional Considerations', *Progress in Neurobiology*, 98, No. 1 (July 2012): 82–98, doi.org/10.1016/j.pneurobio.2012.05.003.

13 Nigel Hamilton, 'Psychospiritual Transformation: Light, Colour, and Symmetry', in Robert J. Hoss and Robert P. Gongloff (eds), *Dreams: Understanding Biology, Psychology, and Culture*, Vol. 2 (Santa Barbara, CA: ABC-CLIO, LLC, 2019), 634–640. Italics in original.

14 Jung, *The Collected Works*, Vol. 14, para. 776.

15 From Matthew Fox (ed.), *Meditations with Meister Eckhart* (Inner Traditions International and Bear & Company © 1983. All rights reserved. http://www.innertraditions.com. Reprinted with permission of publisher), 21.

16 Black Elk in John G. Neihardt, *Black Elk Speaks: The Complete Edition* (Nebraska: The Regents Board of the University of Nebraska, 2014; originally published 1932), 26.

17 David Villaseñor, *Tapestries in Sand: The Spirit of Indian Sand Painting* (Happy Camp, CA: Naturegraph Company Publishers Inc., 1966), 7.

18 David Peat provides a thoughtful integration of Jung's four-function model with the practice of the 'sacred hoop' among the Native American peoples in his *Blackfoot Physics*, 164–170.

19 From Copernicus' *De Revolutionibus Orbium Caelestium*, 1543, quoted in István and Magdolna Hargittai's *Symmetry: A Unifying Concept* (Bolinas, CA: Shelter Publications Inc., 1994), 103.

20 Frank Close, in his book *The Void*, describes the Hartle–Hawking model of the universe in which time takes on the dimensional properties of a sphere (Oxford: Oxford University Press, 2007), 152–156.

21 Jung, *The Collected Works*, Vol. 18, para. 625.

22 If you are puzzled by how light can appear as shining 'black', remember how pure light in a vacuum would, in fact, appear invisible and 'black' (refer to Chapter Five). In lucid dreams, I perceive this radiant darkness as a clear, piercing light. Chapter Ten, 'Journeys into the Deep: Lucid Dreaming and Lucid Surrender', will look at the phenomena of black light.

23 Jung, *The Collected Works*, vol. 14, para. 776.

Chapter Eight – The Power of Healing Presence in Dreams

1   Buber, *I and Thou*, 11.

2   For an enchanting treatise on the art of perfumery and its connection to alchemy, refer to Maggie Aftel, *The Essence of Alchemy: A Book of Perfume* (New York, NY: North Point Press, 1991).

3   *COBUILD Advanced English Dictionary*, s.v. 'presence (*n.*)' ©
    HarperCollins Publishers, accessed 31 July 2019, https://www.collins
    dictionary.com/dictionary/english/presence

4   Carl Rogers, quoted in a 1987 interview with Michèle Baldwin published
    in Baldwin's *The Use of Self in Psychotherapy*, ed. Michèle Baldwin (New
    York, NY: The Haworth Press Inc., 2000), 29.

5   John Welwood, a transpersonal therapist, has developed many teachings
    and practices on unconditional practice. See his chapter on 'The Power
    of Healing Presence' in *Toward a Psychology of Awakening: Buddhism,
    Psychotherapy and the Path of Personal and Spiritual Transformation*
    (Boston, MA: Shambahla Publications Inc., 2002), 141. Italics in original.

6   Cheetham, *All the World's an Icon*, 173.

7   Solrunn Nes gives an exquisite overview of the tradition of icon painting
    using icons that she herself has created in *The Mystical Language of Icons*
    (Canterbury, UK: Canterbury Press, 2004).

8   See Genesis 18:1–15.

9   English Standard Version Bible, Hebrews 13:2.

10 *Stachu* is the nickname for 'Stanislaw' in Polish.

11 This dream comes from a collection of 208 dreams garnered from 147
    survivors of Auschwitz in 1979 by the Kraków Medical Academy, Poland. The
    collection is housed in the Auschwitz-Birkenau Museum Archive. Wojciech
    Owczarski cites this dream in his powerful study of 51 'Therapeutic Dreams
    in Auschwitz' that he identified from among the sample dreams and then
    categorised. See Wojciech Owczarski, 'Therapeutic Dreams in Auschwitz' in
    Jednak Ksiazki, Gdańske Czasopismo Humanistyczne, 6 (2016): 86. Full text
    available at http://cejsh.icm.edu.pl/cejsh/element/bwmeta1.element.desklight-
    623ef4d8-ca2d-4ec9-9295-8c5f5ebac108. I would like to thank Wojciech
    Owczarski for his permission to include this dream.

12 The theologian Rudolf Otto coined this expression and describes it in full in
    his book *The Idea of the Holy*, 2nd edition, trans. John W. Harvey (London:
    Oxford University Press, 1950), particularly pages 13–24.

13 Ibid., 59.

14 The Jersualem Bible 1 John 4:18, 'In love there can be no fear, but fear is
    driven out by perfect love...'.

15 In Greek mythology, the goddess of love, Aphrodite, came out of the sea
    carried on the backs of fish. The fish symbol was used as the twelfth sign
    of the zodiac, Pisces. Early Christians, who viewed Jesus as a 'fisher of
    men', widely used the Greek word *ichthus* (fish) as an acronym for *Iesu
    Christos Theou Uios Soter* (Jesus Christ, Son of God, Saviour). The disciple

Luke reports that Christ ate fish after his resurrection (Luke 24:42). For more associations with fish symbolism, see Chevalier and Gheerbrant, *The Penguin Dictionary of Symbols*, 383–384.

16 My training in psychotherapy was at the Centre for Counselling and Psychotherapy Education in London, accredited by the United Kingdom Council for Psychotherapy. See www.ccpe.org.uk.

17 Robert A. Johnson, *Owning Your Own Shadow* (New York, NY: HarperCollins, 1991), 85.

18 See Werner Herzog's *Lo and Behold, Reveries of the Connected World* (Saville Productions, 2016).

19 Teilhard de Chardin develops the evolution of what he calls *noogenesis*, the development of the mind, in his book *The Phenomenon of Man*, trans. Bernard Wall (New York, NY: Harper & Row Publishers Inc., 1975), particularly pages 180–184.

20 These figures are drawn from two studies, the first by Alfonso Echazarra, 'How has internet use changed between 2012 and 2015?', *PISA in Focus*, No. 83, OECD Publishing, Paris (April 2018): 2, doi.org/10.1787/1e912a10-en, a study supported by the Organization for Economic Cooperation and Development, established in 1961 and representing 34 member countries across the globe. The second study by Ofcom, the UK's communication regulator, focused on the media use of adults in the UK. See Ofcom, 'Adults: Media Use and Attitudes Report, 2019' (30 May 2019): 6, https://www.ofcom.org.uk/__data/assets/pdf_file/0021/149124/adults-media-use-and-attitudes-report.pdf

21 Cited in the Organisation for Economic Cooperation and Development's 'Children & Young People's Mental Health in the Digital Age: Shaping the Future' (OECD, 2018): 8, https://www.oecd.org/els/health-systems/Children-and-Young-People-Mental-Health-in-the-Digital-Age.pdf

22 For more on this theme, see Andrew Powell's thought-provoking essay 'Technology and the Soul in the 21st Century' in his *Conversations with the Soul. A Psychiatrist Reflects: Essays on Life, Death and Beyond* (London: Muswell Hill Press, 2018), 161–179.

23 Google calls this creative programming 'inceptionalism'. For more examples of this computer-generated artform, see https://ai.googleblog.com/2015/06/inceptionism-going-deeper-into-neural.html

24 From George MacDonald's *The Golden Key and Other Fantasy Stories* (Grand Rapids, MI: Wm. B. Eerdmans Publishing Co., 1980), 6–7. The book's 'Publisher's Note' quotes MacDonald as having said that he did not write for children, 'but for the childlike, whether of five, or fifty, or seventy-five', x.

25 Ibid., 11–12.

26 In Lewis, *George MacDonald*, No. 1295, 139.

27 Welwood, *Toward a Psychology of Awakening*, 143.

28 The development of fifth generation (5G) high-speed technologies, operating at speeds 20,000 times faster than the now archaic third generaton (3G), may not only hasten our distractedness but may also harm us and the environment by means of the electromagnetic pollution in which they immerse all life. For a summary of the potential health and environmental effects of 5G EMF, see Priyanka Bandara's and David O. Carpenter's 'Planetary Electromagnetic Pollution: It is Time to Assess its Impact' in *The Lancet Planetary Health*, vol. 2 © 2018 The Author(s). Published by Elsevier Ltd. (December 2018): 512–514, doi.org/10.1016/S2542-5196(18)30221-3. For a detailed meta-study see Martin L. Pall's comprehensive '5G: Great risk for EU, U.S. and International Health! Compelling Evidence for Eight Distinct Types of Great Harm Caused by Electromagnetic Field (EMF) Exposures and the Mechanism that Causes Them' (May 2018), https://www.emfdata.org/en/documentations/detail&id=243

29 Excerpt from *The Way of Life: Lao-Tzu*, trans. Raymond. B. Blakney translation copyright © 1955 by Raymond B. Blakney. Used by permission of New American Library, an imprint of Penguin Publishing Group, a division of Penguin Random House LLC. All rights reserved. (New York, NY: Signet Classics, 2007), No. 21.

30 For more on this topic, see Melinda Powell, 'Metaphoric Presence in Dreams' in *Dreams: Understanding Biology, Psychology, and Culture*, Vol. 2, 628–633.

Chapter Nine – Nightmares: From Fear to Freedom

1   The Holy Bible, NIV ® Proverbs 3:24

2   See Michael Schredl, 'Typical Dream Themes' in Katja Valli and Robert J. Hoss (eds), *Dreams: Understanding Biology, Psychology and Culture*, Vol. 1 (Santa Barbara, CA: ABC-CLIO LLC, 2019), 180–188. Schredl notes that although people commonly report these themes, studies of actual dream accounts show that the theme of being chased actually appears in only 4 to 11 per cent of dreams, and that of falling significantly less. So, although these themes appear less often in dream accounts, people report these types of dreams more readily. This may be because dream scenarios that seemingly pose a direct threat to our existence leave a deep impression and so are more easily remembered.

3   See Andréanne Rousseau and Geneviève Belleville, 'The Mechanisms of Action Underlying the Efficacy of Psychological Nightmare Treatments: A

Systematic Review and Thematic Analysis of Discussed Hypotheses', *Sleep Medicine Review*, 39 (2018): 122–133, doi: 10.1016/j.smrv.2017.08.004

4 Snorre Sturlason, *Heimskringla; or, the Lives of the Norse Kings*, edited with notes by Erling Monsen and translated into English with the assistance of A. H. Smith (New York, NY: Dover Publications Inc., 1990), 9. This tale is cited in a delightful collection of folk legends and traditions compiled by the folklorist Dee L. Ashliman, former Professor Emeritus of German at the University of Pittsburgh, https://www.pitt.edu/~dash/nightmare.html#kuhn2 (last updated May 2005)

5 Ibid., 9.

6 See Ahmed S. BaHammam, Sohaila A. Al-Shimemeri, Reda I. Salama and Munir M. Sharif, 'Clinical and Polysomnographic Characteristics and Response to Continuous Positive Airway Pressure Therapy in Obstructive Sleep Apnea Patients with Nightmares', *Sleep Medicine*, 14, No. 2 (2013): 149–154, doi: 10.1016/j.sleep.2012.07.007. Sleep apnoea can be treated using continuous positive airway pressure (CPAP) therapy and other medical interventions. See your doctor if you think you may have this condition. You can obtain more information about this condition at https://www.mayoclinic.org/diseases-conditions/sleep-apnea/symptoms-causes/syc-20377631

7 For a moving and informative description of nightmares associated with various parasomnias, see Leschziner, *The Nocturnal Brain*.

8 See Virginie Sterpenich, Lampros Perogamvros, Giulio Tononi and Sophie Schwartz, 'Experiencing Fear in Dreams Relates to Brain Response to Aversive Stimuli During Wakefulness', *Sleep Medicine*, 40 Supplement 1 (December 2017): pE259, doi.org/10.1016/j.sleep.2017.11.759 and also the authors' full treatment of this topic in 'Fear in Dreams and in Wakefulness: Evidence for Day/Night Affective Homeostasis', Cold Spring Harbor Laboratory, bioRxiv preprint, posted online 29 January 2019, doi: http://dx.doi.org/10.1101/534099

9 Quoted in 'Bad dreams "help to control fear when awake"' by Sean Coughlan, BBC, 27 November 2019, Family and Education, https://www.bbc.co.uk/news/education-50563835

10 Plato, *Phaedo*, in Edith Hamilton and Huntington Cairns (eds), *The Collected Dialogues, Including the Letters*, Bollingen Series LXXI, 6th edition (Princeton, NJ: Princeton University Press, 1971), 67e, 50.

11 For a collection of similar dream reports in a hospice setting, see Derek Doyle, *The Platform Ticket: Memories and Musings of a Hospice Doctor* (Bakewell, DE: The Pentland Press, Ltd., 1999). See also Jeanne

van Bronkhorst's *Dreams at the Threshold* (Woodbury, MI: Llewellyn Publications, 2015).

12 See Peter and Elizabeth Fenwick, *The Truth in the Light: An Investigation of over 300 Near-Death Experiences* (London: Headline Book Publishing, 1995), 3, 129–140.

13 In a television interview hosted by the BBC's John Freeman on 22 October 1959, Freeman asked Jung, 'Do you believe in God?' After some reflection, Jung replied, 'I don't need to believe; I know.' Later, in a reply to one Valentine Brooke, Jung elaborated on his controversial comment: 'When I say that I don't need to believe in God because I "know", I mean I know of the existence of God-images in general and in particular. I know it is a matter of universal experience and, in so far as I am no exception, I know that I have such experience also, which I call God.' In *Letters*, Vol. 2, 16 November 1959, 'Letter to Valentine Brooke', footnote No. 2, 520–523.

14 See, for example, Martin Ott, Vladimir Gogvadze, Sten Orrenius and Boris Zhivotovsky, 'Mitochondria, Oxidative Stress and Cell Death', *Apoptosis*, 12 (2007): 913–922, doi: 10.1007/s10495-007-0756-2

15 One million centimetres rounds up to 33,000 feet.

16 For an accessible summary of alchemical principles and operations as they relate to psychotherapeutic processes, see Edward F. Edinger, *Anatomy of the Psyche: Alchemical Symbolism in Psychotherapy* (Peru, IL: Open Court Publishing, 1994).

17 Roberto Assagioli, *The Act of Will* (New York, NY: Penguin Group, 1973), 106–122.

18 In his summary of Assagioli's teachings, Mark Thurston uses the following terms to refer to the stages of will outlined in this chapter: 1) Negating Will, 2) Skilful Will, 3) Empowering Will and 4) Transpersonal Will. See Mark Thurston, *Willing to Change: The Journey of Personal Transformation* (Rancho Mirage, CA: We Publish Books, 2005).

19 Charlotte Beradt, 'Dreams Under Dictatorship', Free World (October 1943): 333–337, https://www.museumofdreams.org/third-reich-of-dreams

20 Charlotte Beradt, *The Third Reich of Dreams: The Nightmares of a Nation, 1933–1939* (Great Britain: The Aquarian Press, Thorsons Publishing Group, 1985). I would like to thank Robin Shohet for both preserving this important work by bringing it back into circulation through re-publication in 1985 and for introducing me to it some years ago.

21 Ibid., 9.

22 Ibid., 61.

23 For the complete dream, see Beradt, *The Third Reich of Dreams*, 100–103.

24 Ibid., 169. For a compelling study of dreams as vehicles for political action, see Sharon Sliwinski's, *Dreaming in Dark Times: Six Exercises in Political Thought* (Minneapolis, MI: University of Minnesota Press, 2017). Also, see Kelly Bulkeley's '199 Dreams about Donald Trump' for an overview of social dreaming about a President of the United States, *Huff's Post*, 26 April 2017, www.huffpost.com. You can contribute your own dream at Bulkeley's website at www.idreamoftrump.net.

25 This translation is from B. K. S. Iyengar, *Light on the Yoga Sutra of Patanjali*, I.2 (London: Thonsons, 1996), 45–46.

26 In a novel study on how the brain perceives beauty across the four senses of sight, sound, taste and smell, researchers undertook a meta-analysis of 93 neuroimaging studies. They found that during wakefulness the right anterior insula of the brain, which activates when we are fearful, also becomes stimulated when we perceive beauty. Given that the right anterior insula is normally associated with instinctual aversion to stimuli, no one had foreseen that this area of the brain would become active. Puzzled, the research team investigated further and found that when responding to beauty, the insula works in tandem with the orbital frontal cortex. This part of the brain 'lights up' when we express empathy and receive positive re-enforcement, thus producing a positive emotional response. This research suggests that the insula also plays a part in recognising what does us (and others) good, such as beauty, and, as my dream experience suggests, may help us overcome fear. See Steven Brown, Gao Xiaoqing et al., 'Naturalizing Aesthetics: Brain Areas for Aesthetic Appraisal across Sensory Modalities' in *NeuroImage*, 58, No. 1 (1 September 2011): 250–258, doi.org/10.1016/j.neuroimage.2011.06.012

27 Neurological studies show that gestures made in waking life precede conscious thought, as happened in my dream: the action of kneeling and bowing my head were prompted by a visceral response to the realisation of Beauty. See the section 'The Primacy of the Unconscious Will' in McGilchrist, *The Master*, 186–191.

28 Research on the use of lucid dreaming as a therapeutic intervention for treating nightmares has suggested that directly facing a threatening situation accelerates the reduction of nightmare frequency more quickly than traditional therapeutic methods. See Brigitte Holzinger, Gerhard Klösch and B. Saletu, 'Studies with Lucid Dreaming as Add-On Therapy to Gestalt Therapy', *Acta Neurologica Scandinavica*, 131 (2015): 355–363, doi: 10.1111/ane.12362

29 Krakow, 'Imagery Rehearsal Therapy', 544.

30 See Jaap Lancee, Victor Spoormaker and Jan Van Den Bout, 'Nightmare

Frequency is Associated with Subjective Sleep Quality but not with Psychopathology', *Sleep and Biological Rhythms*, 8 (2010): 187–193, doi. org/10.1111/j.1479-8425.2010.00447.x. Cited in Annika Gieselmann et al., 'Aetiology and Treatment of Nightmare Disorder: State of the Art and Future Perspectives', *Journal of Sleep Research* (July 2018): 7, doi: 10.1111/ jsr.12820

Chapter Ten – Journeys into the Deep: Lucid Dreaming and Lucid Surrender

1   Aristotle, *De Somniis (On Dreams)* in J. A. Smith and W. D. Ross (eds), *The Works of Aristotle Parva Naturalia*, trans. J. I. Beare (Oxford: The Clarendon Press, 1908), 462a.

2   In using the word 'essence', I have in mind a point made by Sarah Young regarding dreams in her article entitled, '"Everything Is What It Is and Not Something Else": A Response to Professor Gion Condrau': 'Phenomenological investigation of the dreaming state should perhaps be regarded as an *attempt* at revealing the essence of dream phenomena and arriving at a correct interpretation, while accepting that this is not a possibility.' In the *Journal of the Society for Existential Analysis*, eds. Ernesto Spinelli, Alessandra Lemma and Simon Du Plock (July 1993): 16. I would like to take this opportunity to thank Sarah, a colleague and friend, for always bringing me back to the teachings of Médard Boss and his faithfulness to apprehending the direct essence of the dream.

3   Chögyal Namkhai Norbu, *Dream Yoga and the Practice of Natural Light* (Ithaca, NY: Snow Lion Publications, 1992), 67.

4   See Ursula Voss et al., 'Lucid Dreaming: A State of Consciousness with Features of Both Waking and Non-Lucid Dreaming', *Sleep*, 32, No. 9 (1 September 2009): 1191–1200, https://www.ncbi.nlm.nih.gov/pmc/articles/ PMC2737577/; and J. Allan Hobson 'The Neurobiology of Consciousness: Lucid Dreaming Wakes Up', *The International Journal of Dream Research*, 2, No. 2 (October 2009): 41–44.

5   Voss et al., 'Lucid Dreaming', 1191. Following on from Voss's research, in 2012 the presence of 40Hz brainwave frequency in lucid dreaming was further confirmed using EEG and fMRI scans by Martin Dresler et al., 'Neural Correlates of Dream Lucidity Obtained from Contrasting Lucid versus Non-Lucid REM Sleep: A Combined EEG/fMRI Case Study', *Sleep*, 35, No. 7 (2012): 1017–1020, http://dx.doi.org/10.5665/ sleep.1974

6   See Elisa Filevich, Martin Dresler, Timothy R. Brick and Simone Kuhn, 'Metacognitive Mechanisms Underlying Lucid Dreaming', *The Journal of*

Neuroscience, 35, No. 3 (21 January 2015): 1082–1088, doi: 10.1523/ JNEUROSCI.3342-14.2015

7   See James F. Pagel, 'The Synchronous Electrophysiology of Conscious States', *Dreaming*, 22, No. 3 (2012): 179, doi: 10.1037/a0029659

8   Voss and Hobson, 'What is the State-of-the-Art on Lucid Dreaming? – Recent Advances and Further Questions' in *Open MIND*, eds. Thomas Metzinger and Jennifer M. Windt (Frankfurt am Main: MIND Group, 2015): 4, doi: 10.15502/9783958570306

9   Ibid., 9–10.

10 For a thought-provoking presentation on using a 'virtual reality' as a model for understanding the relationship between dreaming and the waking state, see Hobson et. al., 'Virtual Reality and Consciousness Inference in Dreaming', 2014: 1–18, doi: 10.3389/fpsyg.2014.01133

11 An expression used by Dean Radin for his book *The Conscious Universe: The Truth of Psychic Phenomena* (San Francisco, CA: HarperOne Publishers, 1997).

12 For a paper at the vanguard of studies on this topic, see Ed Kellogg, 'The Lucidity Continuum', presented at the Eighth Annual Conference of the Lucidity Association, Santa Cruz, 28 June 1992, http://www.driccpe.org.uk/ portfolio-view/the-lucidity-continuum-ed-kellogg

13 For an article on creative writing and lucid dreaming, see Clare Johnson, 'Magic, Meditation and the Void: Creative Dimension of Lucid Dreaming' in Kelly Bulkeley and Ryan Hurd (eds), *Lucid Dreaming: New Perspectives on Consciousness in Sleep*, Vol. 2 (Santa Barbara, CA: Praeger, 2014), 61–64.

14 See Melanie Schädlich and Daniel Erlacher, 'Lucid Music – A Pilot Study Exploring Experiences and Potentials of Music-Making in Lucid Dreams', *Dreaming*, 28, No. 3 (September 2018): 276–286, doi: 10.1037/ drm0000073

15 As an example of sports psychology in lucid dreaming, see Tadas Stumbrys, Daniel Erlacher and Michael Schredl, 'Effectiveness of Motor Practice in Lucid Dreams: A Comparison with Physical and Mental Practice', *Journal of Sports Sciences*, 34, No. 1 (April 2015): 27–34, https://doi. org/10.1080/02640414.2015.1030342. See also Daniel Erlacher and Michael Schredl, 'Practicing a Motor Task in a Lucid Dream Enhances Subsequent Performance: A Pilot Study', *The Sport Psychologist*, 24, No. 2 (2010): 157–167, doi: 10.1123/tsp.24.2.157. See also Melanie Schädlich, Daniel Erlacher and Michael Schredl, 'Improvement of Darts Performance Following Lucid Dream Practice Depends on the Number of Distractions While Rehearsing within the Dream – A Sleep Laboratory Pilot

Study', *Journal of Sports Sciences*, 35, No. 23 (2017): 2365–2372, doi: 10.1080/02640414.2016.1267387

16 See LaBerge et. al., 'Lucid Dreaming Verified by Volitional Communication in REM Dreaming', 1981 and Hearne, 'Lucid Dreams', 1978.

17 For an introduction to the range of experiences within the lucid state, see Stephen LaBerge and Howard Rheingold, *Exploring the World of Lucid Dreaming* (New York, NY: Ballantine Books 1990), and Robert Waggoner, *Lucid Dreaming: Gateway to the Inner Self* (Needham, MA: Moment Point Press Inc., 2009).

18 To obtain these statistics, David T. Saunders et al. undertook a meta-analysis of numerous lucid dreaming studies on lucid dreaming prevalence and frequency. See David T. Saunders, Chris Roe, Graham Smith and Helen Clegg, 'Lucid Dreaming Incidence: A Quality Effects Meta-Analysis of 50 Years of Research', *Consciousness and Cognition*, 43 (2016): 210, http://dx.doi.org/10.1016/j.concog.2016.06.002

19 Interestingly, using electrical stimulation on the brain, Voss et. al. report having had some success inducing lucid dreams at 40Hz. A 25Hz stimulus also succeeded in inducing lucidity. However, such dreams were associated with control over the dream plot, whereas this was not the case in lucid dreams at 40Hz. Much remains to be learned about how the different frequencies manifest in dreams, how they are experienced by the dreamer, and the types of cognition evident in each. Voss et al., 'What is the State-of-the-Art in Lucid Dreaming?', 14.

20 Researchers drew this conclusion from reviewing 35 studies on lucid dream induction. See Tadas Stumbrys, Daniel Erlacher, Melanie Schädlich and Michael Schredl, 'Induction of Lucid Dreams: A Systematic Review of Evidence', *Consciousness and Cognition*, 21 (2012): 1473, http://dx.doi.org/10.1016/j.concog.2012.07.003

21 This conclusion is based on the survey results of 386 lucid dreamers. See Tadas Stumbrys, Daniel Erlacher and Peter Malinowski, 'Meta-Awareness During Day and Night: The Relationship Between Mindfulness and Lucid Dreaming', *Imagination, Cognition and Personality: Consciousness in Theory, Research, and Clinical Practice*, 34, No. 4 (2015): 415, doi: 10.1177/0276236615572594

22 An allusion to the alchemical precept from 'Emblem XLII' in H. M. E. de Jong, *Michael Maier's Atalanta Fugiens: Sources of an Alchemical Book of Emblems* (York Beach, ME: Nicolas-Hays Inc., 2002), 266.

23 In an online survey of 301 lucid dreamers, 81 per cent reported 'having fun' as the main application of their lucid dreaming. See Melanie Schädlich

and Daniel Erlacher, 'Applications of Lucid Dreams: An Online Study', *International Journal of Dream Research*, 5, No. 2 (2012): 134–138.

24 For one of the few studies on lucid dreaming and personal development, see Karen Konkoly and Christopher T. Burke, 'Can Learning to Lucid Dream Promote Personal Growth?', *Dreaming*, 29, No. 2 (June 2019): 113–126, doi: 10.1037/drm0000101. The researchers note that participants who were better adjusted to begin with experienced more personal growth as a result of their lucid dreams, and those who had lucid dreams more frequently reported more satisfaction with their lives.

25 From a *hadith* or teaching of the Prophet Mohammed cited in Henry Corbin, *Alone with the Alone: Creative Imagination in the Sufism of Ibn Arabī*, trans. Willard Trask (Princeton: Princeton University Press, 1969), 114.

26 Stephen LaBerge, *Lucid Dreaming: A Concise Guide to Awakening in Your Dreams and in Your Life* (Boulder, CO: Sounds True Inc., 2004, 2009), 65.

27 For examples of research into this type of lucid dreaming, see Fariba Bogzaran, 'Hyperspace Lucidity, and Creative Consciousness' in Kelly Bulkeley and Ryan Hurd (eds), *Lucid Dreaming: New Perspectives on Consciousness in Sleep*, Vol. 2 (Santa Barbara, CA: Praeger, 2014), 209–231. See also Ted Esser's fascinating summary of his research on 'Kundalini and Non-Duality in the Lucid Dreaming State' in the same volume, 233–263. Ryan Hurd has explored 'Spontaneous Emergence: A Phenomenology of Lucid Dreaming' (Master's thesis, R. D. Hurd, 2008), http://www.driccpe. org.uk/?s=hurd. For seminal work on light in lucid dreaming, see Scott Sparrow, *Lucid Dreaming: Dawning of the Clear Light* (Virginia Beach, VA: Edgar Cayce Foundation, 1976) and George Gillespie, 'Light and Lucid Dreams: A Review' in *Dreaming*, Vol. 2, No. 3 (1992): 167–179, which provides an overview of his findings. Gillespie has recently published a personal account of his lucid experiences, *Seeing: Beyond Dreaming to Religious Experiences of Light* (Exeter, UK: Imprint Academic, 2019). Further, for a dynamic, personal exploration of ecstatic lucid experiences, see Patricia Garfield, *Pathways to Ecstasy: The Way of the Dream Mandala* (New York, NY: Prentice Hall Press, 1979).

28 This teaching has been a touchstone for me in relation to dreams and waking life. Gibran, *The Prophet*, 1951.

29 Cited in Chittick, *Imaginal Worlds*, 27.

30 I have written many articles about Lucid Surrender for the Lucid Dream Exchange (www.dreaminglucid.com) under my maiden name of Ziemer. I have also published a book chapter on the subject from a Jungian

perspective, entitled 'Lucid Surrender and the Alchemical Coniunctio', in Ryan Hurd and Kelly Bulkeley (eds), *Lucid Dreaming: New Perspectives on Consciousness in Sleep*, Vol. 1 (Santa Barbara, CA: Praeger, 2015), 145–146. I look forward to publishing a more detailed book on the experience of Lucid Surrender in the near future.

31 Corbin, *The Man of Light in Iranian Sufiism*, 105. From a *hadith* or teaching of the Prophet Mohammed.

32 Hadrat Abd al-Qadir al-Jilani, *The Secret of Secrets*, interpreted by Shaykh Tosun Bayrak al-Jerrahi al-Halveti (The Islamic Texts Society: Cambridge, UK, 2010), 56.

33 A quote from Andrew Powell's *The Ways of the Soul*, xvii.

Epilogue: For a World in Need of Dreams

1 From the title of Mark Thurston's book, *Dreams: Tonight's Answers for Tomorrow's Questions*, on the teachings of Edgar Cayce, ed. Charles Thomas Cayce (New York, NY: St Martin's Press, 1996).

2 Michael Collins, *Carrying the Fire: An Astronaut's Journeys*, 50th Anniversary Edition (London: Pan Books, 2009), 402.

3 See Stephen Emmet's powerful *10 Billion* (London: Penguin Press Classics, 2008), and David Wallace-Wells' *The Uninhabitable Earth: A Story of the Future* (London: Penguin Random House, UK, 2019).

4 For a compilation of time-lapse films tracking environmental changes, see the collection by the scientist Johnathan Hester, 'Before Our Eyes: Evidence of the Changing Earth We Can See', accessed 4 October 2019, http://www. rescuethatfrog.com/before-our-eyes/#BOE-13

5 For a positive exhortation to action, be inspired by Greta Thunberg's *No One is Too Small to Make a Difference* (London: Penguin Random House UK, 2018–2019).

6 The Alister Hardy Religious Experience Research Centre archive, Account 000128.

Bibliography

'Abd al-Qadir al-Jilani, Hadrat. *The Secret of Secrets*. Interpreted by Shaykh Tosun Bayrak al-Jerrahi al-Halveti. The Islamic Texts Society: Cambridge, UK, 2010.

Adler, Gerhard. *Studies in Analytical Psychology*. London: Routledge Taylor & Frances Group, 1999. (Originally published 1948.)

Aftel, Maggie. *The Essence of Alchemy: A Book of Perfume*. New York, NY: North Point Press, 2001.

Alighieri, Dante. *Divina Commedia*. In *The Divine Comedy of Dante Alighieri, Vol. 3, Paradiso*. Translated and with a commentary by Courtney Langdon. Cambridge: Harvard University Press, 1921. Last updated 26 November 2019. https://oll.libertyfund.org/titles/212

Allen James. *As a Man Thinketh*. Public Domain, 1903.

'Amsterdam Declaration on Earth System Science'. Presented at 'Challenges of a Changing Earth: Global Change Open Science Conference, Amsterdam, The Netherlands, July 2001'. Global International Geosphere-Biosphere Programme Change. http://www.igbp.net/about/history/2001amsterdam declarationonearthsystem science.4.1b8ae20512db692f2a680001312.html

Aristotle. *De Somniis (On Dreams)*. In *The Works of Aristotle Parva Naturalia*. Edited by J. A. Smith and W. D. Ross. Translated by J. I. Beare. Oxford: Clarendon Press, 1908.

Aserinsky, Eugene, and Nathaniel Kleitman. 'Regularly Occurring Periods of Eye Motility, and Concomitant Phenomena, During Sleep'. *Science*, 118, No. 3062 (1953): 273–274. doi: 10.1126/science.118.3062.273

Ashliman, D. L. 'Night-mares: Legends or Superstitions About the Demons that Cause Nightmares'. University of Pittsburgh (website), 'Professor D. L. Ashliman Home Page' (May 2005). https://www.pitt.edu/~dash/nightmare.html#kuhn2

Assagioli, Roberto. *The Act of Will*. New York, NY: Penguin Group, 1973.

Bach, Richard. *Illusions: The Adventures of a Reluctant Messiah*. New York, NY: Dell Publishing Co. Inc., 1977.

BaHammam, Ahmed S., Sohaila A. Al-Shimemeri, Reda I. Salama and Munir M. Sharif, 'Clinical and Polysomnographic Characteristics and Response to Continuous Positive Airway Pressure Therapy in Obstructive Sleep Apnea Patients with Nightmares'. *Sleep Medicine*, 14, No. 2 (2013): 149–154. doi: 10.1016/j.sleep.2012.07.007

Baldwin, Michèle. 'Interview with Carl Rogers on the Use of the Self in Therapy'. In *The Use of Self in Psychotherapy*, 29–38. Edited by Michèle Baldwin. New York, NY: The Haworth Press Inc., 2000.

Bandara, Priyanka, and David O. Carpenter. 'Planetary Electromagnetic Pollution: It is Time to Assess its Impact'. *The Lancet Planetary Health*, Vol. 2 © 2018 The Authors. Published by Elsevier Ltd. (December 2018): 512–514. doi.org/10.1016/S2542-5196(18)30221-3

Baring, Anne. *The Dream of the Cosmos: A Quest for the Soul*. Dorset, UK: Archive Publishing, 2013.

———. 'Dreams: Messages of the Soul'. Reflections 11. Accessed 8 August 2019. https://www.annebaring.com/anbar16_reflections011_dreams.htm

Benson, Herbert. *The Relaxation Response*. New York, NY: William Morrow, 2000.

Beradt, Charlotte. *The Third Reich of Dreams: The Nightmares of a Nation 1933–1939*. Great Britain: The Acquarian Press, Thorsons Publishing Group, 1985.

———. 'Dreams Under Dictatorship'. Free World (October 1943): 333–337. Accessed 27 August 2019. https://www.museumofdreams.org/third-reich-of-dreams

Bértolo, Helder. 'Visual Imagery without Visual Perception?' *Psicológica*, 26 (2005): 173–188.

———, Teresa Paiva, Lara Pessoa, Tiago Mestre, Rachel Marques and Rosa Santos. 'Visual Dream Content, Graphical Representation and EEG Alpha Activity in Congenitally Blind Subjects'. *Cognitive Brain Research*, 15, No. 3 (February 2003): 277–284. doi: 10.1016/s0926-6410(02)00199-4

Billington, Dave. 'Client Experience of the Waking Dream Process'. Master's thesis, D. Billington, 2014. http://www.driccpe.org.uk/?portfolio-view=1575-2

Blagrove, Mark, Sioned Hale, Julia Lockheart, Michelle Carr, Alex Jones and Katja Valli. 'Testing the Empathy Theory of Dreaming: The Relationships Between Dream Sharing and Trait and State Empathy'. *Frontiers in Psychology* (20 June 2019). doi.org/10.3389/fpsyg.2019.01351

Blake, William. 'The Little Black Boy'. In *Songs of Innocence and Experience*. Edited by Sir Geoffrey Keynes. Oxford: Oxford University Press, 1970.

Bogzaran, Fariba. 'Hyperspace Lucidity, and Creative Consciousness'. In *Lucid Dreaming: New Perspectives on Consciousness in Sleep*, Vol. 2, 209–231. Edited by Kelly Bulkeley and Ryan Hurd. Santa Barbara, CA: Praeger, 2014.

Botha, Marlene. 'The Transformative Effects of Colours in Transpersonal Dreamwork'. Master's thesis, M. Botha, 2010. http://www.driccpe.org.uk/?portfolio-view=the-transformative-effect-of-colours-in-transpersonal-dreamwork-m-botha

Brown, Steven, Gao Xiaoqing, Loren Tisdelle, Simon R. Eickhoff and Mario Liotti. 'Naturalizing Aesthetics: Brain Areas for Aesthetic Appraisal across Sensory Modalities'. *NeuroImage*, 58, No. 1 (1 September 2011): 250–258. doi.org/10.1016/j.neuroimage.2011.06.012

Brugaletta, John J. 'A Day of Color'. In *John J. Brugaletta: Selected Poems*. Athens, GA: Futurecycle Press, 2019.

Buber, Martin. *I and Thou*. Translated by Ronald Gregor Smith. New York, NY: MacMillan Publishing Group, 1958. (Originally published 1937.)

Bulkeley, Kelly. '199 Dreams about Donald Trump'. *Huff's Post*, 26 April 2017. www.huffpost.com.

——. *Dreaming in the World's Religions: A Comparative History*. New York, NY: New York University Press, 2008.

Campbell, Dennis. 'NHS Prescribed Record Number of Antidepressants Last Year'. *The Guardian*, 29 June 2017. https://www.theguardian.com/society/2017/jun/29/nhs-prescribed-record-number-of-antidepressants-last-year

Campbell, Joseph, with Bill D. Moyers. *The Power of Myth*. Edited by Sue Betty Flowers. New York, NY: Doubleday, 1988.

——. *The Mythic Image*. Bollingen Series C. Princeton, CT: Princeton University Press, 1974.

Carman, Elizabeth, and Neil Carman. *The Cosmic Cradle: Spiritual Dimensions of Life Before Birth*. Berkeley, CA: North Atlantic Books, 2013.

Cartwright, Rosalind D. *The Twenty-Four Hour Mind: The Role of Sleep and Dreaming in Our Emotional Lives*. New York, NY: Oxford University Press, 2010.

——. 'Dreams that Work: The Relation of Dream Incorporation to Adaptation to Stressful Events'. *Dreaming*, 1, No. 1 (1991): 3–9. https://doi.org/10.1037/h0094312

Caruso, Claire. 'Negative Impacts of Shiftwork and Long Work Hours'. *Rehabilitation Nursing: The Official Journal of the Association of Rehabilitation Nurses*, 39, No. 1 (January–February 2014): 16–25. doi: 10.1002/rnj.107

Cheetham, Tom. *All the World's an Icon: Henry Corbin and the Angelic Function of Beings*. Berkeley, CA: North Atlantic Books, 2012.

Childre, Doc and Howard Martin. *The Heartmath Solution: Proven Techniques for Developing Emotional Intelligence*. London, UK: Judy Piatkus Publishers Limited, 1999.

Chittick, William C. *Imaginal Worlds: Ibn al-'Arabī and the Problem of Religious Diversity*. Albany, NY: State University of New York Press, 1994.

Clark, Andy, and David Chalmers. 'The Extended Mind'. *Analysis*, Oxford

Journals, Oxford University Press, 58, No. 1 (January 1998): 7–19. http://www.jstor.org/stable/3328150

Clemmer, Jim. *The Leader's Digest: Timeless Principles for Team and Organization Success*. Toronto, Canada: TCG Press, 2003.

Close, Frank. *NOTHING: A Very Short Introduction*. Oxford: Oxford University Press, 2009.

——. *The Void*. Oxford: Oxford University Press, 2007.

COBUILD Advanced English Dictionary. © HarperCollins Publishers. Accessed 31 July 2019. https://www.collinsdictionary.com/dictionary/english/presence

Collins, Michael. *Carrying the Fire: An Astronaut's Journeys, 50th Anniversary Edition*. London: Pan Books, 2009.

Cook, Roger. *The Tree of Life: Symbol of the Centre*. London, UK: Thames & Hudson, 1974.

Corbin, Henry. *Swedenborg and Esoteric Islam: Comparative Spiritual Hermeneutics*. Translated by Leonard Fox. West Chester, PA: Swedenborg Foundation, 1999.

——. *The Man of Light in Iranian Sufiism*. Translated by Nancy Pearson. New Lebanon, NY: Omega Publications Inc., 1994.

——. *Alone with the Alone: Creative Imagination in the Sufism of Ibn Arabī*. Translated by Willard Trask. Princeton: Princeton University Press, 1969.

Coughlan, Sean. 'Bad dreams "help to control fear when awake"'. BBC, 27 November 2019, Family and Education. https://www.bbc.co.uk/news/education-50563835

Cox, David. 'David Karnazes: The Man Who Can Run Forever'. *The Guardian*, 30 August 2013. https://www.theguardian.com/lifeandstyle/the-running-blog/2013/aug/30/dean-karnazes-man-run-forever

Damasio, Antonio R. *Descartes' Error: Emotion, Reason and the Human Brain*. New York, NY: Avon Books, 2006.

D'Acquisto, Fulvio. 'Dreaming Autoimmunity: Exploring Dreams in Patients Suffering from Autoimmune Diseases'. Master's thesis, F. D'Acquisto, 2017.

de Broglie, Louis. 'The Aspiration Towards Spirit'. In *Quantum Questions*, 117–129. Edited by Ken Wilber. Boston, MA: Shambala Press, 2001.

de Chardin, Teilhard. *The Phenomenon of Man*. Translated by Bernard Wall. New York, NY: Harper & Row Publishers Inc., 1975. (Originally published 1959.)

Dinesen, Isak. 'The Young Man with the Carnation'. In *Winter's Tales*. London, UK: Penguin Books, 2001.

Doyle, Derek. *The Platform Ticket: Memories and Musings of a Hospice Doctor*. Bakewell, DE: The Pentland Press Ltd., 1999.

Dresler, Renate Wehrle, Victor I. Spoormaker, Stefan P. Koch, Florian Holsboer, Axel Steiger, Hellmuth Obrig, Philipp G. Sämann and Michael Czisch. 'Neural Correlates of Dream Lucidity Obtained from Contrasting Lucid versus Non-Lucid REM Sleep: A Combined EEG/fMRI Case Study'. *Sleep*, 35, No. 7 (2012): 1017–1020. http://dx.doi.org/10.5665/sleep.1974

Echazarra, Alfonso. 'How has internet use changed between 2012 and 2015?' *PISA in Focus*, No. 83, OECD Publishing, Paris (April 2018). doi. org/10.1787/1e912a10-en

Edinger, Edward F. *Anatomy of the Psyche: Alchemical Symbolism in Psychotherapy*. Peru, IL: Open Court Publishing, 1994.

Edwards, Christopher L., Josie E. Malinowski, Shauna L. McGee, Paul D. Bennett, Ruby M. Perrine and Mark T. Blagrove. 'Comparing Personal Insight Gains due to Consideration of a Recent Dream and Consideration of a Recent Event Using the Ullman and Schredl Dream Group Methods'. *Frontiers in Psychology*, 6, No. 831 (June 2015). doi: 10.3389/fpsyg.2015.00831

——, Josie E. Malinowski, Shauna L. McGee, Paul D. Bennett, Ruby M. Perrine and Mark T. Blagrove. 'Dreaming and Insight'. *Frontiers in Psychology* (24 December 2013). doi: 10.3389/fpsyg.2013.00979

Eliade, Mircea. *Images and Symbols: Studies in Religious Symbolism*. Translated by Philip Mairet. Princeton, NJ: Princeton University Press, 1991.

——. *Shamanism: Archaic Techniques in Ecstasy*. Translated by Willard R. Trask. London: Arkana, Penguin Books, 1989.

——. *The Forge and the Crucible: The Origins and Structures of Alchemy*, 2nd edition. Translated by Stephen Corrin. Chicago and London: University of Chicago Press, 1978.

——. *The Quest: History and Meaning in Religion*. Chicago, Illinois: University of Chicago Press, 1969.

Emmet, Stephen. *10 Billion*. London: Penguin Press Classics, 2008.

Emmons, Robert A., and Michael. E. McCullough. 'Counting Blessings Versus Burdens: An Experimental Investigation of Gratitude and Subjective Well-Being in Daily Life'. *Journal of Personality and Social Psychology*, 84, No. 2 (2003): 377–389. doi: 10.1037/0022-3514.84.2.377

Erlacher, Daniel, and Michael Schredl. 'Practicing a Motor Task in a Lucid Dream Enhances Subsequent Performance: A Pilot Study'. *The Sport Psychologist*, 24, No. 2 (2010): 157–167. doi: 10.1123/tsp.24.2.157

Erren, Thomas C., Puran Falaturi, Peter Morefeld, Peter Knauth, Russell J. Reiter and Claus Piekarski. 'Shift Work and Cancer: The Evidence and the Challenge'. *Deutsches Arzteblatt International*, 107, No. 38 (2010): 657–62. doi: 10.3238/arztebl.2010.0657

Esser, Ted. 'Kundalini and Non-Duality in the Lucid Dreaming State'. In *Lucid Dreaming: New Perspectives on Consciousness in Sleep*, Vol. 2, 233–263. Edited by Kelly Bulkeley and Ryan Hurd. Santa Barbara, CA: Praeger, 2014.

Eugene, Andy R., and Jolanta Masiak. 'The Neuroprotective Aspects of Sleep'. *MEDtube Science*, 3, No. 1 (March 2015): 35–40. PMID: 26594659.

Evan-Wentz, W. Y. (ed.) *The Tibetan Book of the Dead*. Translated by Lama Kazi Dawa-Samdup. New York, NY: Oxford University Press, 1968. (Originally published 1927.)

Fenwick, Peter, and Elizabeth Fenwick. *The Truth in the Light: An Investigation of over 300 Near-Death Experiences*. London: Headline Book Publishing, 1995.

Filevich, Elisa, Martin Dresler, Timothy R. Brick and Simone Kuhn. 'Metacognitive Mechanisms Underlying Lucid Dreaming'. *The Journal of Neuroscience*, 35, No. 3 (21 January 2015): 1082–1088, doi: 10.1523/JNEUROSCI.3342-14.2015

Finkel, M. 'The Science of Sleep'. *National Geographic Magazine*, August 2018, 40–77.

Flood, Josephine. *Archaeology of the Dreamtime: The Story of Prehistoric Australia and Its People*. New Haven, CT: Yale University Press, 1990.

Forshaw, Peter J. 'Curious Knowledge and Wonder-Working Wisdom in the Occult Work of Heinrich Khunrath'. In *Curiosity and Wonder from the Renaissance to the Enlightenment*, 107–129. Edited by Robert J. W. Evans and Alexander Marr. New York, NY: Routledge, 2016.

——. '"Behold, the dream cometh": Hyperphysical Magic and Deific Visions in an Early-Modern Theosophical Lab-Oratory'. In *Conversations with Angels: Essays Towards a History of Spiritual Communication, 1100–1700*, 175–200. Edited by Joad Raymond. Hampshire, UK: Palgrave Macmillan, 2011.

Fox, Matthew (trans.). *Meditations with Meister Eckhart*. Santa Fe, NM: Bear & Company, 1983.

Freud, Sigmund. *The Interpretation of Dreams* (First and Second Part), Vols V–VI. In *The Standard Edition of the Complete Psychological Works of Sigmund Freud*, Vols I–24. Edited and translated by James Strachey in collaboration with Anna Freud. London: The Hogarth Press and The Institute of Psychoanalysis, 1981. (Originally published 1900.)

Garfield, Patricia. *Pathways to Ecstasy: The Way of the Dream Mandala*. New York, NY: Prentice Hall Press, 1979.

Gibran, Khalil. *The Prophet*. New York, NY: Alfred A. Knopf, 1951. (Originally published 1923.)

Gieselmann, Annika, Malik Ait Aoudia, Michelle Carr, Anne Germaine, Robert Gorzka, Brigette Holzinger et al. 'Aetiology and Treatment of Nightmare Disorder: State of the Art and Future Perspectives'. *Journal of Sleep Research* (July 2018): 7. doi: 10.1111/jsr.12820.

Gillespie, George. *Seeing: Beyond Dreaming to Religious Experiences of Light.* Exeter, UK: Imprint Academic, 2019.

——. 'Light and Lucid Dreams: A Review'. *Dreaming,* Vol. 2, No. 3 (1992): 167–179.

Glouberman, Dina. *Life Choices, Life Changes: Develop Your Personal Vision for the Life You Want.* London: Hodder & Stoughton, 2003.

Goswámí, Amit. 'Quantum Psychology: An Integral Science for the Ecology of the Psyche'. Paper presented at the International Transpersonal Conference, Prague, 30 September 2017.

Grigg-Damberger, Madeleine M., and Kathy M. Wolfe. 'Infants Sleep for Brain'. *Journal of Clinical Sleep Medicine, Official Publication of the American Academy of Sleep Medicine,* 13, No. 11 (15 November 2017): 1233–1234. doi: 10.5664/jcsm.6786

Grønlie, Janne, Jonathan Soulé and Clive R. Bramham. 'Sleep and Protein Synthesis-Dependent Synaptic Plasticity: Impacts of Sleep Loss and Stress'. *Frontiers in Behavioral Neuroscience,* 7, Article 224 (21 January 2014). doi: 10.3389/fnbeh.2013.00224

Gujar, Ninad, Stephen A. McDonald, Masaki Nishida and Matthew P. Walker. 'A Role for REM Sleep in Recalibrating the Sensitivity of the Human Brain to Specific Emotions'. *Cerebral Cortex,* 21, No. 1 (January 2011): 115–123. doi. org/10.1093/cercor/bhq064

Guo, Bisong and Andrew Powell. *Listen to Your Body: The Wisdom of the Dao.* Honolulu, HI: The University of Hawaii Press, 2001.

Hamilton, Nigel. 'Psychospiritual Transformation: Light, Colour, and Symmetry'. In *Dreams: Understanding Biology, Psychology, and Culture,* Vol. 2. Edited by Robert J. Hoss and Robert P. Gongloff, 634–640. Santa Barbara, CA: ABC-CLIO LLC, 2019.

——. 'The Personal and Therapeutic Significance of Directional Movement within the Space of a Lucid Dream'. Paper presented at International Association for the Study of Dreams Conference, Anaheim, California, June 2017. http://www.driccpe.org.uk/?portfolio-view=the-personal-and-therapeutic-significance-of-moving-and-interacting-within-the-space-of-a-lucid-dream-nigel-hamilton-phd

——. *Awakening Through Dreams: The Journey Through the Inner Landscape.* London: Karnac Books Ltd., 2014.

Hansen, M.C., P. V. Potapov, R. Moore, M. Hancher, S. A. Turubahova, A. Tyukavina, D. Thau and S. V. Stehman. 'High-Resolution Global Maps of 21st-Century Forest Cover Change'. *Science*, 342, No. 6160 (15 November 2013): 850–853. doi: 10.1126/science.1244693

Hargittai, István, and Magdolna Hargittai. *Symmetry: A Unifying Concept*. Bolinas, CA: Shelter Publications Inc., 1994.

Harvey, Andrew. *The Essential Mystics: Selections from the World's Great Wisdom Traditions*. San Francisco, CA: HarperSanFrancisco, 1997.

Hearne, Keith. 'Lucid Dreams: An Electro-Physiological and Psychological Study'. Ph.D. thesis, University of Liverpool, England, 1978. https://www.keithhearne.com/phd-download/

Herzog, Werner. *Lo and Behold, Reveries of the Connected World*. Saville Productions, 2016.

Hester, Johnathan. 'Before Our Eyes: Evidence of the Changing Earth we can See'. Accessed 4 October 2019. http://www.rescuethatfrog.com/before-our-eyes/#BOE-13

Hillman, James. *Archetypal Psychology Uniform Edition of the Writings of James Hillman*, Vol. 1. Putnam, CT: Spring Publications, 2013.

Hobson, J. Allan, Charles C.-H. Hong and Karl J. Friston. 'Virtual Reality and Conscious Inference in Sleep'. *Frontiers in Psychology*, 5, No. 1133 (9 October 2014): 1–18. doi: 10.3389/fpsyg.2014.01133.

—— and Karl J. Friston. 'Waking and Dreaming Consciousness: Neurobiological and Functional Considerations'. *Progress in Neurobiology*, 98, No. 1 (July 2012): 82–98. doi.org/10.1016/j.pneurobio.2012.05.003

——. 'REM Sleep and Dreaming: Towards a Theory of Protoconsciousness'. *Nature Reviews Neuroscience*, 10, No. 11 (November 2009): 803–13. doi: 10.1038/nrn2716

——. 'The Neurobiology of Consciousness: Lucid Dreaming Wakes Up'. *The International Journal of Dream Research*, 2, No. 2 (October 2009): 41–44.

——'.Sleep and Dreaming'. *The Journal of Neuroscience*, 10, No. 2 (1 February 1990): 371–372. doi.org/10.1523/JNEUROSCI

Holzinger, Brigitte, Gerhard Klösch and B. Saletu. 'Studies with Lucid Dreaming as Add-On Therapy to Gestalt Therapy'. *Acta Neurologica Scandinavica*, 131 (2015): 355–363. doi: 10.1111/ane.12362

Hooft Graafland, Julie. 'New Technologies and 21st Century Children: Recent Trends and Outcomes'. *OECD Education Working Papers*, No. 179, OECD Publishing, Paris (12 September 2018): 1–60. doi.org/10.1787/e071a505-en

Horikawa, T., T. Tamaki, Y. Miyawaki and Y. Kamitani. 'Neural Decoding of Visual Imagery During Sleep'. *Science*, 340, No. 6132 (3 May 2013): 639–642. doi: 10.1126/science.1234330

Hoss, Robert J., Katja Valli and Robert P. Gongloff (eds). *Dreams: Understanding Biology, Psychology, and Culture*. Vols 1–2. Santa Barbara, CA: ABC-CLIO LLC, 2019.

——. 'Somatic and Health-Related Dreams'. In *Dreams: Understanding Biology, Psychology, and Culture*, Vol. 1, 292–301. Edited by Katja Valli and Robert J. Hoss. Santa Barbara, CA: ABC-CLIO LLC, 2019.

—— and Robert P. Gongloff (eds). *Dreams That Change Our Lives*. Ashville, NC: Chiron Publications, 2016.

——. *Dream Language: Self-Understanding through Imagery and Color*. Ashland, Oregon: Inner Source, 2005.

Hurd, Ryan. *Sleep Paralysis: A Guide to Hypnagogic Visions and Visitors of the Night*. Los Altos, CA: Hyena Press, 2011.

——. 'Spontaneous Emergence: A Phenomenology of Lucid Dreaming'. Master's thesis, R. D. Hurd, 2008. http://www.driccpe.org.uk/?s=hurd

Huxley, Aldous. *The Doors of Perception*. London: Flamingo, 1994. (Originally published 1954.)

Independent Mental Health Taskforce to the NHS in England. 'The Five Year Forward View of Mental Health'. (February 2016): 10. https://www.england. nhs.uk/wp-content/uploads/2016/02/Mental-Health-Taskforce-FYFV-final.pdf

Isaacson, Walter. *Einstein: His Life and Universe*. London: Simon & Schuster UK Ltd., 2007.

Iyengar, B. K. S. *Light on the Yoga Sutra of Patanjali*. London: Thonsons, 1996.

Jeans, James Sir. 'A Universe of Pure Thought'. In *Quantum Questions: Mystical Writings of the World's Greatest Physicists*, 133–153. Edited by Ken Wilber. Boston, MA: Shambhala Publications Inc., 2001.

Johnson, Clare. 'Magic, Meditation and the Void: Creative Dimension of Lucid Dreaming'. In *Lucid Dreaming: New Perspectives on Consciousness in Sleep*, Vol. 2, 61–64. Edited by Kelly Bulkeley and Ryan Hurd. Santa Barbara, CA: Praeger, 2014.

Johnson, Robert A. *Inner Gold: Understanding Psychological Projection*. Kihei, HI: Koa Books, 2008.

——. *Owning Your Own Shadow*. New York, NY: Harper Collins, 1991.

Julian of Norwich. *Revelations of Divine Love*. Edited by Halcyon Backhouse and Rhona Pipe. London: Hodder & Stoughton, 1997.

Jung, C. G. *The Collected Works*. Translated by R. F. C. Hull. Bollingen Series XX, Vols 1–20. Edited by Herbert Read, Michael Fordham and Gerhard Adler. Princeton, NJ: Princeton University Press, 1955–1992.

——. *Modern Man in Search of a Soul*. Translated by W. S. Dell and Cary F. Baynes. London and New York: Routledge Classics, 2002. (Originally published 1933.)

——. *C.G. Jung: Word and Image*. Edited by Aniela Jaffé. Bollingen Series XCVII, Vol. 2. Princeton: Princeton University Press, 1979.

——. 'To Valentine Brooke'. In *C. G. Jung's Letters: Vol. 2, 1951–1961*. Selected and edited by Gerhard Adler in collaboration with Aniela Jaffé. Translated by R. F. C Hull. London: Routledge & Kegan Paul, 1976.

Khan, Hazrat Inayat. *The Sufi Message of Hazrat Inayat Kahn: The Unity of Religious Ideals*. Vol. 9. Geneva, Switzerland: International Headquarters of the Sufi Movement, 1979.

Kahn, Tracey L., and Stephen P. LaBerge. 'Dreaming and Waking: Similarities and Differences Revisited'. *Consciousness and Cognition*, 20 (2011): 494–514. doi: 10.1016/j.concog.2010.09.002

Kandinsky, Wassily. *Concerning the Spiritual in Art*. Translated by M. T. H. Sadler. New York, New York: Dover Publications Inc., 1977.

Kelsey, Morton T. *God, Dreams, and Revelation*. Minneapolis, MN: Augsburg Fortress, 1991.

Klee, Paul. *Pedagogical Sketchbook*. Translated by Moholy-Nagy. London: Faber & Faber, 1977.

Konkoly, Karen, and Christopher T. Burke. 'Can Learning to Lucid Dream Promote Personal Growth?' *Dreaming*, 29, No. 2 (June 2019): 113–126. doi: 10.1037/drm0000101

Kozmová, Miloslava. 'Emotions During Non-Lucid Problem-Solving Dreams as Evidence of Secondary Consciousness'. *Comprehensive Psychology* (1 January 2015). doi.org/10.2466/09.CP.4.6.

Krakow, Barry, Michael Hollifield, Lisa Johnston, Mary Koss, Ron Schrader, Teddy D. Warner et al. 'Imagery Rehearsal Therapy for Chronic Nightmares in Sexual Assault Survivors with Posttraumatic Stress Disorder: A Randomized Controlled Trial'. *The Journal of the American Medical Association (JAMA)*, 286, No. 5 (1 August 2019): 537–545. doi: 10.1001/jama.286.5.537

Krippner, Stanley, Fariba Bogzaran and André Percia de Carvalho. *Extraordinary Dreams and How to Work with Them*. Albany, NY: State University of New York Press, 2002.

LaBerge, Stephen, Benjamin Baird and Philip G. Zimbardo. 'Smooth Tracking of Visual Targets Distinguishes Lucid REM Sleep Dreaming and Waking Perception from Imagination'. *Nature Communications*, 9, No. 3298 (2018). doi: 10.1038/s41467-018-05547-0/

——. *Lucid Dreaming: A Concise Guide to Awakening in Your Dreams and in Your Life.* Boulder, CO: Sounds True Inc., 2004, 2009.

—— and Howard Rheingold. *Exploring the World of Lucid Dreaming.* New York, NY: Ballantine Books, 1990.

—— Lynn E. Nagel, William. C. Dement and Vincent P. Zarcone Jr. 'Lucid Dreaming Verified by Volitional Communication During REM Sleep'. *Perceptual and Motor Skills*, 52 (1981): 727–732.

Ladinsky, Daniel. 'You Are With the Friend Now'. *I Heard God Laughing: Poems of Hope and Joy, Renderings of Hafiz by Daniel Ladinsky.* London: Penguin Books Ltd., 2006.

Lancee, Jaap, Victor Spoormaker and Jan Van Den Bout. 'Nightmare Frequency is Associated with Subjective Sleep Quality but not with Psychopathology'. *Sleep and Biological Rhythms*, 8 (2010): 187–193. doi.org/10.1111/j.1479-8425.2010.00447.x

Lemley, Brad. 'Where did everything come from?: Guth's Grand Guess'. *Discover*, 23, No. 4. April 2002, 32–39.

Leschziner, Guy. *The Nocturnal Brain: Nightmares, Neuroscience and the Secret World of Sleep.* London: Simon & Schuster Ltd., 2019.

Lesku, John, Anne Aulsebrook and Erika Zaid. 'Evolutionary Perspectives on Sleep'. In *Dreams: Understanding Biology, Psychology and Culture*, Vol. 1, 3–26. Edited by Katja Valli and Robert J. Hoss. Santa Barbara, CA: ABC-CLIO LLC, 2019.

Leu-Semenescu, Smaranda, Ginevra Uguccioni, Jean-Louis Golmard, Virginie Czernecki, Jerome Yelnik, Bruno Dubois, Baudouin Forgeot d'Arc, David Grabli, Richard Levy and Isabelle Arnulf. 'Can we still dream when the mind is blank? Sleep and Dream Mentations in Auto-Activation Deficit'. *Brain*, 136, No. 10 (1 October 2013): 3076–3084. doi.org/10.1093/brain/awt229

Lewis, C. S. *George MacDonald: An Anthology 365 Readings.* Edited by C. S. Lewis. San Francisco, CA: HarperSanFranscisco, 1973.

Libby, Walter. 'The Scientific Imagination'. *Scientific Monthly*, 15, No. 263 (1922): 269. https://archive.org/details/jstor-6552/page/n7

Liberman, Jacob Israel. *Light: Medicine of the Future.* Santa Fe, NM: Bear & Company, 1991.

Lindbergh, Anne Morrow. *Gift from the Sea.* New York, NY: Random House Inc., 1978. (Originally published 1955.)

Linnett, Pauline, and Chris Roe. 'Spontaneous cases of psi within accounts submitted to the Alister Hardy Religious Experience Research Centre'. Paper presented at the British Psychological Society (BPS) Transpersonal Section, 20th Annual Conference, 16–18 September 2016.

Littlehales, Nick. *Sleep: The Myth of 8 Hours, the Power of Naps...and the New Plan to Recharge Your Body and Mind*. UK: Penguin Random House, 2016.

MacDonald, George. 'Truth'. In *George MacDonald: An Anthology 365 Readings*, No. 187. Edited by C. S. Lewis. San Francisco, CA: HarperSanFranscisco, 1973.

——. *The Golden Key and Other Fantasy Stories*. Grand Rapids, MI: Wm. B. Eerdmans Publishing Co., 1980. (Originally published 1867.)

Maclean, Katherine A., Jeannie-Marie S. Leoutsakos, Matthew W. Johnson and Roland R. Griffiths. 'Factor Analysis of the Mystical Experience Questionnaire: A Study of Experiences Occasioned by the Hallucinogen'. *Journal for the Scientific Study of Religion*, 51, No. 4 (December 2012): 721–737. doi: 10.1111/j.1468-5906.2012.01685.x

Maier, Michael. 'Emblem XLII'. In *Michael Maier's Atalanta Fugiens: Sources of an Alchemical Book of Emblems*, written and translated by H. M. E. de Jong. York Beach, ME: Nicolas-Hays Inc., 2002.

Malinowski Josie E., and Chris Edwards. 'Evidence of Insight from Dreamwork'. In *Dreams: Biology, Psychology and Culture*, Vol. 2, 469–478. Edited by Robert J. Hoss and Robert P. Gongloff. Santa Barbara, CA: ABC-CLIO LLC, 2019.

Markowitsch, Hans J., and Angelica Staniloiu. 'Amygdala in Action: Relaying Biological and Social Significance to Autobiographical Memory'. *Neuropsychologia*, 49, No. 4 (March 2011): 718–733. doi: 10.1016/j.neurophsychologia.2010.10.007

—— and Harold Welzer. *The Development of Autobiographical Memory*. Translated by David Emmans. New York, NY: Psychology Press, 2010.

McLean, Adam. *The Alchemical Mandala: A Survey of the Mandala in the Western Esoteric Traditions*. Grand Rapids, MI: Phanes Press Inc., 2002.

McGilchrist, Iain. *The Master and His Emissary: The Divided Brain and the Making of the Western World*. New Haven, CT and London: Yale University Press, 2009.

Meaidi, Amani, Poul Jennum, Maurice Ptito and Ron Kupers. 'The Sensory Construction of Dreams and Nightmare Frequency in Congenitally Blind and Late Blind Individuals'. *Sleep Medicine*, 15 (2014): 585–595. doi.org/10.1016/S0926-6410(02)00199-4.

Naked Science. 'Science and Technology Documentary Series'. Last updated 31 July 2019. https://www.youtube.com/playlist?list=PLpWCFDSTg8dvapwbRd7AVbpNAkFXhqtyo

NASA. 'Dark Energy, Dark Matter'. Accessed 2 August 2019. https://science.nasa.gov/astrophysics/focus-areas/what-is-dark-energy

National Health Service (NHS). 'How to get to Sleep: Sleep and Tiredness'. Last updated 22 July 2019. https://www.nhs.uk/live-well/sleep-and-tiredness/how-to-get-to-sleep/

Neihardt, John G. *Black Elk Speaks: The Complete Edition.* Nebraska: The Regents Board of the University of Nebraska, 2014. (Originally published 1932.)

Nes, Solrunn. *The Mystical Language of Icons.* Canterbury, UK: Canterbury Press, 2004.

Nicholls, Christine Judith. '"Dreamtime" and "The Dreaming": Who dreamed up these terms?' The Conversation UK (28 January 2014). http://theconversation.com/dreamtime-and-the-dreaming-who-dreamed-up-these-terms-20835

Nieminen, Jaakko, Olivia Gosseries, Marcello Massimini et al. 'Consciousness and Cortical Responsiveness: A Within-State Study During Non-Rapid Eye Movement Sleep'. *Scientific Reports*, 6, No. 30932 (August 2016): 1–10. doi: 10.1038/srep30932

Nir, Yuval, Marcello Massimini, Melanie Boly, Giulio Tononi, Elyana Saad, Andrew D. Sheldon, Francesca Siclari and Bradley R. Postle. 'Sleep and Consciousness'. In *Neuroimaging of Consciousness*, 133–182. Edited by Andrea Eugenio Cavanna, Andrea Nani, Hal Blumenfeld and Steven Laureys. © Springer-Verlag Berlin Heidelberg, 2013. doi: 10.1007/978-3-642-37580-4_9

Norbu, Chögyal Namkhai. *Dream Yoga and the Practice of Natural Light.* Ithaca, NY: Snow Lion Publications, 1992.

North Carolina State University, College of Agriculture and Life Sciences, Department of Horticulture Science (webpage) 'Tree Facts'. Accessed 8 August 2019. https://projects.ncsu.edu/project/treesofstrength/treefact.htm

Novalis. *Henry Von Ofterdingen: A Romance.* Dover Thrift Editions. Mineola, NY: Dover Publications Inc., 2015. (Originally Published 1842.)

OECD, Organisation for Economic Cooperation and Development. 'Children & Young People's Mental Health in the Digital Age: Shaping the Future' (2018): 1–16. https://www.oecd.org/els/health-systems/Children-and-Young-People-Mental-Health-in-the-Digital-Age.pdf

Ofcom. 'Adults: Media Use and Attitudes Report, 2019' (30 May 2019): 1–22. https://www.ofcom.org.uk/__data/assets/pdf_file/0021/149124/adults-media-use-and-attitudes-report.pdf

Ott, Martin, Vladimir Gogvadze, Sten Orrenius and Boris Zhivotovsky. 'Mitochondria, Oxidative Stress and Cell Death'. *Apoptosis*, 12. ©Springer Science + Business Media, LLC (2007): 913–922. doi: 10.1007/s10495-007-0756-2

Otto, Rudolph. *The Idea of the Holy*, 2nd edition. Translated by John W. Harvey. London: Oxford University Press, 1950.

Owczarski, Wojciech. 'Therapeutic Dreams in Auschwitz'. In *Jednak Ksiazki. Gdańske Czasopismo Humanistyczne*, 6 (2016), 85–92. http://cejsh.icm. edu.pl/cejsh/element/bwmeta1.element.desklight-623ef4d8-ca2d-4ec9-9295-8c5f5ebac108

Pagel, James F. 'The Synchronous Electrophysiology of Conscious States'. *Dreaming*, 22, No. 3 (2012): 173–19. doi: 10.1037/a0029659

Pall, Martin L. '5G: Great risk for EU, U.S. and International Health! Compelling Evidence for Eight Distinct Types of Great Harm Caused by Electromagnetic Field (EMF) Exposures and the Mechanism that Causes Them'. (May 2018) https://www.emfdata.org/en/documentations/detail&id=243

Parmeggiani, Pier Luigi. 'Interaction Between Sleep and Thermoregulation: An Aspect of the Control of Behavioral States'. *Sleep*, 10, No. 5 (1987): 426–435.

Pascal, Blaise. *Blaise Pascal's Penseés: Thoughts on God, Religion and Wagers*. Translated by William F. Trotter. Greenwood, WI: Suzeteo Enterprises. (Originally published 1660.)

Pascoe, Judy. 'Drawing Dreams: The Transformation Experience of Expressing Dream Imagery as Art'. Master's thesis, J. Pascoe, 2016. http://www.driccpe. org.uk/?portfolio-view=drawing-dreams-the-transformational-experience-of-expressing-dream-imagery-as-art

Peat, David. *Blackfoot Physics: A Journey into the Native American Universe*. London: Fourth Estate Limited, 1996.

Plato. *Phaedo*. In *The Collected Dialogues, Including the Letters*. Edited by Edith Hamilton and Huntington Cairns, Bollingen Series LXXI. Princeton, 6th edition. Princeton, NJ: Princeton University Press, 1971.

Polkinghorne, John. *Quantum Theory: A Very Short Introduction*. London: Oxford University Press, 2002.

Powell, Andrew. *Conversations with the Soul: A Psychiatrist Reflects: Essays on Life, Death and Beyond*. London: Muswell Hill Press, 2018.

——. *The Ways of the Soul: A Psychiatrist Reflects: Essays on Life, Death and Beyond*. London: Muswell Hill Press, 2017.

Powell, Melinda. 'Metaphoric Presence in Dreams'. In *Dreams: Understanding Biology, Psychology, and Culture*, Vol. 2, 628–633. Edited by Robert J. Hoss and Robert P. Gongloff. Santa Barbara, CA: ABC-CLIO LLC, 2019.

Powers, Richard. *The Overstory*. London: Penguin Random House, 2018.

Puhle, Annekatrin. *Light Changes: Experiences in the Presence of Transforming Light*. Guildford, UK: White Crow Books, 2013.

Puttonen, Eetu, Christian Briese, Gottfried Mandlburger, Martin Wieser, Martin Pfennigbauer, András Zlinszky and Norbert Pfeifer. 'Quantification of Overnight Movement of Birch (Betula pendula) Branches and Foliage with Short Interval Terrestrial Laser Scanning'. *Frontiers in Plant Science*, 7, Article 222 (29 February 2016). doi: 10.3389/fpls.2016.00222

Radin, Dean. *The Conscious Universe: The Truth of Psychic Phenomena*. San Francisco, CA: HarperOne Publishers, 1997.

Rilke, Rainer Maria. *Rainer Maria Rilke, Die Gedichte*. Frankfurt am Main and Leipzig: Insel Verlag GmbH, 2006.

Rousseau, Andréanne, and Geneviève Belleville. 'The Mechanisms of Action Underlying the Efficacy of Psychological Nightmare Treatments: A Systematic Review and Thematic Analysis of Discussed Hypotheses'. *Sleep Medicine Review*, 39 (2018): 122–133. doi: 10.1016/j.smrv.2017.08.004

Royal Society for Public Health (website). 'Waking Up to the Health Benefits of Sleep' (March 2016): 1–30. https://www.rsph.org.uk/uploads/assets/uploaded/a565b58a-67d1-4491-ab9112ca414f7ee4.pdf

Saunders, David T., Chris A. Roe, Graham Smith and Helen Clegg. 'Lucid Dreaming Incidence: A Quality Effects Meta-Analysis of 50 years of Research'. *Consciousness and Cognition*, 43 (2016): 197–215. http://dx.doi.org/10.1016/j.concog.2016.06.002

Schädlich, Melanie and Daniel Erlacher. 'Lucid Music – A Pilot Study Exploring Experiences and Potentials of Music-Making in Lucid Dreams'. *Dreaming*, 28, No. 3 (September 2018): 276–286. doi: 10.1037/drm0000073

——, Daniel Erlacher and Michael Schredl. 'Improvement of Darts Performance Following Lucid Dream Practice Depends on the Number of Distractions While Rehearsing within the Dream – A Sleep Laboratory Pilot Study'. *Journal of Sports Sciences*, 35, No. 23 (2017): 2365–2372. doi: 10.1080/02640414.2016.1267387

—— and Daniel Erlacher. 'Applications of Lucid Dreams: An Online Study'. *International Journal of Dream Research*, 5, No. 2 (2012): 134–138.

Scholem, Gershom. *Kabbalah*. New York, NY: Meridian, 1978.

Schredl, Michael. 'Typical Dream Themes'. In *Dreams: Understanding Biology, Psychology and Culture*, Vol. 1, 180–188. Edited by Katja Valli and Robert J. Hoss. Santa Barbara, CA: ABC-CLIO LLC, 2019.

Schweber, S. Silvan. *Einstein, Oppenheimer and the Meaning of Genius*. Cambridge, Massachusetts: Harvard University Press, 2008.

Seligman, Kurt (trans.). *The Mirror of Magic.* New York, 1948. In *The Penguin Dictionary of Symbols.* Edited by Jean Chevalier and Alain Gheerbrant. Translated by John Buchanan-Brown. London, UK: Penguin Books, 1996.

Shainberg, Catherine. *Kabbalah and the Power of Dreaming: Awakening the Visionary Life.* Rochester, NY: Inner Traditions, 2005.

Sheldrake, Rupert. *Science and Spiritual Practices: Reconnecting through Direct Experience.* London: Coronet, 2017.

Shohet, Robin. *Dream Sharing: A Guide to Understanding Dreams by Sharing and Discussion.* Northamptonshire, England: Crucible, 1985.

Shokri-Kojori, Ehsan, Gene-Jack Wang, Corinda E. Wiers, Sukru B. Demiral, Min Guo, Sung Won Kim, Elsa Lindgren et al. 'ß-Amyloid Accumulation in the Human Brain after One Night of Sleep Deprivation'. *Proceedings of the National Academy of Sciences,* USA, PNAS, 115, No. 17 (24 April 2019): 4483–4488. doi: 10.1073/pnas.1721694115

Sleep Council. 'The Great British Bedtime Report'. Chapel Hill, Skipton, UK (2017): 2–7. https://sleepcouncil.org.uk/wp-content/uploads/2018/04/The-Great-British-Bedtime-Report-2017.pdf

Sliwinski, Sharon. *Dreaming in Dark Times: Six Exercises in Political Thought.* Minneapolis, MI: University of Minnesota Press, 2017.

Somers, Barbara, with Ian Gordon Brown. *The Journey in Depth: A Transpersonal Perspective.* Edited by Hazel Marshall. Leicestershire, UK: Archive Publishing, 2002.

Sparrow, Scott G. 'Imagery Change Analysis: Working with Imagery from the Standpoint of Co-Creative Dream Theory' (2013). http://www.driccpe.org.uk/?portfolio-view=imagery-change-analysis-working-with-imagery-from-the-standpoint-of-co-creative-dream-theory-scott-sparrow

——. *Lucid Dreaming: Dawning of the Clear Light.* Virginia Beach, VA: Edgar Cayce Foundation, 1976.

Stafford, William. 'Glances'. *In Travelling Through the Dark.* New York, NY: Harper & Row Publishing, 1962.

Steele, Robert, and Dorothea Waley Singer. 'The Emerald Table'. In *Proceedings of the Royal Society of Medicine,* 21, No. 3 (January 1928): 485–501. https://www.ncbi.nlm.nih.gov/pmc/articles/PMC2101974/?page=1

Stickgold, Robert, J. Allan Hobson and R. Fosse. 'Sleep, Learning, and Dreams: Off-Line Memory Reprocessing'. *Science,* 294, No. 5544 (2 November 2001): 1052–1057. doi: 10.1126/science.1063530

Stirling, John Myer, Yoshiki Ishikawa, Takashi Hata and Ismet Karacan. 'Cerebral Blood Flow in Normal and Abnormal Sleep and Dreaming'. *Brain and Cognition*, 6, No. 3 (July 1987): 266–294. doi.org/10.1016/0278-2626(87)90127-8

Sterpenich, Virginie, Lampros Perogamvros, Giulio Tononi and Sophie Schwartz. 'Experiencing Fear in Dreams Relates to Brain Response to Aversive Stimuli During Wakefulness'. *Sleep Medicine*, 40, Supplement 1 (December 2017): E259-pE259. doi.org/10.1016/j.sleep.2017.11.759

——. 'Fear in Dreams and in Wakefulness: Evidence for Day/Night Affective Homeostasis'. Cold Spring Harbor Laboratory, bioRxiv preprint, posted online 29 January 2019. doi: http://dx.doi.org/10.1101/534099

Stumbrys, Tadas, Daniel Erlacher and Peter Malinowski. 'Meta-Awareness During Day and Night: The Relationship Between Mindfulness and Lucid Dreaming'. *Imagination, Cognition and Personality: Consciousness in Theory, Research, and Clinical Practice*, 34, No. 4 (2015): 415. doi: 10.1177/0276236615572594

——, Daniel Erlacher and Michael Schredl, 'Effectiveness of Motor Practice in Lucid Dreams: A Comparison with Physical and Mental Practice'. *Journal of Sports Sciences*, 34, No. 1 (April 2015): 27–34. https://doi.org/10.1080/02640414.2015.1030342

——, Daniel Erlacher, Melanie Schädlich and Michael Schredl, 'Induction of Lucid Dreams: A Systematic Review of Evidence'. *Consciousness and Cognition*, 21 (2012): 1456–1475. http://dx.doi.org/10.1016/j.concog.2012.07.003

Sturlason, Snorre. *Heimskringla; or, the Lives of the Norse Kings*. Edited with notes by Erling Monsen and translated into English with the assistance of A. H. Smith. New York, NY: Dover Publications Inc., 1990.

The Gospel of Thomas. Presented by Hug McGregor Ross. London: Watkins Publishing Inc., 2002.

The Holy Bible, American King James Version. AKJV. Edited by Michael Peter (Stone) Engelbrite. Public Domain, 1999.

The Holy Bible, English Standard Version. ESV® Text Edition: 2016. Copyright © 2001 by Crossway Bibles, a publishing ministry of Good News Publishers.

The Holy Bible, New International Version. NIV ® Copyright © 1973, 1978, 1984, 2011 by Biblica Inc.™

The Jerusalem Bible: Reader's Edition. Edited by Alexander Jones. Garden City, New York, NY: Doubleday & Company, Inc., 1968.

Thunberg, Greta. *No One is Too Small to Make a Difference*. London: Penguin Random House UK, 2018–2019.

——. 'I'm striking from school to protest inaction on climate change – you should too'. *The Guardian*, 26 November 2018. https://www.theguardian.

com/commentisfree/2018/nov/26/im-striking-from-school-for-climate-change-too-save-the-world-australians-students-should-too

Thurston, Mark. *Willing to Change: The Journey of Personal Transformation.* Rancho Mirage, CA: We Publish Books, 2005.

——. *Dreams: Tonight's Answers for Tomorrow's Questions: Edgar Cayce's Wisdom for the New Age,* edited by Charles Thomas Cayce. New York, NY: St. Martin's Press, 1996.

Tzu, Lao. *The Way of Life.* Translated by R. B. Blakney. New York, NY: Signet Classics, 2007.

Ullman, Montague, Stanley Krippner and Alan Vaughan. *Dream Telepathy: Experiments in Nocturnal Extrasensory Perception.* Charlottesville, VA: Hampton Roads Publishing Company, 2001.

University of Oxford. 'Our World in Data'. Global Change Data Lab (website) (Published May 2018 and updated April 2019). https://ourworldindata.org/global-mental-health

van Bronkhorst, Jeanne. *Dreams at the Threshold.* Woodbury, MI: Llewellyn Publications, 2015.

van de Castle, Robert L. *Our Dreaming Mind.* New York and Toronto: Ballantine Books, 1994.

van der Helm, E., and Matthew P. Walker. 'Overnight Therapy? The Role of Sleep in Emotional Brain Processing'. *Psychological Bulletin,* 135, No. 5 (September 2009): 731–748. doi: 10.1037/a0016570

van Dusen, Wilson. *Swedenborg's Journal of Dreams: 1743–1744.* Translated by J. J. G. Wilkinson. Edited by G. E. Klemming. New York, NY: Swedenborg Foundation Inc., 1996. (Originally published 1860.)

Viereck, George Sylvester. 'What Life Means to Einstein'. *The Saturday Evening Post,* 26 October 1929. http://www.saturdayeveningpost.com/wp-content/uploads/satevepost/what_life_means_to_einstein.pdf

Villaseñor, David. *Tapestries in Sand: The Spirit of Indian Sand Painting.* Happy Camp, CA: Naturegraph Company Publishers Inc., 1966.

Virtanen, Marianna, Katrina Heikkilä, Marcus Jokela, Angelae E. Ferrie, G. David Batty, Jussi Vahtera and Miki Kivimäki. 'Long Working Hours and Coronary Heart Disease: A Systematic Review and Meta-Analysis'. *American Journal of Epidemiology,* 176, No.7 (2012): 586–596. doi: 10.1093/aje/kws139

von Bingen, Hildegard. *Mystical Visions.* Translated from *Scivias* by Bruce Hozeski and introduced by Matthew Fox. Santa Fe, NM: Bear & Company, 1995.

von Goethe, Johann Wolfgang. *Faust*. Translated by Albert G. Latham. New York: E. P. Dutton & Co., 1908.

——. *Theory of Colours*. Translated by Charles Lock Eastlake. Mineola, NY: Dover Publications Inc., 2016. (Originally published 1810.)

Voss, Ursula, Romain Holzmann, Inka Tuin and J. Allan Hobson. 'Lucid Dreaming: A State of Consciousness with Features of Both Waking and Non-Lucid Dreaming'. *Sleep*, 32, No. 9 (1 September 2009): 1191–1200. https://www.ncbi.nlm.nih.gov/pmc/articles/PMC2737577/

——, and Allan Hobson. 'What is the State-of-the-Art on Lucid Dreaming? – Recent Advances and Further Questions'. In *Open MIND*, edited by Thomas Metzinger and Jennifer M. Windt. Frankfurt am Main: MIND Group, 2015: 1–20. doi: 10.15502/9783958570306

Waggoner, Robert. *Lucid Dreaming: Gateway to the Inner Self*. Needham, MA: Moment Point Press Inc., 2009.

Walker, Matthew. *Why We Sleep: The New Science of Sleep and Dreams*. UK: Penguin Random House, 2018.

Wallace-Wells, David. *The Uninhabitable Earth: A Story of the Future*. London: Penguin Random House, UK, 2019.

Wamsley, Erin J. 'Dreaming and Offline Memory Consolidation'. *Current Neurology and Neuroscience Reports*, 14, No. 3 (March 2014): 433. doi.org/10.1007/s11910-013-0433-5

Watson, Andrew J., and James E. Lovelock. 'Biological Homeostasis of the Global Environment: The Parable of Daisyworld'. *Tellus*, 35B (September 1983): 284–289. doi.org/10.1111/j.1600-0889.1983.tb00031.x

Welwood, John. *Toward a Psychology of Awakening: Buddhism, Psychotherapy and the Path of Personal and Spiritual Transformation*. Boston, MA: Shambahla Publications Inc., 2002.

Wittgenstein, Ludwig. *Remarks on Colour*. Edited by G. E. M. Anscombe. Translated by Linda L. McAlister and Margarete Schättle. Oxford: Blackwell Publishers Ltd., 1977.

——. *Philosophical Investigations*, 2nd edition. Translated by G. E. Anscombe. Oxford: Basil Blackwell, 1986.

Wohlleben, Peter. *The Hidden Life of Trees*. Vancouver, BC: Greystone Books Ltd., 2015.

World Health Organization. World Health Assembly. 'Global Burden of Mental Disorders and the Need for a Comprehensive, Coordinated Response from Health and Social Sectors at the Country Level: Report by the Secretariat'. No. 65 (20 January 2012). https://apps.who.int/iris/handle/10665/78898

World Health Organization. *Investing in Mental Health*. Geneva: World Health Organization, 2003. https://www.who.int/mental_health/media/investing_mnh.pdf

Xie, Lulu, Hongyi Kang, Qiwu Xu, Michael J. Chen, Yonghong Liao, Meenakshisundaram Thiyagara et al. 'Sleep Drives Metabolite Clearance from the Adult Brain'. *Science*, 342, No. 6156 (18 October 2013): 373–377. doi: 10.1126/science.1241224

Yeats, William Butler. 'Two Trees'. In *William Butler Yeats: Selected Poems and Three Plays*, 3rd edition. Edited by M. L. Rosenthal. New York, NY: Scribner Paperback Poetry Edition, Simon & Schuster Inc., 1996.

Young, Sarah. '"Everything Is What It Is and Not Something Else": A Response to Professor Gion Condrau'. In Ernesto Spinelli, Alessandra Lemma and Simon Du Plock (eds), *Journal of the Society for Existential Analysis* (July 1993): 13–18.

Zadra, Antonio. 'Chronic Nightmares'. In *Dreams: Understanding Biology, Psychology, and Culture*, Vol. 2, 480–486. Edited by Robert J. Hoss and Robert P. Gongloff. Santa Barbara, CA: ABC-CLIO LLC, 2019.

Zajonc, Arthur. *Catching the Light: The Entwined History of Light and Mind*. New York and Oxford: Oxford University Press, 1993.

Ziemer, Mary [Melinda Powell], 'Lucid Surrender and the Alchemical Coniunctio'. In *Lucid Dreaming: New Perspectives on Consciousness in Sleep*, Vol. 1, 145–146. Edited by Ryan Hurd and Kelly Bulkeley. Santa Barbara, CA: Praeger, 2014.

Zlinszky, András, and Norbert Pfeifer. 'Quantification of Overnight Movement of Birch (Betula pendula) Branches and Foliage with Short Interval Terrestrial Laser Scanning'. *Frontiers in Plant Science*, 7, Article 222 (29 February 2016). doi: 10.3389/fpls.2016.00222

Image Credits

Text Credits

Index

About the author

Inspired by dreams, Melinda Powell co-founded the Dream Research Institute, at the Centre for Counselling and Psychotherapy Education, London, to promote research into the relationship between dreams and wellbeing. Melinda has served as past vice-president of the International Association for the Study of Dreams and as director of Help Counselling Centre. She works as a psychotherapist and teaches the art of Lucid Dreaming. Melinda has published and lectured widely on dreams and lucidity. Born in Southern California, she lived for a number of years in Poland and Switzerland before making her home in the United Kingdom.